#republic

#republic

DIVIDED DEMOCRACY IN THE AGE OF SOCIAL MEDIA

CASS R. SUNSTEIN

PRINCETON UNIVERSITY PRESS

Princeton and Oxford

Published by Princeton University Press,
41 William Street, Princeton, New Jersey 08540

In the United Kingdom: Princeton University Press,
6 Oxford Street, Woodstock, Oxfordshire OX20 1TR

press.princeton.edu

Jacket design by Amanda Weiss

Library of Congress Cataloging-in-Publication Data

Names: Sunstein, Cass R., author.
Title: #Republic : divided democracy in the age
of social media / Cass R. Sunstein.
Other titles: Hashtag republic
Description: Princeton : Princeton University Press, 2017. | Includes index.
Identifiers: LCCN 2016038668 | ISBN 9780691175515 (hardback)
Subjects: LCSH: Information society—Political aspects. | Internet—
Political aspects. | Social media—Political aspects. | Polarization
(Social sciences) | Political participation—Technological innovations.
| Democracy. | Political culture. | BISAC: POLITICAL SCIENCE /
Political Ideologies / Democracy. | POLITICAL SCIENCE /
Political Freedom & Security / General. | POLITICAL SCIENCE /
Censorship. | POLITICAL SCIENCE / Public Policy / General.
Classification: LCC HM851 .S869 2017 | DDC 303.48/33—dc23
LC record available at https://lccn.loc.gov/2016038668

British Library Cataloging-in-Publication Data is available

This book has been composed in Adobe Text Pro and Gotham

Printed on acid-free paper. ∞

Printed in the United States of America

10 9 8 7 6 5 4 3 2 1

I think, when the people have chosen a representative, it is his duty to meet others from the different parts of the Union, and consult, and agree with them on such acts as are for the general benefit of the whole community.

💬 **ROGER SHERMAN, 1789**

It is hardly possible to overrate the value, in the present low state of human improvement, of placing human beings in contact with persons dissimilar to themselves, and with modes of thought and action unlike those with which they are familiar. . . . Such communication has always been, and is peculiarly in the present age, one of the primary sources of progress.

💬 **JOHN STUART MILL, 1848**

Now even as we speak, there are those who are preparing to divide us—the spin masters, the negative ad peddlers who embrace the politics of "anything goes." Well, I say to them tonight, there is not a liberal America and a conservative America—there is the United States of America. There is not a Black America and a White America and Latino America and Asian America—there's the United States of America.

💬 **BARACK OBAMA, 2004**

If you could look through thousands of stories every day and choose the 10 that were most important to you, which would they be? The answer should be your News Feed. It is subjective, personal, and unique—and defines the spirit of what we hope to achieve.

💬 **FACEBOOK, 2016**

CONTENTS

PREFACE

In a well-functioning democracy, people do not live in echo chambers or information cocoons. They see and hear a wide range of topics and ideas. They do so even if they did not, and would not, choose to see and hear those topics and those ideas in advance. These claims raise serious questions about online behavior and uses of social media, and the astonishing growth in the power to choose—to screen in and screen out.

Louis Brandeis, one of America's greatest Supreme Court justices, insisted that the biggest threat to freedom is "an inert people." To avoid inertness, a democratic public must certainly be free from censorship. But the system of free expression must do far more than avoid censorship; it must ensure that people are exposed to competing perspectives. The idea of free speech has an affirmative side. It imposes constraints on what government may do, but it requires a certain kind of culture as well—one of curiosity, openness, and humility.

Members of a democratic public will not do well if they are unable to appreciate the views of their fellow citizens, if they believe "fake news," or if they see one another as enemies or adversaries in some kind of war. Learned Hand, a lower court judge from many decades ago, put his finger on the point when he said that the "spirit of liberty" is "that spirit which is not too sure that it is right."

The English language has two enduring accounts of democratic dystopia. George Orwell's *Nineteen Eighty-Four*, with its omnipresent, choice-denying Big Brother, is the most familiar vision of democracy's defeat. Orwell's novel depicts a triumph of authoritarianism, symbolized by the boot in the face, and reflected in Adolf Hitler's Germany, Joseph Stalin's Soviet Union, and Mao Tse-tung's China. His is a tale of the triumph of fascism or communism. Many authoritarians are censors, and they silence those who disagree with them. To them, the Internet can be a great threat, and they are nervous about social media, which they also attempt to censor (except when it suits their purposes).

A much subtler and equally chilling vision is Aldous Huxley's *Brave New World*, with its pacified, choice-happy, formally free citizenry. Huxley's world lacks the most obvious authoritarians. People are controlled with pleasure, not with prisons and guns. In a sense, people are allowed to do exactly what they want—but the government succeeds in controlling people's very desires. Consider the plea of Huxley's hero, John the Savage, who resists the pursuit of pleasure: "But I don't want comfort. I want God, I want poetry, I want real danger, I want freedom, I want goodness. I want sin."[1]

With the help of its constitution, the United States has not come close to *Nineteen Eighty-Four*, and it has managed to avoid anything like *Brave New World*. True, there have been authoritarian actions (such as the internment of Japanese Americans on the West Coast during World War II), and pleasure seeking plays a major role in American culture. But for the United States at least, neither Orwell nor Huxley can be said to be prescient. Their novels are instructive political nightmares, not depictions of a past or future reality.

What both authors missed is another kind of dystopia, produced by the power to create one's very own echo chamber: the power of personalization, or gated communities, which can diminish individual freedom and endanger self-government itself. For all its horrors, *Brave New World* was a community of sorts, unified by shared activities and concerns. What is coming, and my concern in this book, is quite different.

For a preview, consider the words of John Stuart Mill, speaking of the value of international trade:

> It is hardly possible to overrate the value, in the present low state of human improvement, of placing human beings in contact with persons dissimilar to themselves, and with modes of thought and action unlike those with which they are familiar. . . . Such communication has always been, and is peculiarly in the present age, one of the primary sources

of progress. To human beings, who, as hitherto educated, can scarcely cultivate even a good quality without running it into a fault, it is indispensable to be perpetually comparing their own notions and customs with the experience and example of persons in different circumstances from themselves: and there is no nation which does not need to borrow from others, not merely particular arts or practices, but essential points of character in which its own type is inferior.[2]

It is now child's play to compare notions and customs; learning is instantaneous. For people all over the planet, that is good news. Actually it is great news. For that reason, we might be celebrating what Mill rightly identifies as a primary source of progress. In some ways, a celebration is very much in order, and a book could easily be written about it.

That is not this book. My goal here is instead to explore contemporary obstacles to achieving what Mill deemed "indispensable"—and to see what might be done to remove them.

#republic

THE DAILY ME

In 1995, MIT technology specialist Nicholas Negroponte prophesied the emergence of "the Daily Me." With the Daily Me, he suggested, you would not rely on the local newspaper to curate what you saw, and you could bypass the television networks. Instead, you could design a communications package just for you, with each component fully chosen in advance.[1]

If you want to focus only on basketball, you could do exactly that. If your taste runs to William Shakespeare, your Daily Me could be all Shakespeare, all the time. If you like to read about romances—perhaps involving your favorite celebrities—your newspaper could focus on the latest love affairs, or who's breaking up with whom. Or suppose that you have a distinctive point of view. Maybe your views are left of center, and you want to read stories fitting with what you think about climate change, equality, immigration, and the rights of labor unions. Or maybe you lean to the right, and you want to see conservative perspectives on those issues, or maybe on just one or two, and on how to cut taxes and regulation, or reduce immigration.

Perhaps what matters most to you are your religious convictions, and you want to read and see material with a religious slant (your own). Perhaps you want to speak to and hear from your friends, who mostly think as you do; you might hope that all of you will share the same material. What matters is that with the Daily Me, everyone could enjoy an *architecture of control*. Each of us would be fully in charge of what we see and hear.

In countless domains, human beings show "homophily": a strong tendency to connect and bond with people who are like them. The tendency to homophily is dampened if people live within social architectures that expose them to diverse types of people—in terms of perspectives, interests, and convictions. But with an architecture of control, birds of a feather can easily flock together.

In the 1990s, the idea of a Daily Me seemed more than a little absurd. But it's looking astoundingly good. If anything, Negroponte understated what was coming, what has now arrived, and what is on the horizon. Is that a promise or a threat? I think it's both—and that the threatening part is what needs to be emphasized, not least because so many people see it as pure promise.

True, there's no Daily Me, at least not quite yet. But we're getting there. Most Americans now receive much of their news from social media, and all over the world, Facebook has become central to people's experience of the world. It used to be said that the "Revolution Will Not Be Televised"; maybe or maybe not, but you can be pretty sure that the revolution will be tweeted (#Revolution). In 2016, for example, the military attempted a coup in Turkey. It succeeded in seizing the nation's major television network. But it failed to take over social media, which the government and its supporters successfully used to call the public to the streets and, in short order, to stabilize the situation. Coup attempts often stand or fall on public perceptions of whether they are succeeding, and social media played a major role in combating the perception that the government was falling.

When people use Facebook to see exactly what they want to see, their understanding of the world can be greatly affected. Your Facebook friends might provide a big chunk of the news on which you focus, and if they have a distinctive point of view, that's the point of view that you'll see most. I worked in the Obama administration, and so did a number of my Facebook friends, and what I see on my Facebook page often fits the interests and views of the kind of people who worked in the Obama administration. Is that an unalloyed good? Probably not. And I have conservative friends whose Facebook pages look radically different from mine, and in ways that fit with their political convictions. We are living in different political universes—something like science fiction's parallel worlds. A lot of the supposed news is fake.

Your Twitter feed might well reflect your preferred topics and convictions, and it might provide much of what you see about politics—taxes, immigration, civil rights, and war and peace. What comes in your feed is your choice, not anyone else's. You might well choose to include topics that interest you, and points of view that you find congenial. In fact that seems quite natural. Why would you want topics that bore you and perspectives that you despise?

ALGORITHMS AND HASHTAGS

As it turns out, you do not need to create a Daily Me. Others are creating it for you right now (and you may have no idea that they're doing it). Facebook itself does some curating, and so does Google. We live in the age of the algorithm, and the algorithm knows a lot.[2] With the rise of artificial intelligence, algorithms are bound to improve immeasurably. They will learn a great deal about you, and they will know what you want or will like, before you do, and better than you do. They will even know your emotions, again before and better than you do, and they will be able to mimic emotions on their own.

Even now, an algorithm that learns a little bit about you can discover and tell you what "people like you" tend to like. It can create something close to a Daily Me, just for you, in a matter of seconds. In fact that's happening every day. If the algorithm knows that you like certain kinds of music, it might know, with a high probability, what kinds of movies and books you like, and what political candidates will appeal to you. And if it knows what websites you visit, it might well know what products you're likely to buy, and what you think about climate change and immigration.

A small example: Facebook probably knows your political convictions, and it can inform others, including candidates for public office, of what it knows. It categorizes its users as very conservative, conservative, moderate, liberal, and very liberal. It does so by seeing what pages you like. If you like certain opinions but not others, it is easy to put together a political profile. If you mention certain candidates favorably or unfavorably, categorization is easier still. By the way, Facebook doesn't hide what it is doing. On the Ad Preferences page on Facebook, you can look under "Interests," and then under "More," and then under "Lifestyle and culture," and finally under "US Politics," and the categorization will come right up.

Machine learning can be used (and probably is being used) to produce fine-grained distinctions. It is easy to imagine a great deal of sorting—not just from the political right to the political left, but also with specifics about the issues that you care most about, and your likely views on those issues (immigration, national security, equality, and the environment). To say the least, this information can be useful to others—campaign managers, advertisers, fund-raisers and liars, including political extremists.

Or consider the hashtag. With #Ireland, #SouthAfrica, #DemocratsAreCommunists, or #ClimateChangeIsAHoax, you can find in an instant a large number of items that interest you, or that fit with or even fortify your convictions. The whole idea of the hashtag is to enable people to find tweets and information that interests them. It's a simple and fast sorting mechanism. You can create not merely a Daily Me but rather a MeThisHour or a MeNow. (#MeNow? I thought I just made that up, but of course it's in common use.) Many people act as *hashtag entrepreneurs*; they create or spread hashtags as a way of promoting ideas, perspectives, products, persons, supposed facts, and eventually actions.

Many of us are applauding these developments, which can obviously increase fun, convenience, learning, and entertainment. Almost no one wants to see advertisements for products that don't interest them. If they're bored by stories about France's economy, why should they have to see such stories on their computer screen or their phone?

It is a fair question, but the architecture of control has a serious downside, raising fundamental questions about freedom, democracy, and self-government. What are the social preconditions for a well-functioning system of democratic deliberation or individual liberty itself? Might serendipity be important, even if people do not want it? Might a perfectly controlled communications universe—a personalized feed—be its own kind of dystopia? How might social media, the explosion of communications options, machine learning, and artificial intelligence alter the capacity of citizens to govern themselves?

As we will see, these questions are closely related. My largest plea here, in fact, is for an *architecture of serendipity*—for the sake of individual lives, group behavior, innovation, and democracy itself. To the extent that social media allow us to create our very own feeds, and essentially live in them, they create serious problems. And to the extent that providers are able to create something like personalized experiences or gated communities for each of us, or our favorite topics and preferred groups, we should be wary. Self-insulation and personalization are solutions to some genuine problems, but they also spread falsehoods, and promote polarization and fragmentation. An architecture of serendipity counteracts homophily, and promotes both self-government and individual liberty.

There is an important clarification. These are claims about the nature of freedom, personal and political, and the kind of communications system that best serves a democratic order. These are not claims about what all or most people are doing. As we will see, many people do like echo chambers, and they very much want to live in them. Many other people dislike echo chambers; they are curious, even intensely so, and they want to learn about all sorts of topics and many points of view. Many people simply gravitate, by default, to the most well-known or popular sites, which do not have a clear ideological orientation. Empirical work confirms these claims, showing that many members of the public are keenly interested in seeing perspectives that diverge from their own, and also that with online browsing, most people spend their time on mainstream sites lacking identifiable political convictions.[3] Many people are open-minded, and their views shift on the basis of what they learn. Such people have an identifiable civic virtue; they are not too sure that they are right, and they want to discover the truth.

Many other people much prefer to hear opinions that are consistent with their own, but they are also perfectly willing to hear opinions that challenge them; they do not love the idea of an echo chamber, and they do not create one for themselves. In due course, I will have a fair bit to say about how people are actually using websites and social media, and the extent to which people are moving toward an architecture of control. But my central claims are not empirical; they are about individual and social ideals. They are about the kind of culture that is best suited to a well-functioning democracy.

TWO REQUIREMENTS

What I will be emphasizing, then, is *people's growing power to filter what they see*, and also *providers' growing power to filter for each of us, based on what they know about us*. In the process of discussing these powers, I will attempt to provide a better understanding of the meaning of freedom of speech in a self-governing society. A large part of my aim is to explore what makes for a well-functioning system of free expression. Above all, I urge that in a diverse society, such a system requires far more than restraints on government censorship and respect for individual choices. For the last several decades, this has been the preoccupation of American law and politics, and in fact the law and politics of many other nations as well, including, for example, Germany, France, England, Italy, South Africa, and Israel. Censorship is indeed the largest threat to democracy and freedom. But an exclusive focus on government censorship produces serious blind spots. In particular, a well-functioning system of free expression must meet two distinctive requirements.

First, people should be exposed to materials that they would not have chosen in advance. Unplanned, unanticipated encounters are central to democracy itself. Such encounters often involve topics and points of view that people have not sought out and perhaps find quite irritating—but that might nevertheless change their lives in fundamental ways. They are important to ensure against fragmentation, polarization, and extremism, which are predictable outcomes of any situation in which like-minded people speak only with themselves. In any case, truth matters.

I do not suggest that government should force people to see things that they wish to avoid. But I do contend that in a democracy deserving the name, lives—including digital ones—should be structured so that people frequently come across views and topics that they have not specifically selected. That kind of structuring is, in fact, a form of *choice architecture* from which individuals and groups greatly benefit. Here, then, is my plea for serendipity.

Second, many or most citizens should have a wide range of common experiences. Without shared experiences, a heterogeneous society will have a much more difficult time addressing social problems. People may even find it hard to understand one another. Common experiences, emphatically including the common experiences made possible by social media, provide a form of social glue. A national holiday is a shared experience. So is a major sports event (the Olympics or the World Cup), or a movie that transcends individual and group differences (*Star Wars* is a candidate). So is a celebration of some discovery or achievement. Societies need such things. A system of communications that radically diminishes the number of such experiences will create a range of problems, not least because of the increase in social fragmentation.

As preconditions for a well-functioning democracy, these requirements—chance encounters and shared experiences—hold in any large country. They are especially important in a heterogeneous nation—one that faces an occasional danger of fragmentation. They have even more importance as many nations become increasingly connected with others (Brexit or no Brexit) and each citizen, to a greater or lesser degree, becomes a "citizen of the world." That is a controversial idea, but consider, for example, the risks of terrorism, climate change, and infectious diseases. A sensible perspective on these risks and others like them is impossible to obtain if people sort themselves into echo chambers of their own design. And at a national level, gated communications communities make it extremely difficult to address even the most mundane problems.

An insistence on chance encounters and shared experiences should not be rooted in nostalgia for some supposedly idyllic past. With respect to communications, the past was hardly idyllic. Compared to any other period in human history, we are in the midst of many extraordinary gains, not least from the standpoint of democracy itself. For us, nostalgia is not only unproductive but also senseless. Things are getting better, not worse.

Nor should anything here be taken as a reason for "optimism" or "pessimism"—two potential obstacles to clear thinking about new technological developments. If we must choose between them, by all means let us choose optimism.[4] But in view of the many potential gains and losses inevitably associated with massive technological change, any attitude of optimism or pessimism is far too general to be helpful. Automobiles are great, but in the United States alone, many thousands of people die every year in car crashes. Plastics are a huge advance, but they have created a serious waste disposal problem. What I mean to provide is not a basis for pessimism but instead a lens through which we might understand, a bit better than before, what makes a system of freedom of expression successful in the first place, and what a well-functioning democracy requires. That improved understanding will equip us to understand a free nation's own aspirations, and thus help us to evaluate continuing changes in the system of communications. It will also point the way toward a clearer understanding of the nature of citizenship and its cultural prerequisites.

As we will see, it is much too simple to say that any system of communications is desirable if and because it allows individuals to see and hear what they choose. Increased options are certainly good, and the rise of countless niches has many advantages. But unanticipated, unchosen exposures and shared experiences are important too.

WHY THIS MATTERS: VIOLENCE, PARTYISM, AND FREEDOM

Do echo chambers matter? Exactly why? Some people might not love it if their fellow citizens are living in information cocoons, but in the abstract, that is up to each of us, a reflection of our freedom to choose. If people like to spend their time with Mozart, football, climate change deniers, or *Star Wars*, so what? Why worry?

The most obvious answer is also the narrowest: violent extremism. If like-minded people stir one another to greater levels of anger, the consequences can be literally dangerous. Terrorism is, in large part, a problem of hearts and minds, and violent extremists are entirely aware of that fact. They use social media to recruit people, hoping to increase their numbers or inspire "lone wolves" to engage in murderous acts. They use social media to promote their own view of the world, hoping to expand their reach. The phenomena to be discussed here are contributors to many of the most serious threats we face in the world today.

More broadly, echo chambers create far greater problems for actual governance, even if they do not produce anything like violence or criminality. Most important, they can lead to terrible policies or a dramatically decreased ability to converge on good ones. Suppose (as I believe) that the United States should enact reasonable controls on gun purchases—saying, for example, that those on terrorist watch lists should not be allowed to buy guns, unless they can show that they present no danger. Or suppose (as I also believe) that some kind of legislation controlling greenhouse gas emissions would be a good idea. (Perhaps you disagree with these illustrations; if so, choose your own.) In the United States, political polarization on such issues is aggravated by voters' self-segregation into groups of like-minded people, which can make it far more difficult to produce sensible solutions. Even if the self-segregation involves only a small part of the electorate, they can be highly influential, not least because of the intensity of their beliefs. Public officials are accountable to the electorate, and even if they would much like to reach some sort of agreement, they might find that if they do so, they will put their electoral future on the line. Social media certainly did not cause the problem, but in #Republic, things are worse than they would otherwise be.

I have worked in various capacities with the federal government and met on many occasions with members of Congress. With respect to important issues, Republicans have said to me, "Of course we would like to vote with the Democrats on that one, but if we did, we would lose our jobs." There is no question that behind closed doors, Democrats would on occasion say the same thing about working with Republicans. Both sides are worried about the effects of echo chambers—about an outburst of noisy negativity from segments of constituents, potentially producing serious electoral retribution. Social media increase the volume of that noise, and to that extent, they heighten polarization.

Over the last generation, the United States has seen an explosion in "partyism"—a kind of visceral, automatic dislike of people of the opposing political party. Partyism certainly isn't as horrible as racism; no one is enslaved or turned into a lower caste. But according to some measures, partyism now exceeds racism. In 1960, just 5 percent of Republicans and 4 percent of Democrats said that they would feel "displeased" if their child married outside their political party.[5] By 2010, those numbers had reached 49 and 33 percent, respectively—far higher than the percentage of people who would be "displeased" if their child married someone with a different skin color.[6] In hiring decisions, political party matters: many Democrats do not want to hire Republicans, and vice versa, to such an extent that they would favor an inferior candidate of their preferred political party.[7] Here as elsewhere, we should be cautious before claiming causation; it would be reckless to say that social media and the Internet more generally are responsible for the remarkable increase in partyism. But there is little doubt that a fragmented media market is a significant contributing factor.

By itself, partyism is not the most serious threat to democratic self-government. But if it decreases government's ability to solve serious problems, then it has concrete and potentially catastrophic consequences for people's lives. I have offered the examples of gun control and climate change; consider also immigration reform and even infrastructure—issues on which the United States has been unable to make progress in recent years, in part because of the role of echo chambers. To be sure, the system of checks and balances is designed to promote deliberation and circumspection in government, and prevent insufficiently considered movement. But paralysis was hardly the point—and a fragmented communications system helps to produce paralysis.

There is another problem. Echo chambers can lead people to believe in falsehoods, and it may be difficult or impossible to correct them. Falsehoods take a toll. One illustration is the belief that President Barack Obama was not born in the United States. As falsehoods go, this one is not the most damaging, but it both reflected and contributed to a politics of suspicion, distrust, and sometimes hatred. A more harmful example is the set of falsehoods that helped produce the vote in favor of "Brexit" (the exodus of the United Kingdom from the European Union) in 2016. Even if Brexit was a good idea (and it wasn't), the vote in its favor was made possible, in part, by uses of social media that badly misled the people of the United Kingdom. In the 2016 presidential campaign in the United States, falsehoods spread like wildfire on Facebook. Fake news is everywhere. To date, social media have not helped produce a civil war, but that day will probably come. They have already helped prevent a coup (in Turkey in 2016).

These are points about governance, but, as I have suggested, there is an issue about individual freedom as well. When people have multiple options and the liberty to select among them, they have freedom of choice, and that is exceedingly important. As Milton Friedman emphasized, people should be "free to choose." But freedom requires far more than that. It requires certain background conditions, enabling people to expand their own horizons and to learn what is true. It entails not merely satisfaction of whatever preferences and values people happen to have but also circumstances that are conducive to the free formation of preferences and values.

The most obvious way to curtail those circumstances is censorship and authoritarianism—the boot on the face, captured by George Orwell's *Nineteen Eighty-Four*: "If you want a vision of the future, imagine a boot stamping on a human face—forever." A world of limitless choices is incalculably better than that. But if people are sorting themselves into communities of like-minded types, their own freedom is at risk. They are living in a prison of their own design.

DEATH AND LIFE

Let me now disclose a central inspiration for this book, one that might seem far afield: *The Death and Life of Great American Cities* by Jane Jacobs.[8] Among many other things, Jacobs offers an elaborate tribute to the sheer diversity of cities—to public spaces in which visitors encounter a range of people and practices that they could have barely imagined, and that they could not possibly have chosen in advance. As Jacobs describes great cities, they teem and pulsate with life:

> It is possible to be on excellent sidewalk terms with people who are very different from oneself and even, as time passes, on familiar public terms with them. Such relationships can, and do, endure for many years, for decades. . . . The tolerance, the room for great differences among neighbors—differences that often go far deeper than differences in color—which are possible and normal in intensely urban life . . . are possible and normal only when streets of great cities have built-in equipment allowing strangers to dwell in peace together. . . . Lowly, unpurposeful and random as they may appear, sidewalk contacts are the small change from which a city's wealth of public life may grow.[9]

Jacobs's book is about architecture, not communications. But with extraordinary vividness, Jacobs helps show, through an examination of city architecture, why we should be concerned about a situation in which people are able to create communications universes of their own liking. Her "sidewalk contacts" need not occur only on sidewalks. The idea of "architecture" should be taken broadly rather than narrowly. Websites have architectures, and so do Facebook, Twitter, YouTube, and Reddit. And acknowledging the benefits that Jacobs finds on sidewalks, we might seek to discover those benefits in many other places. At its best, I believe, a system of communications can be for many of us a close cousin or counterpart to a great urban center (while also being a lot safer, more convenient, and quieter). For a healthy democracy, shared public spaces, online or not, are a lot better than echo chambers.

In a system with robust public forums, such as streets and parks, and general-interest intermediaries, such as daily newspapers and network television, self-insulation is more difficult; echo chambers are much harder to create; and people will frequently come across views and materials that they would not have chosen in advance. For diverse citizens, this provides something like a common framework for social experience. "Real-world interactions often force us to deal with diversity, whereas the virtual world may be more homogeneous, not in demographic terms, but in terms of interest and outlook. Place-based communities may be supplanted by interest-based communities."[10] Consider here the finding that communities that believed the apocalypse was near, and thought the attacks on September 11, 2001, were a clear sign to that effect, used the Internet so as "to insulate" themselves "from the necessarily divergent ideas that might generate more constructive public discussion."[11]

To be sure, we do not yet know whether anything can or should be done about fragmentation and excessive self-insulation. I will take up that topic in due course. For purposes of obtaining understanding, few things are more important than to separate the question of whether there is a problem from the question of whether anything should be done about it. Dangers that cannot be alleviated continue to be dangers. They do not go away if or because we cannot, now or ever, think of decent solutions. It is much easier to think clearly when we appreciate that fact.

WHAT FACEBOOK WANTS

On June 29, 2016, Facebook made a significant announcement, under a post called "Building a Better News Feed for You."[12] It didn't exactly say that it had found a way to produce a Daily Me, but it came fairly close, and it made clear its aspirations.

The post emphasizes that "the goal of News Feed is to show people the stories that are most relevant to them." With that point in mind, why does Facebook rank stories in its News Feed? "So that people can see what they care about first, and don't miss important stuff from their friends." In fact, the News Feed is animated by "core values," starting with "getting people the stories that matter to them most." Facebook therefore asks this question: "If you could look through thousands of stories every day and choose the 10 that were most important to you, which would they be? The answer should be your News Feed. It is subjective, personal, and unique—and defines the spirit of what we hope to achieve." (It's worth pausing over that.) I should note that I like Facebook and use it regularly—but it can improve.

Consistent with that spirit, Facebook says, "To help make sure you don't miss the friends and family posts you are likely to care about, we put those posts toward the top of your News Feed. We learn from you and adapt over time. For example, if you tend to like photos from your sister, we'll start putting her posts closer to the top of your feed so you won't miss what she posted while you were away." In this way and others, personalization matters: "Something that one person finds informative or interesting may be different from what another person finds informative or interesting." The News Feed is designed so that different people get what they want.

Facebook says that it does not play favorites. Its business is "connecting people and ideas—and matching people with the stories they find most meaningful." (The word "meaningful" is interesting here. What does it mean?) It follows that "as News Feed evolves, we'll continue building easy-to-use and powerful tools to give you the most personalized experience." That "we" is unduly confident that "the most personalized experience" is what is most desirable.

From the post, it is not exactly clear what Facebook did to improve the situation, but the company appears to have altered its algorithm to ensure that at the top of your News Feed, you will see items from your friends, thus increasing the likelihood that what you will see will be what most interests you. The post concludes: "We view our work as only 1 percent finished—and are dedicated to improving along the way." That's good news.

We do not know for sure, but Facebook probably made this change for three reasons. First, it had recently faced allegations of political bias, in the form of suppression of conservative news sources. An algorithm that emphasizes family and friends, and seemingly puts users in full control, can claim political neutrality. Second, Facebook has an obligation to its shareholders, and if its News Feed really can be turned into a Daily Me, it might well get more clicks, which means more revenue. Third, many users had been merely posting news articles of various sorts, which meant a reduction in original posts. People might find the reposted articles less interesting, and if so, there are fewer clicks, making for a less attractive product. (I speculate that the third reason might be the most important.)

It is entirely reasonable for Facebook to take these points into account. But we should not aspire to a situation in which everyone's News Feed is perfectly personalized, so that supporters of different politicians—Bernie Sanders, Hillary Clinton, Donald Trump, someone else—see fundamentally different stories, focusing on different topics or covering the same topics in radically different ways. Facebook seems to think that it would be liberating if every person's News Feed could be personalized so that people see only and exactly what they want. Don't believe it. In the 2016 presidential campaign, the News Feed spread a lot of falsehoods.

Facebook is right to underscore the importance of core values, but it might want to rethink its own. True, it is a business, not a public utility. True, it has obligations to its shareholders. But in view of its massive role in determining what kinds of news people see, it is far from ideal if it does not include, among its core values, promoting or at least not undermining democratic self-government. Facebook can do better.

"I'M SCARED; HOW ABOUT YOU?"

I have a friend who has a rule: "You cannot be happier than your spouse." That might be too simple, but he's onto something: emotions are contagious. If you are in a happy family, you'll be happier yourself, and if your partner or your children are enraged about something, or frightened, your own emotions will tend in the same direction.

It stands to reason that the emotional valence of what you read or see will have analogous effects. If your Twitter feed is full of pessimistic people, verging on despair about the economy or the fate of your nation, you'll become more pessimistic as well. A more alarming possibility: if an alienated young person is reading material from a terrorist organization, furious about the supposed misdeeds of the United States or the United Kingdom, he might get furious too—and perhaps be led to commit acts of violence. One consequence of personalization is likely to be not only fragmentation with respect to topics and points of view but also fragmented *feelings*—perhaps in general, or perhaps with respect to specific objects and positions.

Evidence to this effect comes from an important and controversial study by Facebook itself.[13] In the study, Facebook worked with Cornell University to conduct an experiment in which the company deliberately fed certain users sad posts in order to test whether the sadness of those posts would affect the emotions of those users. Of course Facebook did not have direct access to users' emotions—but it could see what they did next. Would their own behavior be affected? Would their posts shift in some way?

Yes and yes. As it turned out, the users who were given the sad posts began posting sad posts themselves. If we measure the effects on their emotions by what they did next, we can fairly say that sadness proved contagious on Facebook pages, just as in families and workplaces. The study is controversial because Facebook users do not exactly love the idea that the company may be manipulating their feelings. (If Facebook really wanted to make its users, or some subcategories of them, mad or sad, it could easily do that.) But to its credit, Facebook made a genuine contribution to science, producing as it did strong evidence that the emotional valence of what you read on social media will affect not only what you think but also how you feel. And if people are sorting themselves into different groups, or being sorted into such groups, it is inevitable that the emotional experiences of those groups will differ—often in response to precisely the same events.

A World Cup game is a benign example; if Germany is playing Argentina, fans of different teams will have different emotional reactions to the same outcome. In many ways, an election is similar. But we could also have radically different emotional responses to an event that is not self-evidently polarizing—a terrorist attack, a natural disaster, or a purely scientific report. In fact that is happening every day, in large part because of the power of echo chambers.

PRECURSORS AND INTERMEDIARIES

To some people, unlimited filtering may seem quite strange—a potential product of recent technologies and perhaps even the stuff of science fiction (come true, as it frequently does). But in many ways, it is continuous with what has come before. Filtering is inevitable, a fact of life. It is as old as humanity itself. It is built into our minds. No human being can see, hear, or read everything. In the course of any hour, let alone any day, every one of us engages in massive filtering, simply in order to make life manageable and coherent. Attention is a scarce commodity, and people manage their own attention in order to ensure that they are not overwhelmed.

Indeed, the entire field of behavioral science can be seen to stem from an insistent focus on the limited nature of attention, and the filters we impose on our thought and experience. Daniel Kahneman, Nobel Prize winner and a founder of the field, is widely known for his 2011 masterpiece, *Thinking, Fast and Slow*. But the arc of his career was nicely signaled by the title of his first book, published in 1973: *Attention and Effort*. Much of behavioral science emphasizes that it is effortful to attend to certain topics and concerns. People often want to minimize that effort. That's built into our species. Sometimes we allocate our attention deliberately: we decide to focus on our children, not on problems in Syria and Iraq. But often we allocate our attention without thinking about it. When you're driving, you concentrate on what's in front of you and what's in back, and many of your motions are automatic. What we "see" and what we notice are frequently outside our conscious control.

With respect to the world of communications, a free society gives people a great deal of power to filter out unwanted materials. Only tyrannies force people to read or watch. In free nations, those who read newspapers do not read the same newspaper; many people do not read any newspaper at all. Every day, people make choices among magazines based on their tastes and point of view. Sports enthusiasts choose sports magazines, and in many nations they select a magazine focused on the sport of their choice—*Basketball Weekly*, say, or the *Practical Horseman*. Conservatives can read *National Review* or the *Weekly Standard*; countless magazines are available for those who like cars; *Dog Fancy* is a popular item for canine enthusiasts; people whose political views are somewhat left of center might like the *American Prospect*; many people like *Cigar Aficionado*.

These are simply contemporary illustrations of a long-standing fact of life in many countries: a diversity of communications options and a wide range of possible choices. But the emerging situation does contain large differences, stemming above all from dramatic increases in individual control over content, the number of available options, the sheer speed with which people can receive information, and corresponding decreases in the power of *general-interest intermediaries*.[14]

General-interest intermediaries include newspapers, magazines, and broadcasters. An appreciation of their social functions will play a large role in this book. As prominent current examples, consider *Time, Newsweek,* the *New York Times,* the *Wall Street Journal,* the

Columbia Broadcasting System, and the *New York Review of Books*. People who rely on such intermediaries have a range of chance encounters, involving shared experiences with diverse others, and also exposure to materials and topics that they did not seek out in advance. The *New York Review of Books* provides you with a lot of material that you would not have chosen in advance; so too with the daily newspaper. You might find a range of stories that you would not have selected if you had the power to include or exclude them. Your eyes might come across a story about tensions over immigration in Germany, crime in Los Angeles, innovative business practices in Tokyo, a terrorist attack in India, or a hurricane in New Orleans, and you might read those stories, although you would hardly have placed them in your Twitter feed or your Daily Me. You might watch a particular television channel—perhaps you prefer channel 4—and when your favorite program ends, you might see the beginning of another show, perhaps a drama or news special that you would not have chosen in advance, but that somehow catches your eye.

Reading *Time* or *Newsweek*, you might come across a discussion of endangered species in Madagascar or genocide in Darfur, and it might interest you, even affect your behavior, maybe change your life, despite the fact that you would not have sought it out in the first instance. A system in which individuals lack control over the particular content that they see has a great deal in common with a public street, where you might encounter not only friends but also a heterogeneous array of people engaged in a wide array of activities (including perhaps bank presidents, political protesters, and panhandlers).

Some people believe that the mass media are dying—that the whole idea of general-interest intermediaries, providing shared experiences and exposure to diverse topics and ideas for millions, was a short episode in the history of human communications. As a prediction, this view seems wrong; even on the Internet, the mass media continue to play a large role. But certainly their significance has been falling over time.

It is an understatement to say that the communications market is in flux. Many of the most important general-interest intermediaries are in serious trouble. We should not forget that from the standpoint of human history, even in industrialized societies, such intermediaries are relatively new and far from inevitable. Newspapers, radio stations, and television broadcasters have particular histories with distinctive beginnings as well as possibly distinctive endings. In fact, the twentieth century should be seen as the great era for the general-interest intermediary, which provided similar information and entertainment to millions of people.

The twenty-first century may well be altogether different on this score. Consider one small fact: in 1930, daily newspaper circulation was 1.3 per household—a rate that had fallen to less than 0.50 by as early as 2003, even though the number of years of education, typically correlated with newspaper readership, rose sharply in that period. At the very least, the sheer volume of options and the power to customize are sharply diminishing the social role of the general-interest intermediary.

Indeed, one of the distinguishing features of the current era, accompanying the Daily Me, is the *special-interest intermediary*. Instead of serving as broad sources of information that cover a variety of topics, online news outlets often take the form of specialized "verticals" that focus on narrower subjects, such as sports, technology, or politics, or use specialized methodologies of interest to niche markets, whether large or small (such as fivethirtyeight .com, which emphasizes statistical approaches to politics and sports). These outlets are proliferating at a rapid rate; they attract capital from investors and are run more like start-ups than established news outlets. The greater specialization of these information sources, such as the various platforms run by Vox Media, will produce some echo chambers—and to that extent, diminish the likelihood of shared experiences.

HER

For a vivid illustration of what's around the corner, consider Spike Jonze's brilliant 2015 film, *Her*. In some ways, I think that it ranks with *Nineteen Eighty-Four* or *Brave New World* as a depiction of a humanly recognizable dystopian future, and it captures a dystopia that Orwell and Huxley could not have envisioned.

Theodore Twombly, the film's protagonist, makes a living by writing highly personalized notes and cards—for example, anniversary notes from wives to husbands—based on a great deal of information about both the sender and the receiver. In Twombly's world, love letters are simultaneously outsourced and customized. Twombly isn't exactly an operating system, but he sure acts like one. He also faces an imminent divorce, and his own life is in shambles, filled with video games and anonymous phone sex (personalized, of course). Everything changes when he purchases an operating system, a form of artificial intelligence (think Siri 4.0) who names "herself" Samantha.

Samantha has access to Twombly's computer, including his e-mails. She is a fast reader: she knows what he likes and dislikes, and she understands his strengths and weaknesses. Perhaps above all, she is interested in him. She listens. She yearns to see the world through his eyes. She is there when he wakes up, and every evening she's the one who says good night to him and to whom he says good night. She watches him while he sleeps.

If that were all, of course, Twombly's interest would wane quickly. Unless you are an impossible narcissist, you can't fall for someone whose only words are "Tell me more!" As she is constructed, Samantha has independent interests and concerns. She likes to write music, she's playful, she's curious, she can be insecure, and she's a tease. We can't know for sure, but perhaps those characteristics are a product of personalization as well. Perhaps they are exactly what Twombly wants and needs. Perhaps the algorithm knows, from a perusal of his browsing habits, how much independence he wants his partner to have, and exactly what kind.

Twombly falls in love with Samantha. How could he avoid that? She knows everything about him. She's his Daily Me, turned into a lover. Maybe that's irresistible. Let's hope that in reality, our operating systems will never become our lovers. (It's not fanciful to predict that they will, at least in some sense, though the movie makes a compelling argument for real human beings, imperfect personalization and all.) Whatever happens, we can take *Her* as a metaphor for processes, occurring every minute, by which our browsing habits—the words we use, the places we go, the friends we make, the things that we "like"—provide countless clues about our tastes and values. You don't have to be Samantha to be able to cater to those tastes and values. You can be some algorithm now in common use.

SOCIAL MEDIA

My topic is online behavior in general, and so much of the discussion will involve uses of big websites—newyorktimes.com, foxnews.com, Amazon.com, pandora.com. But I will also spend a lot of time on social media, which requires some definitional work.

Speaking of pornography, Supreme Court Justice Potter Stewart famously wrote, "I know it when I see it." Do we know social media when we see it? Any particular examples will become dated, but Facebook, Twitter, Instagram, and Snapchat certainly count. According to a helpful definition, social media are "Internet-based platforms that allow the creation and exchange of user-generated content, usually using either mobile or web-based technologies."[15] Wikipedia fits that definition, because people use it to produce content. YouTube must be included, because people share content there; Flickr and Vine are also examples. Blogs (such as Marginal Revolution) and microblogs (such as Twitter) are definitely included. So are social networking sites, most prominently Facebook, but also WhatsApp, Orkut, Yik Yak, Tumbler, and Tuenti. Social media can be used both for social purposes and games (such as Second Life and Pokémon Go). Can apps count? For my purposes, they certainly can, so long as they fit the definition.

It should be clear that we are dealing with a highly protean category, and its content changes rapidly over time. In 2006, blogs and the blogosphere were all the rage; while blogs exist and remain important, they have far less centrality (and the very word "blogosphere" seems to be a relic, a bit like "rotary phone" or "groovy"). Twitter was launched in 2006, Tumbler and WhatsApp in 2010, and Snapchat in 2011. Social media often have nothing at all to do with politics or democracy (indeed, they are a kind of vacation from it), and to that extent, they do not trigger my principal concerns here. But even if they are wholly apolitical, they might create niches, and niches produce fragmentation.

A WORD ON BASELINES

Any assessment of the world of the Internet, and any claims about what's wrong with it, must ask one question: *Compared to what*? We could easily imagine a suggestion that in some prior period— say, 1940, 1965, or 1980—the world of communications was much better. Perhaps there was a golden age of communication; many people think so. But that is not my claim here. I will be comparing the current situation not to some lost utopia but instead to a communications system that has never existed—one in which existing technological capacities and unimaginable improvements are enlisted to provide people with the equivalent of a great city, full of substance, fun, diversity, challenge, comfort, disturbance, colors, and surprise.

That is frustratingly vague, I know. It might help to say what the idealized baseline does *not* include. (It is much easier to speak of injustices than to offer an account of justice.) It does not involve a system of acute political polarization, in which large numbers of people sort themselves into information cocoons. It is not highly fragmented. It involves unanticipated exposures to topics and ideas. It counteracts falsehoods, spread by innocent or not-so-innocent people, misleading their fellow citizens about issues of health and wealth. It promotes deliberation among people who are not of like mind. It recognizes that some people are curious, and it cultivates political curiosity, seeing it as a civic virtue. (Recall that identifiable people have that virtue and like to read material that challenges their own preconceptions.)

These ideas are vague too. We should not offer a conception of an ideal communications market that is sanctimonious or preachy, or hopelessly ill suited to the lives (not to mention the attention spans) of actual human beings. My hope is that the ideal baseline, and departures from it, will emerge as we explore concrete problems.

POLITICS, FREEDOM, AND FILTERING

In the course of the discussion, we will encounter many issues. Each will be treated in some detail, but for the sake of convenience, here is a quick catalog:

- the importance of chance encounters and shared experiences for democratic societies

- the large difference between pure populism, or direct democracy, and a democratic system that attempts to ensure deliberation and reflection as well as accountability

- the intimate relationship between free speech rights and social well-being, which such rights often serve

- the pervasive risk that discussion among like-minded people will breed excessive confidence, extremism, contempt for others, and sometimes even violence

- the potentially dangerous role of social cascades, including "cybercascades," in which information, whether true or false, spreads like wildfire

- the enormous potential of the Internet and other communications technologies for promoting freedom in both poor and rich countries

- the utterly implausible nature of the view that free speech is an "absolute"

- the ways in which information provided to any one of us is likely to benefit many of us

- the difference between our role as citizens and our role as consumers

- the inevitability of regulation of speech, and indeed the inevitability of speech regulation benefiting those who most claim to be opposed to "regulation"

- the potentially destructive effects of intense market pressures on both culture and government

But the unifying issue throughout will be the various problems for a democratic society that might be created by the power to filter. Democracies may or may not be fragile, but polarization can be a serious problem, and it is heightened if people live in different communications universes—as in fact they sometimes seem to do in the United States, the United Kingdom, France, Germany, and elsewhere. There is no doubt that the modern communications environment, including social media, contributes to the rise of partyism.

One question, which I answer in the affirmative, is whether individual choices, innocuous and perfectly reasonable in themselves, might produce a large set of social difficulties. Another question, which I also answer in the affirmative, is whether it is important to maintain the equivalent of "street corners" or "commons" where people are exposed to things quite involuntarily. More specifically, I seek to defend a particular conception of democracy—a deliberative conception—and evaluate, in its terms, the outcome of a system with perfect power of filtering.

My claim is emphatically not that street corners and general-interest intermediaries will or would disappear in a world of perfect filtering. To what degree the market will produce them or their equivalent is an empirical issue. Some people invite general-interest intermediaries by default; if they are looking for news, that is where they go, and they do not much care about ideological disposition. Some people have a strong taste for street corners and their equivalent on television and the Internet. Indeed, the Internet holds out immense promise for allowing people to be exposed to materials that used to be too hard to find, including new topics and new points of view. If you would like to find out about different forms of cancer and different views about possible treatments, you can do so in less than a minute. If you are interested in learning about the safety record of different automobiles, a quick search will tell you a great deal. If you would like to know about a particular foreign country, from its customs to its politics to its weather, you can do better with the Internet than you could have done with the best of encyclopedias.

From the standpoint of those concerned with ensuring access to more topics and more opinions, existing communications technologies are a terrific boon. But it remains true that many apparent "street corners," on the Internet in particular, are highly specialized, limited as they are to particular topics and points of views. What I will argue is not that people lack curiosity or that street corners will disappear but instead that there is an insistent need for them, and that a system of freedom of expression should be viewed partly in light of that need. In particular, I will emphasize the risks posed by any situation in which hundreds of thousands, millions, or even hundreds of millions of people are mainly listening to louder echoes of their own voices.

WHAT ISN'T THE ISSUE

Some clarifications, designed to specify the central issues, are now in order. I will be stressing problems on the "demand" side of the speech market. These are problems that stem not from the actions of producers but instead from the choices and preferences of consumers. I am aware that on one view, the most important emerging problems come from large corporations, and not from the many millions and indeed billions of individuals who make communications choices. In the long run, however, I believe that the most interesting questions, and certainly the most neglected ones, involve consumer behavior. This is not because consumers are usually confused, irrational, or malevolent. It is because choices that seem perfectly reasonable in isolation may, when taken together, end up disserving democratic goals.

Because of my focus on the consumers of information, I will not be discussing a wide range of issues that have engaged attention in recent decades. Many of these issues involve the allegedly excessive power of large corporations or conglomerates.

- I will not deal with the feared disappearance of coverage of issues of interest to small or disadvantaged groups. Every day, that is less of a problem. On the contrary, there has been a tremendous growth in niche markets, serving groups both large and small. With a decrease in scarcity, this trend will inevitably continue. In #Republic, people should be able to find what they want, and should be able to become members of groups that they like. Technological development is a great ally of little groups and minorities, however defined. People with unusual or specialized tastes are not likely to be frozen out of the emerging communications universe. The opposite is much more likely to be true: they will have easy access to their preferred fare—far easier than ever before. If you love *Star Wars*, the 2012 television show *Awake*, or Taylor Swift, you can find people who will share the love.

- I will not be exploring the fascinating increase in people's ability to participate in *creating* widely available information—through art, movies, books, science, and much more. With social media, any one of us might be able to make a picture, a story, or a video clip available to all of us; YouTube is merely one example. In this way, social media have a powerful democratizing function.[16] Countless websites are now aggregating diverse knowledge. For diverse products—books, movies, cars, doctors, and computers—it is easy to find sources that tell you what most people think, and it is easy as well to contribute to that collective knowledge. Prediction markets, for example, aggregate the judgments of numerous forecasters, and they are proving to be remarkably accurate. There is much to be said about the growing ability of consumers to be producers too.[17] But that is not my topic here.

I will provide little discussion of monopolistic behavior by suppliers, or manipulative practices by them. Undoubtedly some suppliers do try to monopolize, and some do try to manipulate; consider, for example, the fact that Google provides paid links for certain sites (but not others) or tailors search algorithms to present certain search results (over others). Every sensible producer of communications knows that a degree of filtering is a fact of life. Producers also know something equally important but less obvious: consumers' attention is the crucial (and scarce) commodity in the emerging market. Companies stand to gain a great deal if they can shift attention in one direction rather than another. This is why many Internet sites supply information and entertainment to consumers for free. Consumers are actually commodities, and they are often "sold" to advertisers in return for money; it is therefore advertisers and not consumers who pay. This is pervasively true of radio and television.[18] It is true of numerous websites too.

Especially in light of the overriding importance of attention, some private companies will attempt to manipulate consumers, and occasionally they will engage in monopolistic practices. Is this a problem? No unqualified answer would make sense. A key question is whether market forces will reduce the adverse effects of efforts at manipulation or monopoly. I believe that to a large extent, they will, because competition for eyeballs is fierce, but that is not entirely clear. For example, Facebook is no ordinary competitor, and it has a lot of market power. But that is not my main concern here. For a democracy, many of the most serious issues raised by new technologies do not involve manipulation or monopolistic behavior by large companies. By contrast, personalization via algorithm will be a central theme.

I will put to one side the active debate over the uses of copyright law to limit the dissemination of material on the Internet and elsewhere. This is an exceedingly important debate, to be sure, but one that raises issues very different from those explored in this book.[19] Nor will I explore the sharply contested question, in some ways related, of "net neutrality," designed to level the playing field among communications providers.

I will not be discussing the "digital divide," at least not as the term is ordinarily understood. People concerned about that problem emphasize the existing inequality in access to new communications technologies—an inequality that divides those with and without access to the Internet. That is indeed an important issue, certainly domestically and even more so internationally, because it threatens to aggravate existing social inequalities, many of them unjust, at the same time that it deprives many millions (perhaps billions) of people of information and opportunities. But in both the domestic and international context, that problem seems likely to diminish over time, as new technologies, above all the Internet, are made increasingly available to people regardless of their income or wealth.

Of course we should do whatever we reasonably can to accelerate the process, which will provide benefits, not least for both freedom and health, for millions and even billions. But what I will describe will operate even if everyone is on the right side of that divide—that is, even if everyone has access to the Internet. My focus will be on the distinctive cultural and political divides, across values and tastes, that are emerging in the presence of universal access—on how reasonable choices by individual consumers might produce both individual and social harm. This point is emphatically connected with inequalities, but not in access to technologies; it does not depend in any way on inequalities there.

The digital divides that I will explore may or may not be a nightmare. But if I am right, there is all the reason in the world to reject the view that free markets, as embodied in the notion of "consumer sovereignty," exhaust the concerns of those who seek to evaluate any system of communications. The imagined world of innumerable, diverse editions of the Daily Me is not a utopian dream, and it would create—is creating—serious problems from the democratic point of view.

AN ANALOGY AND AN IDEAL

The changes now being produced by contemporary communications technologies are understated, not overstated, by the idea of the Daily Me. What is happening goes far beyond the increasingly customized computer screen.

Many of us telecommute instead of going to a workplace; this is a growing trend. Rather than visiting the local bookstore, where we might well end up seeing a number of diverse people, we shop for books on Amazon.com. Others increasingly avoid local restaurants, because seamless.com, or something like it, is entirely delighted to deliver sushi or a pizza to us. Near the dawn of the modern era, media analyst Ken Auletta enthused, "I can sample music on my computer, then click and order. I don't have to go to a store. I don't have to get in a car. I don't have to move. God, that's heaven."[1]

Really? Heaven? True, if you are interested in anything at all—from computers to linens to diamonds to cars to medical advice—an online company will be happy to assist you. Indeed, if you would like to attend college or even get a graduate degree, you may be able to avoid the campus. College education is available online, and if you'd like to perform marriage ceremonies, you can get licensed to do that too.[2]

It would be foolish to claim that this is bad, or a loss, in general or on balance. On the contrary, the dramatic increase in convenience is a wonderful blessing for people. Driving around in search of gifts can be a real bother. (Can you remember what this used to be like? Is it still like that for you?) For many of us, the chance to point and click is an extraordinary improvement. And many people, both rich and poor, take advantage of current technologies to "go" to places that they could not in any sense have visited before—South Africa, Germany, Iran, France, Venice, Beijing, as well as stores everywhere, and an immense variety of specialized doctors' offices. But it is far from foolish to worry that for millions of people, the consequence of this increased convenience is to decrease the set of chance encounters with diverse others—and also to be concerned about the consequence of the decrease for democracy and citizenship.

Or consider the concept of collaborative filtering—a familiar part of daily life online. We take it for granted, but it is worth pausing over how remarkable this is, and how remarkable it is that we no longer find it remarkable. Once you order a book from Amazon, for example, it is in an excellent position to tell you the choices of other people who like that particular book. Once you have ordered a number of books, Amazon.com knows and will tell you the other books—or music and movies—that you are likely to like, based on what people like you have liked. And of course other websites, such as Netflix, are prepared to tell you which new movies you'll enjoy and which you won't—simply by asking you to rate certain movies, then matching your ratings to those of other people, and then finding out what people like you think about movies that you haven't seen. The algorithms are excellent, and they're getting better.

For music and food, there are countless possibilities, and they are becoming more plentiful and more amazing every day. For example, Pandora asks you for your favorite song, and once you disclose it, it will create a channel all for you, based on that song. Pandora doesn't depend mostly on collaborative filtering; it finds songs that *sound* like the ones you like. After it makes an initial cut, it asks you to say whether you do, in fact, like the songs it has chosen for you, and in that way, it can get more and more precise. Its basic goal is to promote personalization—to appeal to your preferences and tastes, and get rid of the "junk." Few of us like "junk," but note well: what first seems to you to fall in that category (Bob Dylan, Bach, Mozart, Taylor Swift), might turn out, after serendipitous exposure, to be among your favorites.

Once Pandora knows what music you like, it probably knows a lot more about you, at least with a high probability. If you like Aimee Mann and Liz Phair, it will know something about your probable demographic, and so too if you like Selena Gomez, Haim, or the Dave Clark 5. Do musical preferences predict political inclinations? Not long ago, an official with Pandora said that its predictions about those inclinations, based on zip code as well as musical choices, are between 75 and 80 percent accurate. And with that level of accuracy, it developed an advertising service "that would enable candidates and political organizations to target the majority of its 73 million active monthly Pandora listeners based on its sense of their political leanings."[3]

Personalized shopping is becoming readily available, and it is intended to match the interests and purchasing patterns of customers with a dazzling array of products, including radios, computers, fabrics, pens, and room designs. Here as well, information about one set of patterns can provide predictions about others. It's not quite Samantha from *Her*, but if you know what socks people like, you might be able to make some extrapolations, and if you know about radio and cell phones as well, the extrapolations might start to become highly accurate. Or consider the suggestion that before long we will "have virtual celebrities. . . . They'll look terrific. In fact, they'll look so terrific that their faces will be exactly what you think is beautiful and not necessarily what your neighbor thinks, because they'll be customized for each home."[4] (Is it surprising to hear that several websites provide personalized romance stories? That at least one asks you for information about "your fantasy lover," and that it designs a story to suit your tastes?)

In many ways what is happening is quite wonderful, and the recommendations from Amazon.com, Netflix, and analogous services can be miraculously good, even uncanny. Countless people have discovered new favorite books, movies, and bands through this route. But it might well be disturbing if the consequence is to encourage people to narrow their horizons or cater to their existing tastes rather than allow them to form new ones. And the concern is amplified because many people aren't even aware that this filtering is happening. The problem is a real one for movies and music, but it is most serious in the democratic domain. Suppose that people with a certain political conviction find themselves learning about more and more authors with the same view, and thus strengthening their preexisting judgments, only because most of what they are encouraged to read says the same thing. In a democratic society, might this not be troubling?

The underlying issues here are best approached through two different routes. The first involves an unusual and somewhat exotic constitutional doctrine, based on the idea of the "public forum." The second involves a general constitutional ideal, indeed the most general constitutional ideal of all: deliberative democracy. As we will see, a decline in common experiences and a system of individualized filtering might compromise that ideal. As a corrective, we might build on the understandings that lie behind the notion that a free society creates a set of public forums, providing speakers' access to a diverse people, and ensuring in the process that each of us hears a wide range of speakers, spanning many topics and opinions.

THE IDEA OF THE PUBLIC FORUM

In the common understanding, the free speech principle is taken to forbid government from "censoring" speech of which it disapproves. In the standard cases, the government attempts to impose penalties, whether civil or criminal, on political dissent, libelous speech, commercial advertising, or sexually explicit speech. The question is whether the government has a legitimate and sufficiently weighty reason for restricting the speech that it seeks to control.

This is indeed what most of the law of free speech is about. In Germany, France, the United States, Mexico, and many other nations, constitutional debates focus on the limits of censorship. But in free countries, an important part of free speech law takes a different form. In the United States, for example, the Supreme Court has ruled that *streets and parks must be kept open to the public for expressive activity.* In the leading case, from the early part of the twentieth century, the Court stated, "Wherever the title of streets and parks may rest, they have immemorially been held in trust for the use of the public and time out of mind, have been used for the purposes of assembly, communicating thought between citizens, and discussing public questions. Such use of the streets and public places has, from ancient times, been a part of the privileges, immunities, rights, and liberties of citizens."[5]

It follows that governments are obliged to allow speech to occur freely on public streets and in public parks—even if many citizens would prefer to have peace and quiet, and even if it seems irritating to come across protesters and dissidents when you are simply walking home or going to the local grocery store. If you see protesters on a local street and wonder why they are allowed to be there (and perhaps to bother you), the answer is that the Constitution gives them a right to do so.

To be sure, the government is allowed to impose restrictions on the "time, place, and manner" of speech in public places. No one has a right to set off fireworks or use loudspeakers on the public streets at 3:00 a.m. in order to complain about crime, racism, climate change, or the size of the defense budget. But time, place, and manner restrictions must be both reasonable and limited. Government is essentially obliged to allow speakers, whatever their views, to use public property to convey messages of their choosing.

A distinctive feature of the public forum doctrine is that it creates *a right of speakers' access, both to places and people.* Another distinctive feature is that the public forum doctrine creates a right, not to avoid governmentally imposed *penalties* on speech, but to ensure government *subsidies* of speech. There is no question that taxpayers are required to support the expressive activity that, under the public forum doctrine, must be permitted on the streets and parks. Indeed, the costs that taxpayers devote to maintaining open streets and parks, from cleaning to maintenance, can be quite high. Thus the public forum represents one area of law in which the right to free speech demands a public subsidy to speakers.

JUST STREETS AND PARKS?
OF AIRPORTS AND THE INTERNET

Simply as a matter of principle, there seems to be good reason to expand the public forum well beyond streets and parks. In the modern era, other places have increasingly come to occupy the role of traditional public forums. The mass media and the Internet have become far more important than streets and parks as arenas in which expressive activity occurs. If you want to reach your friends, you'd do well to use Facebook, not the park around the block. If you want to get to a lot of people, you would probably do best to use Twitter or Instagram, not your local street corner.

Nonetheless, the Supreme Court has been wary of expanding the public forum doctrine beyond streets and parks. One reason is that any serious expansion might involve private institutions, which are not covered by the First Amendment at all. (If Facebook flatly refuses to post certain writings or takes down some accounts, there is no constitutional problem.) And perhaps the Court's wariness stems from a belief that once the historical touchstone is abandoned, lines will be extremely hard to draw, and judges will be besieged with requests for rights of access to both private and public property. Hence the Court has rejected the seemingly plausible argument that many other places—including those owned or overseen by the government—should be seen as public forums too. In particular, it has been urged that airports, more than streets and parks, are crucial to reaching a heterogeneous public; airports are places where diverse people congregate and where it is important to have access if you want to speak to large numbers of people. The Court was not convinced, responding that the public forum idea should be understood by reference to historical practices. Airports certainly have not been treated as public forums from "ancient times."[6]

Nonetheless, some members of the Court have shown considerable uneasiness about a purely historical test. In the most vivid passage on the point, Supreme Court Justice Anthony Kennedy wrote, "Minds are not changed in streets and parks as they once were. To an increasing degree, the more significant interchanges of ideas and shaping of public consciousness occur in mass and electronic media. The extent of public entitlement to participate in those means of communication may be changed as technologies change."[7] What Justice Kennedy recognizes here is the serious problem of how to "translate" the public forum idea into the modern technological environment. And if the Supreme Court is unwilling to do any such translating, it remains open for Congress, state governments, private institutions, and ordinary citizens to consider doing exactly that. In other words, the Court may not be prepared to say that the public forum idea extends beyond streets and parks as a matter of constitutional law. But even if the Court is unprepared to act, Congress and state governments are permitted to conclude that a free society requires a right of access to areas where many people meet.

Indeed, private and public institutions might reach such conclusions without judicial compulsion, and take steps on their own to ensure that people are exposed to a diversity of views. Airports and train stations might decide to remain open for expressive activity—as many now are. Broadcasters might attempt, on their own, to create the functional equivalent of public forums, allowing people with a wide range of views to participate—as many now do. Google, Facebook, Instagram, Twitter, and their successors might think creatively about creating spontaneous, unchosen encounters. An important question, for private institutions at least as much as government, is how to carry forward the goals of old law in the modern era.

WHY PUBLIC FORUMS? OF ACCESS, UNPLANNED ENCOUNTERS, AND IRRITATIONS

The Supreme Court has given little sense of why, exactly, it is important to ensure that the streets and parks remain open to speakers. This is the question that must be answered if we are to know how to understand the relevance of the public forum doctrine to contemporary problems.

We can make some progress here by noticing that the public forum doctrine promotes three important goals.[8] *First*, it ensures that speakers can have access to a wide array of people. If you want to claim that taxes are too high, religious diversity is not being respected, or police brutality is widespread, you are able to press this argument on many people who might otherwise fail to hear the message. The diverse people who walk the streets and use the parks are likely to hear speakers' arguments about taxes, religious plurality, or the police; they might also learn about the nature and intensity of views held by their fellow citizens. Perhaps some people's views change because of what they learn; perhaps they will become curious enough so as to investigate the question on their own. It does not much matter if this happens a little or a lot. What is important is that speakers are allowed to press concerns that might otherwise be ignored by their fellow citizens.

On the speakers' side, the public forum doctrine thus *creates a right of general access to heterogeneous citizens*. On the listeners' side, the public forum creates not exactly a right but rather an opportunity, if perhaps an unwelcome one: *shared exposure to diverse speakers with diverse views and complaints*. It is important to emphasize that the exposure is shared. Many people will be simultaneously exposed to the same views and complaints, and they will encounter views and complaints that some of them might have refused to seek out in the first instance. In fact, the exposure might well be considered, much of the time, irritating or worse.

In nations that are struggling against authoritarian rule, the shared exposure can make a massive difference. People might think that their own objections and fears are merely their own, and there is no sense that real change is possible. They might feel isolated in their discontent or rage. Once they see that dozens, hundreds, or millions of people are unhappy, and prepared to do something about it, major reforms might occur; potentially, a government might be overthrown. The Arab Spring occurred in large part as a result of processes of this kind, and public forums were crucial.[9] (Social media can of course play a major role here; they serve many of the functions of old-style public forums. They can be used for or against rebellions, in large part by giving people a sense of what other people are thinking and doing.)

Second, the public forum doctrine allows speakers not only to have general access to heterogeneous people but also to specific people and specific institutions against which they have a complaint. Suppose, for example, that you believe that the state legislature has behaved irresponsibly with respect to crime or immigration. The public forum ensures that you can make your views heard by legislators, simply by protesting in front of the state legislature itself. It often promotes access to the truth.

The point applies to private as well as public institutions. If a clothing store is believed to have cheated customers or acted in a racist manner, protesters are allowed a form of access to the store itself. This is not because they have a right to trespass on private property—no one has that right—but because a public street is highly likely to be close by, and a strategically located protest will undoubtedly catch the attention of the store and its customers. Under the public forum doctrine, speakers are thus permitted to have access to particular audiences, and particular listeners cannot easily avoid hearing complaints that are directed against them. In other words, listeners have a sharply limited power of self-insulation. If they want to live in gated communities, they might be able to do so, but the public forum will impose a strain on their efforts.

Third, the public forum doctrine increases the likelihood that people generally will be exposed to a wide variety of people and views. When you go to work or visit a park, it is possible that you will have a range of unexpected encounters, however fleeting or seemingly inconsequential. On your way to the office or when eating lunch in the park, you cannot easily wall yourself off from contentions or conditions that you would not have sought out in advance, or that you would have avoided if you could. Here too the public forum doctrine tends to ensure a range of experiences that are widely shared—streets and parks are public property—and also a set of exposures to diverse views and conditions.

What I mean to suggest is that these exposures help promote understanding and in that sense freedom. As we will soon see, all these points can be closely connected to democratic ideals.

UNPLANNED AND UNWANTED

We should also distinguish here between exposures that are *unplanned* and exposures that are *unwanted*. In a park, for example, you might encounter a baseball game or a group of people protesting the conduct of the police. These might be unplanned experiences; you did not choose them and you did not foresee them. But once you encounter the game or the protest, you are hardly irritated; you may even be glad to have stumbled across them. The baseball game might be fun to watch. The protest might be interesting or disturbing; you might agree with it or not, but it could get under your skin. You might be glad that you saw it.

By contrast, you might also encounter homeless people or beggars asking you for money, or perhaps trying to sell you something that you really don't want. (The latter is daily life in New York City.) If you could have filtered out these experiences, you would have chosen to do so. For many people, the category of unwanted—as opposed to unplanned—exposures includes a great many political activities. You might be bored by those activities and wish that they were not disturbing your stroll through the street. You might be irritated or angered by such activities, perhaps because they are disturbing your stroll, perhaps because of the content of what is being said, or perhaps because of who is saying it.

It is also important to distinguish between exposures to *experiences* and exposures to *arguments*. Public forums make it more likely that people will not be able to wall themselves off from their fellow citizens. People will get a glimpse, at least, of the lives of others, as through encountering people from different social classes. Some of the time, however, the public forum doctrine makes it more likely that people will have a sense, however brief, not simply of the experiences but also of the arguments being made by people with a particular point of view. You might encounter written materials, for example, that draw attention to the problem of domestic violence. The most ambitious uses of public forums are designed to alert people to arguments as well as experiences— though the latter sometimes serves as a kind of shorthand reference for the former, as when a picture or a brief encounter has the effect of thousands of words.

In referring to the goals of the public forum doctrine, I aim to approve of encounters that are unwanted as well as unplanned, and also of exposure to experiences as well as arguments. But those who disapprove of unwanted encounters (who wants them?), and welcome people's ability to fence them off, might also agree that unplanned ones are desirable, not least because they can change people's lives. And those who believe that exposure to arguments is too demanding or too intrusive might also appreciate the value, in a heterogeneous society, of exposure to new experiences.

GENERAL-INTEREST INTERMEDIARIES
AS UNACKNOWLEDGED PUBLIC FORUMS

Of course there is a limit to how much can be done on streets and in parks. Even in the largest cities, streets and parks are insistently *local*. But other institutions perform many of the same functions as streets and parks do. In fact, society's general-interest intermediaries— newspapers, magazines, and television broadcasters, whether online or not—can be understood as public forums of an especially import- ant sort. The same is not quite true of social media. Your Facebook News Feed might be a public forum of a kind, but it is not public in the same sense.

The reasons are straightforward. When you read a city news- paper or a national magazine, your eyes will come across a number of articles that you would not have selected in advance. If you are like most people, you will read some of those articles. Perhaps you did not know that you might have an interest in the latest legislative proposal involving national security, Social Security reform, or Somalia, or recent developments in the Middle East, but a story might catch your attention. What is true for topics is also true for points of view.

You might think that you have nothing to learn from someone whose view you abhor. But once you come across the editorial pages, you might well read what they have to say, and you might well benefit from the experience. Perhaps you will be persuaded on one point or another, or informed whether or not you are persuaded. Or perhaps you might clarify and improve your own arguments. Perhaps you will learn the truth.

At the same time, the front-page headline on the daily newspaper or the cover story in a weekly magazine is likely to have a high degree of salience for a wide range of people. While shopping at the local grocery store, you might see the cover of *Time* or *Newsweek*, and the story—about a promising politician, a new risk, a surprising development in Europe—might catch your attention, so you might pick up the issue and learn something even if you had no interest in advance.

Unplanned and unchosen encounters often turn out to do a great deal of good, for individuals and society at large. In some cases, they change people's lives. The same is true, though in a different way, for unwanted encounters. In some cases, an editorial from your least favorite writer might irritate you. You might wish that the editorial weren't there. But despite yourself, your curiosity might be piqued, and you might read it. Perhaps this isn't a lot of fun. But it might prompt you to reassess your own view and even revise it. At the very least, you will have learned what many of your fellow citizens think, and why they think it— as when you encounter, with some displeasure, a series of stories on crime, climate change, Iraq, racism, or alcohol abuse, but find yourself learning a bit, or more than a bit, from what those stories have to say.

Television broadcasters have similar functions. Perhaps the best example is what has long been an institution in many nations: the evening news. If you tune into the evening news, you will learn about a number of topics that you would not have chosen in advance. Because of the speed and immediacy of television, broadcasters performed the functions of public forums even more than general-interest intermediaries in the print media. In some times and places, the lead story on the networks has had a great deal of public salience, helping to define central issues and creating a kind of shared focus of attention for many millions of people. And what happens after the lead story—the coverage of a menu of topics both domestic and international—creates something like a speakers' corner beyond anything ever imagined in Hyde Park.

None of these claims depends on a judgment that general-interest intermediaries always do an excellent job, or even a good one. Sometimes such intermediaries fail to provide even a minimal understanding of topics or opinions. Sometimes they offer a watered-down version of what most people already think. Often they suffer from prejudices and biases of their own. Sometimes they deal little with substance, and veer toward sound bites, supposed scandals, and sensationalism—properly deplored trends in the last decades. At other times they present froth. In any era, and perhaps especially today, they face severe market pressures to do one thing: attract eyeballs. That imperative often leads to coverage that does not (to put it lightly) serve democratic ideals.

What matters for present purposes is that in their best forms, general-interest intermediaries expose people to a range of topics and views at the same time that they provide shared experiences for a heterogeneous public. There are no hashtags, and that's fortunate. Indeed, general-interest intermediaries of this sort have large advantages over streets and parks precisely because most of them tend to be so much less local and so much more national or even international. Typically they expose people to questions and problems in other areas or even other nations. They even offer a form of modest, backdoor cosmopolitanism, ensuring that many people will learn something about diverse areas of the planet, regardless of whether they are much interested, initially or ever, in doing so.

Of course, general-interest intermediaries are not public forums in the technical sense that the law recognizes. These are private rather than public institutions. Most important, members of the public do not have a legal right of access to them. Individual citizens are not allowed to override the editorial and economic choices of private owners. In the 1970s, a sharp constitutional debate on precisely this issue resulted in a resounding defeat for those who claimed a constitutionally guaranteed access right.[10] But the question of legal compulsion is really incidental to my central claim here. Society's general-interest intermediaries, even without legal compulsion, serve many of the functions of public forums. They promote shared experiences; they expose people to information and views that would not have been selected in advance.

TWO KINDS OF FILTERING

The public forum doctrine is an odd and unusual one, especially insofar as it creates a kind of speakers' access right to people and places, subsidized by taxpayers. But the doctrine is closely associated with a long-standing constitutional ideal, one that is far from odd: republican self-government.

From the beginning, the US constitutional order was designed to create a republic, as distinguished from a monarchy, an empire, or a direct democracy. We cannot understand the system of freedom of expression, and the effects of modern communications technologies and filtering, without reference to this ideal. It will therefore be worthwhile to spend some space on the concept of a republic, and on the way the US Constitution embodies it, in terms of a deliberative approach to democracy. And the general ideal is hardly limited to the United States; it plays a role in many nations committed to self-government.

In a republic, the government is not managed by any king or queen; there is no sovereign operating independently of the people.[11] The US Constitution represents a firm rejection of the monarchical heritage, and its framers self-consciously transferred sovereignty from any monarchy (with the explicit constitutional ban on "titles of nobility") to "We the People." This decision represents, in Gordon Wood's illuminating phrase, the "radicalism of the American revolution."[12] At the same time, the founders were extremely fearful of popular passions and prejudices, and they did not want government to translate popular desires directly into law. Indeed, they embraced a form of filtering, though one very different from what I have emphasized thus far. Rather than seeking to allow people to filter what they would see and hear, they attempted to create institutions that would "filter" popular desires so as to ensure policies that would promote the public good.

In that sense, the framers of the Constitution were not simple democrats. They were republicans. And they were republicans of a particular sort. They rejected the long-standing view—pressed by their antifederalist opponents—that a republic could exist only in a small territory of like-minded people. As James Madison put it in the "Federalist No. 10," one salutary effect of size would be

> to refine and enlarge the public views, by passing them through the medium of a chosen body of citizens, whose wisdom may best discern the true interest of their country, and whose patriotism and love of justice will be least likely to sacrifice it to temporary or partial considerations. Under such a regulation, it may well happen that the public voice, pronounced by the representatives of the people, will be more consonant to the public good than if pronounced by the people themselves, convened for the purpose.

That refinement and enlargement was crucial. It offers a cautionary note for all those who celebrate social media in particular and the Internet in general as means for injecting public convictions into public policy. Those convictions may reflect insufficient understanding of complex questions, perhaps above all of fact;

many questions in public policy require engagement with technical matters. In the founding period, the structure of political representation and the system of checks and balances were designed to create a kind of filter between people and law, so as to ensure that what would emerge would be both reflective and well informed. At the same time, the founders placed a high premium on the idea of "civic virtue," which required participants in politics to act as citizens dedicated to something other than their own self-interest, narrowly conceived.

This form of republicanism involved an attempt to create a deliberative democracy. In this system, representatives would be accountable to the public at large. But there was also supposed to be a large degree of reflection and debate, within both the citizenry and government itself.[13] In the history of political thought, the idea of deliberative democracy has had many defenders. Consider Aristotle's suggestion that when diverse groups "all come together . . . they may surpass—collectively and as a body, although not individually—the quality of the few best. . . . When there are many who contribute to the process of deliberation, each can bring his [sic] share of goodness and moral prudence; . . . some appreciate one part, some another, and all together appreciate all."[14] Here, then, is a clear suggestion that many minds, deliberating together, may improve on "the quality of the few best." Centuries later, John Rawls wrote of the same possibility: "The benefits from discussion lie in the fact that even representative legislators are limited in knowledge and the ability to reason. No one of them knows everything the others know, or can make all the same inferences that they can draw in concert. Discussion is a way of combining information and enlarging the range of arguments."[15]

Jürgen Habermas, elaborating these themes, stresses norms and practices designed to allow victory by "the better argument":

Rational discourse is supposed to be public and inclusive, to grant equal communication rights for participants, to require sincerity and to diffuse any kind of force other than the forceless force of the better argument. This communicative structure is expected to create a deliberative space for the mobilization of the best available contributions for the most relevant topics.[16]

Habermas has explored the idea of an "ideal speech situation," in which all participants attempt to seek the truth, do not behave strategically, and accept a norm of equality.[17] The framers of the US Constitution did not speak of an ideal speech situation, but the aspiration to deliberative democracy can be seen in many places in their design. The system of bicameralism, for example, was intended as a check on insufficiently deliberative action from one or another legislative chamber; the Senate in particular was supposed to have a "cooling" effect on popular passions. The long length of service for senators was designed to make deliberation more likely; so too for large election districts, which would reduce the power of small groups over the decisions of representatives. The electoral college was originally a deliberative body, ensuring that the choice of the president would result from some combination of popular will and reflection and exchange on the part of representatives. Most generally, the system of checks and balances had, as its central purpose, the creation of a mechanism for promoting deliberation within the government as a whole.

From these points it should be clear that the Constitution was not rooted in the assumption that direct democracy was the ideal, to be replaced by republican institutions only because direct democracy was impractical in light of what were, by modern standards, extremely primitive technologies for communication. Many recent observers have suggested that for the first time in the history of the world, something like direct democracy has become feasible. It is now possible for citizens to tell their government, every week and even every day, what they would like it to do. Indeed, some websites have been designed to enable citizens to do precisely that.[18] We should expect many more experiments in this direction.

Social media are easily enlisted to figure what large numbers of people want the government to do.

But from the standpoint of constitutional ideals, direct democracy via Twitter or Facebook or imaginable alternatives would be nothing to celebrate; indeed it would be a grotesque distortion of founding aspirations. It would undermine the deliberative goals of the original design. The American system has never been a direct democracy, and a good democratic order attempts to ensure informed and reflective decisions, not simply snapshots of individual opinions, suitably aggregated.[19]

HOMOGENEITY, HETEROGENEITY, AND A TALE OF THE FIRST CONGRESS

There were articulate opponents of the original constitutional plan, and their voices have echoed throughout American history; they spoke in terms that bear directly on modern technologies. The antifederalists believed that the Constitution was doomed to failure on the ground that deliberation would not be possible in a large, heterogeneous republic. Following the great political theorist Baron de Montesquieu, a revered authority for antifederalists and federalists alike, they urged that public deliberation would be possible only where there was fundamental agreement. Consider Montesquieu's own words:

It is natural to a republic to have only a small territory, otherwise it cannot long subsist. In a large republic there are men of large fortunes, and consequently of less moderation; there are trusts too great to be placed in any single subject; he has interest of his own; he soon begins to think that he may be happy, great and glorious, by oppressing his fellow citizens; and that he may raise himself to grandeur on the ruins of his country. In an extensive republic the public good is sacrificed to a thousand private views; it is subordinate to exceptions, and depends on accidents. In a small one, the interest of the public is more obvious, better understood, and more within the reach of every citizen; abuses have less extent, and, of course, are less protected.[20]

The antifederalist who signed himself "Brutus" (probably Robert Yates, a New York judge) much admired Montesquieu, and he was explicit on the importance of homogeneity:

In a republic, the manners, sentiments, and interests of the people should be similar. If this be not the case, there will be a constant clashing of opinions; and the representatives of one part will be continually striving against those of the other. This will retard the operations of government, and prevent such conclusions as will promote the public good.[21]

The founders rejected this time-honored view; the result was a fundamental revision of republican thought. As they saw it, a large republic would be better, not worse, precisely because of the "constant clashing of opinions," from which learning would be possible. In The Federalist No. 70, Alexander Hamilton put it most clearly. He turned Montesquieu on his head, arguing that "the differences of opinion, and the jarring of parties in [the legislative] department of the government, though they may sometimes obstruct salutary plans, yet often promote deliberation and circumspection, and serve to check excesses in the majority." This is a point about the epistemic value of diversity, at least when people are listening to one another. That is filtering of a distinctive sort—the kind of filter that is created when institutions require people to discuss questions with one another and subject themselves to "the jarring of parties."

It was here that the Constitution's framers made a substantial break with conventional republican thought, focusing on the potential *benefits* of diversity for democratic debate. Indeed, it is here that we can find the framers' greatest and most original contribution to political theory. For them, heterogeneity, far from being an obstacle, would be a creative force, improving deliberation and producing better outcomes. If everyone agreed, what would people need to talk about? Why would they want to talk at all?

In an often-forgotten episode in the first Congress, the nation rejected a proposed part of the original Bill of Rights, a "right" on the part of citizens "to instruct" their representative on how to vote. The proposed right was justified on republican (what we would call democratic) grounds. To many people, it seemed a good way of ensuring accountability on the part of public officials. But the early Congress decided that such a "right" would be a betrayal of republican principles. Senator Roger Sherman's voice was the sharpest and most forceful:

> The words are calculated to mislead the people, by conveying an idea that they have a right to control the debates of the Legislature. This cannot be admitted to be just, because it would destroy the object of their meeting. I think, when the people have chosen a representative, it is his duty to meet others from the different parts of the Union, and consult, and agree with them to such acts as are for the general benefit of the whole community. If they were to be guided by instructions, there would be no use in deliberation.[22]

Sherman's words reflect the founders' general receptivity to deliberation among people who are quite diverse, and who disagree on issues both large and small. In fact, it was through deliberation among such persons that "such acts as are for the general benefit of the whole community" would emerge. Of course the framers were not naive. Sometimes some regions as well as some groups would gain while others would lose. What was and remains important is that the resulting pattern of gains and losses would themselves have to be defended by reference to reasons. The Constitution might well be seen as intended to create a "republic of reasons," in which the use of governmental power would have to be justified, not simply supported, by those who asked for it. And the justification would have to take place among diverse people, not within echo chambers.

We can even take Sherman's understanding of the task of the representative to have a corresponding understanding of the task of the idealized citizen in a well-functioning republic. Citizens are not supposed merely to press their own self-interest, narrowly conceived, nor are they to insulate themselves from the judgments of others. Even if they are concerned with the public good, they might make errors of fact or value—errors that can be reduced or corrected through the exchange of ideas. Insofar as people are acting in their capacity as citizens, their duty is to "meet others" and "consult," sometimes through face-to-face discussions, and if not, through other routes, as, for example, by making sure to consider the views of those who think differently.

This is hardly to say that most people should be devoting most of their time to politics. In a free society, people have a range of things to do. But to the extent that both citizens and representatives are acting on the basis of diverse encounters and experiences, and benefiting from heterogeneity, they are behaving in accordance with the highest ideals of the constitutional design.

E PLURIBUS UNUM, AND JEFFERSON VERSUS MADISON

Any heterogeneous society faces a risk of fragmentation. This risk has been serious in many periods in American history, most notably during the Civil War, but often in the twentieth century and the twenty-first as well. The institutions of the Constitution were intended to diminish the danger, partly by producing a good mix of local and national rule, partly through the system of checks and balances, and partly through the symbol of the Constitution itself. Thus the slogan "e pluribus unum," or "from many, one," can be found on ordinary currency, in a brief, pervasive reminder of a central constitutional goal.

Consider in this regard the instructive debate between Thomas Jefferson and Madison about the value of a bill of rights. In the founding era, Madison, the most important force behind the Constitution itself, sharply opposed such a bill on the ground that it was unnecessary and was likely to sow confusion. Jefferson thought otherwise, and insisted that a bill of rights, enforced by courts, could be a bulwark of liberty. Madison was eventually convinced of this point, but he emphasized a different consideration: the unifying and educative functions of a bill of rights.

In a letter to Jefferson on October 17, 1788, Madison asked, "What use, then, . . . can a bill of rights serve in popular Government?" His basic answer was that the "political truths declared in that solemn manner acquire by degrees the character of fundamental maxims of free Government, and as they become incorporated with the National sentiment, counteract the impulses of interest and passion."[23] He spoke of culture, not courts. In Madison's view, the Bill of Rights, along with the Constitution itself, would eventually become a source of shared understandings and commitments among extremely diverse people. The example illustrates the founders' belief that for a diverse people to be self-governing, it was essential to provide them a range of common values and commitments.

TWO CONCEPTIONS OF SOVEREIGNTY, AND HOLMES VERSUS BRANDEIS

We are now in a position to distinguish between two conceptions of sovereignty, bearing directly on debates about the Internet and social media. The first involves consumer sovereignty—the idea behind free markets. The second involves political sovereignty—the idea behind free nations. The two conceptions cut in radically different directions.

The notion of consumer sovereignty underlies enthusiasm for the Daily Me. It is the underpinning of any utopian vision of the unlimited power to filter. Writing as early as 1995, Bill Gates cheerfully predicted,

> Customized information is a natural extension. . . . For your own daily dose of news, you might subscribe to several review

services and let a software agent or a human one pick and choose from them to compile your completely customized "newspaper." These subscription services, whether human or electronic, will gather information that conforms to a particular philosophy and set of interests.[24]

Gates's prediction is a reality. With social media, it is easy to gather information that precisely fits your interests and preexisting views. Or consider Gates's celebratory and prescient words in 1999: "When you turn on DirectTV and you step through every channel—well, there's three minutes of your life. When you walk into your living room six years from now, you'll be able to just say what you're interested in, and have the screen help you pick out a video that you care about. It's not going to be 'Let's look at channels 4, 5, and 7.'"[25]

That is true, more or less, and it is the principle of consumer sovereignty in action. With its focus on "what interests you," Facebook is picking up on the same idea. In a way, that is the political philosophy or even theology of Silicon Valley. Consider these more recent words from Google's brilliant Eric Schmidt: "It will be very hard for people to watch or consume something that has not in some sense been tailored for them."[26] What is perhaps most interesting is that Gates, Facebook, Schmidt, and others seem unself-conscious about such ideas. They appear not to see that it takes a kind of stand, and that there are other ways of evaluating the communications market.

The notion of political sovereignty underlies the democratic alternative, which poses a challenge to Gates's vision on the ground that it might undermine both self-government and freedom, properly conceived. Recall here philosopher John Dewey's words:

Majority rule, just as majority rule, is as foolish as its critics charge it with being. But it never is *merely* majority rule. . . . The important consideration is that opportunity be given that idea to spread and to become the possession of the multitude. . . . The essential need, in other words, is the improvement of the methods and conditions of debate, discussion, and persuasion. That is *the* problem of the public.[27]

Consumer sovereignty means that individual consumers are permitted to choose exactly as they wish, subject to any constraints provided by the price system as well as their current holdings and requirements. This idea plays a significant role in thinking about not only economic markets but also both politics and communications. When we talk as if politicians are "selling" a message and even themselves, we are treating the political domain as a kind of market, subject to the forces of supply and demand. And when we act as if the purpose of a system of communications is to ensure that people can see exactly what they "want," the notion of consumer sovereignty is very much at work. The idea of political sovereignty stands on different foundations. It does not take individual tastes as fixed or given; it does not see people as simply "having" tastes and preferences.

For those who value political sovereignty, "We the People" reflect on what we want by exchanging diverse information and perspectives. (Recall Hamilton's plea for the "jarring of parties" as a way of promoting circumspection and deliberation.) The political process shapes what we want, as individuals and a community. The idea of political sovereignty embodies democratic self-government, understood as a requirement of "government by discussion," accompanied by reason-giving in the public domain, where different people speak with one another and listen respectfully, even when in intense conflict. Political sovereignty comes with its own distinctive preconditions, and these are violated if government power is not backed by justifications, and instead represents the product of force or simple majority will.

It should be clear that the two conceptions of sovereignty are in potential tension. If laws and policies are "bought," in the same way that soap and cereal are bought, the idea of political sovereignty is badly compromised. The commitment to consumer sovereignty will also undermine political sovereignty if free consumer choices result in insufficient understanding of public problems, or if they make it difficult to have anything like a shared or deliberative culture. We will disserve our own aspirations if we confound consumer sovereignty with political sovereignty. If the latter is our governing ideal, we will evaluate the system of free expression at least partly by seeing whether it promotes democratic goals. If we care only about consumer sovereignty, the only question is whether consumers are getting what they want—a question that seems, unfortunately, to be dominating discussions of the Internet and other new technologies.

With respect to the system of freedom of speech, the conflict between consumer sovereignty and political sovereignty can be found in an unexpected place: the great constitutional dissents of Supreme Court Justices Oliver Wendell Holmes and Louis Brandeis. In the early part of the twentieth century, Holmes and Brandeis were the twin heroes of freedom of speech, dissenting, usually together, from Supreme Court decisions allowing the government to restrict political dissent. Sometimes Holmes wrote for the two dissenters; sometimes the author was Brandeis. But the two spoke in quite different terms. Holmes wrote of "free trade in ideas," and treated speech as part of a great political market with which government could not legitimately interfere. Consider the defining passage from Holmes's greatest free speech opinion:

> When men have realized that time has upset many fighting faiths, they may come to believe even more than they believe the very foundations of their own conduct that the ultimate good desired is better reached by free trade in ideas—that the best test of truth is the power of the thought to get itself accepted in the competition of the market, and that truth is the only ground upon which their wishes safely can be carried out. That at any rate is the theory of our Constitution.[28]

Brandeis's language, in his greatest free speech opinion, was altogether different:

Those who won our independence believed that the final end of the state was to make men free to develop their faculties, and that in its government the deliberative forces should prevail over the arbitrary. . . . They believed that . . . without free speech and assembly discussion would be futile; . . . that the greatest menace to freedom is an inert people; that public discussion is a political duty; and that this should be a fundamental principle of the American government.[29]

Note Brandeis's suggestion that the greatest threat to freedom is an "inert people," and his insistence, altogether foreign to Holmes, that public discussion is not only a right but also "a political duty." Brandeis regards self-government as something dramatically different from an exercise in consumer sovereignty. He does not speak of free trade in ideas. His conception of free speech is self-consciously republican, with its emphasis on the obligation to engage in public discussion. On the republican conception, unrestricted consumer choice is not an appropriate foundation for policy in a context in which the very formation of preferences and the organizing processes of the democratic order are at stake.

In fact, Brandeis can be taken to have offered a conception of the social role of the idealized citizen. For such a citizen, active engagement in politics, at least some of the time, is a responsibility, not just an entitlement. If citizens are "inert," freedom itself is at risk. If people are constructing a Daily Me that is restricted to sports or the personal lives of celebrities, they are not operating in the way that citizenship requires. This does not mean that people have to be thinking about public affairs all, most, or even much of the time. But it does mean that each of us has rights and duties as citizens, not simply as consumers.

As we will see, active citizen engagement is necessary to promote not only democracy but social well-being too. And in the modern era, one of the most pressing obligations of a citizenry that is not inert is to ensure that "deliberative forces should prevail over the arbitrary." For this to happen, it is indispensable to ensure that the system of communications promotes democratic goals. Achievement of those goals emphatically requires both unchosen exposures and shared experiences.

REPUBLICANISM WITHOUT NOSTALGIA

These are abstractions; it is time to be more concrete. I will identify three problems in the hypothetical world of perfect filtering. These difficulties would beset any system in which individuals have complete control over their communications universe, and exercised that control so as to create echo chambers or information cocoons.

The first difficulty involves *fragmentation*. The problem here comes from the creation of diverse speech communities whose members talk and listen mostly to one another. A likely consequence is considerable difficulty in mutual understanding. When society is fragmented, diverse groups will tend to polarize in a way that can breed extremism, and even hatred and violence. Modern technologies and social media are dramatically increasing people's ability to hear echoes of their own voices and wall themselves off from others. An important result is the existence of *cybercascades*— processes of information exchange in which a certain supposed fact or point of view becomes widespread, simply because so many people seem to believe it. Cybercascades often promote fragmentation, because they occur with some groups and not others. Indeed, cybercascades are frequently a prime source of fragmentation— and of belief in falsehoods.

The second difficulty involves a distinctive characteristic of information. Information is a public good in the technical sense that once one person knows something, other people are likely to benefit as well. If you learn about crime in the neighborhood or the problem of climate change, you might well tell other people too, and they will benefit from what you have learned. In a system in which each person can customize their own communications universe, or in which that universe is customized for them, there is a risk that people will make choices that generate too little information. An advantage of a system with general-interest intermediaries and public forums—with broad access by speakers to diverse publics—is that it ensures a kind of social spreading of information. At the same time, an individually filtered speech universe is likely to produce too few of what the philosopher Edna Ullmann-Margalit has called *solidarity goods*—goods whose value increases with the number of people who are consuming them.[30] A presidential debate is a classic example of a solidarity good.

The third and final difficulty has to do with the proper understanding of freedom and the relationship between consumers and citizens. If we believe in consumer sovereignty, and if we celebrate the power to filter, we are likely to think that freedom consists in the satisfaction of private preferences—in an absence of restrictions on individual choices. This is a widely held view about freedom. Indeed, it is a view that underlies much current thinking about free speech. It is mostly right. But it is also inadequate—a big part of the picture, true, but hardly the whole thing.

Of course free choice is important. But freedom, properly understood, consists not simply in the satisfaction of whatever preferences people have, but also in the chance to have preferences and beliefs formed under decent conditions—in the ability to have preferences formed after exposure to a sufficient amount of information as well as an appropriately wide and diverse range of options. There can be no assurance of freedom in a system committed to the Daily Me.

POLARIZATION

The Internet can bring people together rather than draw them apart. Countless people are using social media to build larger and more diverse communities. But there is narrowing as well, in the form of communities of niches. One of my own fields is behavioral science, and with the help of Twitter, those of us who are interested in that field can easily find each other. If you want to learn about the latest developments, Twitter is a great help. For example, behavioral scientists are interested in "loss aversion," which means that people dislike losses more than they like corresponding gains. If you're interested in new examples, exceptions, or elaborations of the behavioral finding, Twitter is terrific. And yes, there is a #lossaversion.

That's great, but for academics in any particular field, there's a risk that Twitter will contain echo chambers just for them. And of course people can find hashtags to signal topics or points of view of many different kinds. In 2015, #NeverTrump was popular for a time, in opposition to #MakeAmericaGreatAgain, and Clinton supporters favored #ImWithHer, which was opposed by #LockHerUp. Those who wanted genetically modified organism (GMO) labels on food looked for #JustLabelIt, and #BlackLivesMatter competed with #AllLivesMatter.

Many people are using the Internet in exactly the sense prophesied by those who celebrate the Daily Me, and in a way that invites the continuing emergence of highly specialized websites, discussion groups, and feeds of innumerable sorts. What problems would be created as a result?

FLAVORS, FILTERS, AND VOTES

It is obvious that if there is only one flavor of ice cream and only one kind of toaster, a wide range of people will make the same choice. (Some people will refuse ice cream, and some will rely on something other than toasters, but that is another matter.) It is also obvious that as choice is increased, different individuals and different groups will make increasingly different choices. It is obvious, finally, that as the costs of reaching people with particular interests, and of interacting with them, as well as interacting start to shrink, then we will see a massive increase in niche markets of multiple kinds. This has been the growing pattern over time with the proliferation of communications options.

On YouTube, like-minded people can, in a sense, congregate to discuss and focus on one or more of those possibilities—not least when the clip casts ridicule on a particular person or point of view. Consider the celebratory words of David Bohnett, founder of geocities.com (no longer in service, but at one time the third most visited website): "The Internet gives you the opportunity to meet other people who are interested in the same things you are, no matter how specialized, no matter how weird, no matter how big or how small."[1] This is undoubtedly true, but it is not only an occasion for celebration.

To see this point, it is necessary to think a bit about why people are likely to engage in filtering. The simplest reason is that people often know, or think they know, what they like and dislike. A friend of mine is keenly interested in Russia; he subscribes to a service that provides him with some two dozen stories about Russia each day. If you are bored by news stories involving Russia or the Middle East, or if you have no interest in Wall Street, you might turn your mind off when these are discussed, and if you can filter your communications universe accordingly, you might think that it's even better. In addition, many people like hearing discussions that come from a perspective that they find sympathetic. If you are a

Republican, you might prefer a newspaper with a Republican slant, or at least without a Democratic one. And indeed, many Americans with conservative leanings prefer to get their news from avowedly conservative sources, such as Fox News or the *Wall Street Journal*, whereas many Americans with liberal leanings work hard to avoid those very sources.

Does that matter? An ingenious study by Gregory J. Martin and Ali Yurukoglu of Stanford University explores whether people's voting behavior really is influenced by what they see on cable news.[2] Their research starts with the fact that in different parts of the United States, the stations found on specific channels vary. It turns out that when it comes to the total number of viewers, channel location matters a lot. People are more likely to watch stations in the lower positions. For historical reasons, Fox News and MSNBC have sometimes received advantageous channel positions—but sometimes have not.

Across recent time periods and in various parts of the country, Martin and Yurukoglu examined the relationships among channel positions, people's intended votes, county-level presidential vote shares, and individual viewership. With several large data sets, they tested the effects on voting of watching Fox News and MSNBC. One of their findings is that Fox and MSNBC have both grown more ideologically defined, and Republicans and Democrats alike are aware of that. In 2000 and 2004, a typical Democrat was no more likely than a typical Republican to watch MSNBC. By 2008, a typical Democrat was 20 percentage points more likely to watch MSNBC. In 2004, a Republican was only 11 points more likely than a Democrat to watch Fox. By 2008, the gap had widened to more than 30 points.

The authors also found that both Fox and MSNBC have real effects on people's likely votes. For those who end up watching Fox because of channel position, just four additional minutes of weekly viewing increases the probability of intending to vote for the Republican presidential candidate by 0.9 percentage points. For those who watch MSNBC, four such extra minutes decreases the likelihood of intending to vote for the Republican presidential candidate by about 0.7 percentage points.

With one hour of viewing per week, the effects are greater. In 2008, an hour of MSNBC decreased the likelihood of a Republican vote by about 3.6 percentage points. In the same year, watching Fox for an hour increased the probability of a Republican vote by 3.5 points. At the level of individual voters, that may not be such a huge deal. But considered across the United States, the effects are large. The researchers estimate that in 2004 and 2008, if there had been no Fox News on cable television, the Republican vote share (as measured by voters' expressed intentions) would have been 4 percentage points lower. And if MSNBC had had CNN's more moderate ideology, the Republican share of the 2008 presidential vote intention would have been about 3 percentage points higher. (In general, Fox has more success in converting viewers than MSNBC does; it also has a much larger audience.)

These are disturbingly big numbers. Fox News and MSNBC do not merely attract like-minded people. They also heighten divisions among voters, contributing to political polarization—and they affect people's ultimate votes. We're speaking here of television rather than websites or social media, but the phenomenon is quite general.

APPROPRIATELY SLANTED

Many people are most willing to trust, and most enjoy, "appropriately slanted" stories about the events of the day. Their particular choices are designed to ensure that they can trust what they read. Or maybe they want to insulate themselves from opinions that they find implausible, indefensible, or invidious. Everyone considers some points of view beyond the pale, and we filter those out if this is at all possible. For many years, I lived in Chicago, and I loved the Chicago Bears. (I still love them—just a bit less.) When they were on national television, I turned off the sound and listened to the local announcers. I did this not only because the local announcers were better but also because they were biased in the Bears' favor, and when the Bears did badly, their hearts broke along with mine.

Or consider the fact that after people buy a new car, they often love to read advertisements that speak enthusiastically about the same car that they have just obtained. Those advertisements tend to be comforting because they confirm the wisdom of the decision to purchase that particular car. If you are a member of a particular political party or have strong convictions, you might want support, reinforcement, and ammunition, not criticism.

We can make some distinctions here. Members of some groups want to wall themselves off from most or all others simply in order to maintain a degree of comfort and possibly a way of life. For the same reason, some religious groups self-segregate. Such groups tolerate pluralism and are interested largely in self-protection; they do not have large ambitions or seek to proselytize to others. Political regimes can act similarly. In 2016, the Chinese government took new steps to restrict the activities of foreign nonprofits in China. An evident goal was to protect its own interests. Its focus was on China and its environs, not on remote lands.

Other groups have a self-conscious social project or even a kind of "combat mission" to convert others, and their desire to self-segregate is intended to strengthen their members' convictions in order to promote long-term recruitment and conversion plans. Terrorists operate in just this way. That is one reason that they use social media. Political parties sometimes think in similar terms, and they frequently ignore the views of others, except when they hold those views up to ridicule. When links are provided to other sites, it is often to show how dangerous or contemptible competing views really are. Tweeters and bloggers routinely do exactly this.

OVERLOAD, GROUPISM, AND *E PLURIBUS PLURES*

In the face of dramatic increases in communications options, there is an omnipresent risk of information overload—too many options, too many topics, too many opinions, a cacophony of voices. Indeed the risk of overload and the need for filtering go hand in hand. In my view, Bruce Springsteen's music is timeless, but his hit from the 1990s, "57 Channels and Nothing On," is hilariously out of date in light of the number of current programming options (just 57?!). Filtering, often in the form of narrowing, is inevitable in order to avoid overload and impose some order on an overwhelming number of sources of information. Your Twitter feed will be restricted to what you want to see, and your Facebook friends will be a small subset of humanity.

By itself, this is not a problem. But when options are so plentiful, many people will take the opportunity to listen only or mostly to those points of view that they find most agreeable. For many of us, of course, what matters is that we enjoy what we see or read, or learn from it, and it is not necessary that we are comforted by it. But there is a natural human tendency to make choices with respect to entertainment and news that do not disturb our preexisting view of the world.

I am not suggesting that the Internet is a lonely or antisocial domain; it is hardly that. In contrast to television, many of the current options are extraordinarily social, dramatically increasing people's capacity to form bonds with individuals and groups that would otherwise have been entirely inaccessible. Facebook, Twitter, Instagram, Medium, and Vine provide increasingly remarkable opportunities, not for isolation, but for the creation of new groups and connections. This is the foundation for the concern about the risk of fragmentation.

Consider in this regard a revealing little experiment from a number of years ago.[3] Members of a nationally representative group of Americans were asked whether they would like to read news stories from one of four sources: Fox (known to be conservative), National Public Radio (NPR, known to be liberal), CNN (often thought to be liberal), and the British Broadcasting Network (whose politics are not widely known to Americans). The stories came in different news categories: US politics, the war in Iraq, "race in America," crime, travel, and sports. For the first four categories, Republicans chose Fox by an overwhelming margin. In contrast, Democrats split their "votes" among NPR and CNN—and showed a general aversion to Fox. For travel and sports, the divide between Republicans and Democrats was much smaller. And independents showed no preference for any particular source.

That's not exactly amazing, but there was a more surprising finding: *people's level of interest in the same exact news stories was greatly affected by the network label.* For Republicans, the identical headline became far more interesting and the story became far more attractive if it carried the Fox label. In fact, the Republican "hit rate" for the same news stories was three times higher when it was labeled "Fox." (Interestingly, the hit rate was doubled when sports and travel stories were so labeled.) Democrats showed a real aversion to stories labeled "Fox," and the CNN and NPR labels created a modest increase in their interest.

The overall conclusion is that Fox attracts substantial Republican support, and that Democratic viewers and readers take pains to avoid Fox—while CNN and NPR have noticeable but weak brand loyalty among Democrats. There is every reason to suspect that the result would generalize to online behavior—that people with identifiable leanings are consulting sources, including websites, that match their predilections, and are avoiding sources that do not cater to those predilections.

All this is just the tip of the iceberg. To cite some wise words from long ago:

> Because the Internet makes it easier to find like-minded individuals, it can facilitate and strengthen fringe communities that have a common ideology but are dispersed geographically. Thus, particle physicists, Star Trek fans, and members of militia groups have used the Internet to find each other, swap information and stoke each others' passions. In many cases, their heated dialogues might never have reached critical mass as long as geographical separation diluted them to a few parts per million.[4]

It is worth underlining the idea that people are working to "stoke each others' passions," because that notion will play a large role in the discussion to follow. Of course, many of those with committed views on one or another topic—gun control, abortion, or immigration—are speaking mostly with each other. Social media feeds and linking behavior follow a similar pattern.

All this is perfectly natural and even reasonable. Those who visit what they see as appropriately slanted sites are likely to want to visit similarly slanted sites, and people who create a site with one point of view are unlikely to want to promote their adversaries. (Recall that collaborative filtering works because people tend to like what people like them tend to like.) And many people who consult sites with a distinctive perspective hardly restrict themselves to like-minded sources of information. But what we now know about individual behavior supports the general view that many people are mostly hearing more and louder echoes of their own voices. To say the least, this is undesirable from the democratic standpoint.

I do not mean to deny the obvious fact that any system that allows for freedom of choice will create some balkanization of opinion. Long before the advent of the Internet, and in an era of a handful of television stations, people made self-conscious choices among newspapers and radio stations. In any era, many people want to be comforted rather than challenged. Magazines and newspapers, for example, often cater to people with definite interests in certain points of view. Since the early nineteenth century, African American newspapers have been widely read by African Americans, and these newspapers offer significantly different coverage of common issues than white-oriented newspapers and also make dramatically different choices about what issues are important.[5] Whites rarely read such newspapers.

What is emerging nonetheless counts as a significant change. With a dramatic increase in options and a greater power to customize comes a corresponding increase in the range of actual choices, and those choices are likely, in many cases, to match demographic characteristics, preexisting political convictions, or both. Of course this has many advantages; among other things, it greatly increases the aggregate amount of information, the entertainment value of choices, and the sheer fun of the options. But there are problems too. If diverse groups are seeing and hearing quite different points of view, or focusing on quite different topics, mutual understanding might be difficult, and it might be increasingly hard for people to solve problems that society faces together.

Consider a few examples. Many Americans fear that certain environmental problems—abandoned hazardous waste sites, genetic engineering of food, climate change—are extremely serious and require immediate government action. But others believe that the same problems are imaginative fictions, generated by zealots and self-serving politicians. Many Americans think that most welfare recipients are indolent and content to live off the work of others. On this view, "welfare reform," to be worthy of the name, consists of reduced handouts—a step necessary to encourage people to fend for themselves. But many other Americans believe that welfare recipients generally face severe disadvantages and would be entirely willing to work if decent jobs were available. On this view, welfare reform, understood as reductions in benefits, is an act of official cruelty. Many people believe that the largest threat to American security remains terrorism, and that if terrorism is not a top priority, catastrophic attacks are likely to ensue. Many others believe that while terrorism presents serious risks, the threat has been overblown, and that other problems, including climate change, deserve at least equal attention.

To say the least, it will be difficult for people armed with such opposing perspectives to reach anything like common ground or make progress on the underlying questions. People might believe opposing "facts." Consider how these difficulties will increase if people do not know the competing view, consistently avoid speaking with one another, and are unaware how to address divergent concerns of fellow citizens.

Numerous websites are created and run by hate groups and extremist organizations. They appear to be achieving a measure of success, at least if we measure this by reference to "hits." Some such groups have had hundreds of thousands or even millions of visitors. What is also striking is that many extremist organizations and hate groups provide links to one another, and expressly attempt to encourage both recruitment and discussion among like-minded people.

We can sharpen our understanding here if we attend to the phenomenon of *group polarization*. This phenomenon raises serious questions about any system in which individuals and groups make diverse choices, and many people end up in echo chambers of their own design. On the Internet, polarization is a real phenomenon; we might even call it "cyberpolarization." To understand how it works, we need to investigate a little social science.

AN EXPERIMENT IN COLORADO

The term "group polarization" refers to something simple: after deliberation, people are likely to move toward a more extreme point in the direction to which the group's members were originally inclined. With respect to the Internet and social media, the implication is that groups of like-minded people, engaged in discussion with one another, will typically end up thinking the same thing that they thought before—but in a more extreme form.

For an initial glimpse of the problem, let us put the Internet to one side and consider a small experiment in democracy that was held in Colorado in 2005.[6] About sixty US citizens were brought together and assembled into ten groups, each consisting of six people. Members of each group were asked to deliberate on three of the most controversial issues of the day: *Should states allow same-sex couples to enter into civil unions? Should employers engage in "affirmative action" by giving a preference to members of traditionally disadvantaged groups? Should the United States sign an international treaty to combat global warming?*

As the experiment was designed, the groups consisted of "liberal" and "conservative" members—the former from Boulder, the latter from Colorado Springs. It is widely known that Boulder tends to be liberal and that Colorado Springs tends to be conservative. The groups were screened to ensure that their members conformed to these stereotypes. In the parlance of election years, there were five "blue state" groups and five "red state" ones—five groups whose members initially tended toward liberal positions on the three issues, and five whose members tended toward conservative positions on those issues. People were asked to state their opinions individually and anonymously both before and after fifteen minutes of group discussion, and also try to reach a public verdict before making their final anonymous statements as individuals. What was the effect of discussion?

The results were simple. In almost every group, members ended up with more extreme positions after they spoke with one another. Discussion made civil unions more popular among liberals; discussion made civil unions less popular among conservatives. Liberals favored an international treaty to control global warming before discussion; they favored it more strongly after discussion. Conservatives were neutral on that treaty before discussion; they strongly opposed it after discussion. Mildly favorable toward affirmative action before discussion, liberals became strongly favorable toward it after discussion. Firmly negative about affirmative action before discussion, conservatives became even more negative about it afterward.

Aside from increasing extremism, the experiment had an independent effect: it made both liberal and conservative groups significantly more homogeneous—and thus squelched diversity. Before members started to talk, many groups displayed a fair bit of internal disagreement. The disagreements were reduced as a result of a mere fifteen-minute discussion. Even in their anonymous statements, group members showed far more consensus after discussion than before. It follows that discussion helped to widen the rift between liberals and conservatives on all three issues. Before discussion, some liberal groups were, on some issues, fairly close to some conservative groups. The result of discussion was to divide them far more sharply.

GROUP POLARIZATION

The Colorado experiment is vivid evidence of group polarization. The basic phenomenon has been found in over a dozen nations.[7] Consider a few examples:

- Members of a group of moderately profeminist women became more strongly profeminist after discussion.[8]

- After discussion, citizens of France, initially critical of the United States and its intentions with respect to economic aid, became more critical still.[9]

- After discussion, whites predisposed to show racial prejudice offered more negative responses to the question of whether white racism is responsible for conditions faced by African Americans in US cities.[10]

- After discussion, whites predisposed not to show racial prejudice offered more positive responses to the same question.[11]

- Republican appointees, on three-judge panels, show especially conservative voting patterns when they sit only with fellow Republican appointees; Democratic appointees show especially liberal voting patterns when they sit only with fellow Democratic appointees.[12]

The phenomenon of group polarization has conspicuous importance for social media and the Internet more generally, at least to the extent that groups with distinctive identities engage in within-group discussion. Effects of the kind just described should be expected with terrorist and hate groups as well as less extreme organizations of all sorts. If the public is balkanized, and if different groups are designing their own preferred communications packages, the consequence will be not merely the same but still more balkanization, as group members move one another toward more extreme points in line with their initial tendencies. At the same time, different deliberating groups, each consisting of like-minded people, will be driven increasingly far apart, simply because most of their discussions are with one another.

It is true, of course, that most of us do not use the power to filter so as to become walled off from other points of view. (Even so, some people will do, and are doing, exactly that. I will turn to empirical issues in due course, but for now, let's just reiterate that on Facebook and Twitter, many people create something like echo chambers; they want their own views to be confirmed. Something similar is true for the millions of people who select newspapers, radio stations, and television channels because they can hear some version of their own voices.

This is sufficient for significant polarization to occur, and cause serious social risks. In general, *it is precisely the people most likely to filter out opposing views who most need to hear them.* Social media make it easier for people to surround themselves (virtually) with the opinions of like-minded others and insulate themselves from competing views. For this reason alone, they are a breeding ground for polarization, and potentially dangerous for both democracy and social peace.

WHY POLARIZATION?

There have been three main explanations for group polarization. Massive evidence now supports all of them.

Persuasive arguments and information. The first explanation emphasizes the role of persuasive arguments and information. The intuition here is simple. Any individual's position on any issue is a function, at least in part, of which arguments seem convincing. On balance, that is good news. People *should* pay attention to arguments. If you are like most people, you are likely to notice the information held and revealed by those with whom you interact. And if your position is going to move as a result of group discussion, it is likely to move in the direction of the most persuasive position defended within the group, taken as a whole. The most persuasive position will be defined, in large part, by the reasonableness and number of arguments offered in its favor.

Here's the central point: if the group's members are already inclined in a certain direction, they will offer a disproportionately large number of arguments tending in that same direction, and a disproportionately small number of arguments tending the other way. The consequence of discussion will naturally be to move people further in the direction of their initial inclinations. Thus, for example, a group whose members lean in favor of the nation's current leader will, in discussion, provide a wide range of arguments in that leader's favor, and the arguments made in opposition to them will be both fewer and weaker. The group's members, to the degree that they shift, will shift toward a more extreme position in favor of the current leader. And the group as a whole, if a group decision is required, will move not to the median position but instead to a more extreme point.

On this account, the central factor behind group polarization is the existence of a *limited argument pool*—one that is skewed (speaking purely descriptively) in a particular direction. It is easy to see how shifts might happen with discussion groups online; consider a group of Democrats or Republicans, terrorists, or environmentalists. The point helps to explain what happens every day on social networks. If your Twitter feed consists of people who think as you do, or if your Facebook friends share your convictions, the argument pool will be sharply limited. Indeed, shifts should occur with individuals not engaged in discussion but instead consulting only ideas—on radio, television, or the Internet—to which they are predisposed. The tendency of such consultations will be to entrench and reinforce preexisting positions—often resulting in extremism. If people who watch Fox News are drawn further in a conservative direction, or if people who watch Russian state television end up with less enthusiasm for the United States, the relevant argument pool is probably playing a large role.

Reputational considerations. The second mechanism, involving people's concern for their reputations, begins with the reasonable suggestion that people want to be perceived favorably by other group members and also perceive themselves favorably. Once they hear what others believe, they frequently adjust their positions in the direction of the dominant position. The German sociologist Elisabeth Noell-Neumann has used this idea as the foundation for a general theory of public opinion, involving a "spiral of silence" in which people with minority positions silence themselves, potentially excising those positions from society over time.[13] That happens in authoritarian societies, but it can also take place in democracies. Sometimes it is a good thing; people who believe that the sun goes around the earth, or that slavery was a fine idea, may end up self-silencing, as societies converge on scientific and moral truths, making false or invidious beliefs disappear (or nearly so). But the spiral of silence is not always benign. For present purposes, the central point is that when people care about their reputations, what they say within group discussions will be affected. As a result, groups can become more extreme.

Suppose, for instance, that people in a certain group tend to be sharply opposed to a certain war, continued reliance on fossil fuels, and gun ownership, and that they also want to be seen as sharply opposed to all these policies. If they are in a group whose members are also sharply opposed to these things, they might well shift in the direction of even stronger opposition after they see what other group members think. In countless studies, exactly this pattern is observed. Of course people will not shift if they have a clear sense of what they think and will not let the opinions of others move them. But most people, most of the time, are not so fixed in their views.

The point offers an account of the likely effects of exposure to ideas and claims on television, radio, and social media—even in the absence of a chance for interaction. Note that group polarization occurs *merely on the basis of exposure to the views of others*. Discussion is not necessary. The "mere exposure" effect means that polarization is likely to be a common phenomenon in a balkanized speech market.

Imagine that conservatives are visiting conservative sites; that liberals are visiting liberal sites; that environmentalists are visiting sites dedicated to establishing the risks of genetic engineering and climate change; that critics of environmentalists are visiting sites whose purpose is to expose frauds allegedly perpetrated by environmentalists; and that people inclined to racial hatred are visiting sites that express racial hatred. To the extent that these exposures are not complemented by exposure to competing views, group polarization will be the inevitable consequence.

Confidence, extremism, and corroboration. The most intriguing explanation of group polarization stresses the close links among confidence, extremism, and corroboration by others.[14] On many issues, including political ones, people are really not sure what they think, and their lack of certainty inclines them toward the middle. We might feel tentative about complex matters—the effects of an increase in the minimum wage, the proper approach to climate change, or what to do about some dangerous international situation. Our views are moderate and provisional.

It is only as people gain confidence that they become more extreme in their beliefs. For better or worse, they can be radicalized, even if the ultimate conclusion is not all that radical. Agreement from others tends to increase confidence, and for this reason like-minded people, having deliberated with one another, become more convinced that they are right—and hence more extreme. Even in mundane contexts, involving the attractiveness of people in slides and the comfort of chairs, the opinions of ordinary people in experiments become more extreme simply because their views have been corroborated, and because they become more confident after learning that others share their views.[15]

This is a quite-fundamental point, and it helps explain what happens on Twitter every day. If you learn that other "people like you" like a certain band, a particular movie, an identifiable political position, or a specific candidate, you might well follow their lead. Indeed, if you learn that "people like you" tend to have a certain position on national security or Social Security reform, you might well end up adopting their position, and perhaps doing so with great confidence, even if you haven't much thought about the question independently. When people find that others share their initial inclination, they often become more confident and therefore more extreme. Consider in this regard the effects of social media platforms on which people's views end up being constantly reaffirmed by like-minded types.

I am using the idea of radicalization pretty loosely here. You can become radicalized in the sense that you come to believe, firmly, a position that is within the political mainstream—for example, that your preferred political candidate is not just the best but immeasurably better than the alternatives, and that any other choice would be catastrophic. On both sides, this happened in the 2016 campaign between Donald Trump (#CrookedHillary) and Hillary Clinton (#NeverTrump). Of course you can become radicalized in more disturbing ways; we will get to that in due course.

THE ENORMOUS IMPORTANCE OF GROUP IDENTITY

With respect to polarization, perceptions of identity and group membership are important, both for communications in general and social media in particular. Group polarization will significantly increase if people think of themselves as part of a group having a shared identity and a degree of solidarity. If they think of themselves in this way, group polarization is both more likely and more extreme.[16] If, say, a number of people in an online discussion group think of themselves as opponents of high taxes, advocates of animal rights, or critics of the Supreme Court, their discussions are likely to move them in extreme directions, simply because they understand each other as part of a common cause. Similar movements should be expected for those who listen to a radio show known to be conservative, or who watch a television program dedicated to traditional religious values or exposing white racism. A lot of evidence so suggests.[17]

Group identity matters in another way. Suppose that you are participating in an online discussion, but you think that other group members are significantly *different* from you. If so, you are less likely to be moved by what they say. If, for example, other group members are styled "Republicans," and you consider yourself a Democrat, you might not shift at all—even if you would indeed shift as a result of the same arguments if you were all styled "voters," "jurors," or "citizens." Thus a perception of shared group identity will heighten the influence of others' views on your own, whereas a perception of unshared identity and relevant differences will reduce that effect, and possibly even eliminate it.

These findings should not be surprising. Recall that in ordinary cases, group polarization is a product of limited argument pools, reputational considerations, and the effects of corroboration. If this is so, it stands to reason that when group members think of one another as similar along a salient dimension, or if some external factor (politics, geography, race, or sex) unites them, group polarization will be heightened. If identity is shared, persuasive arguments are likely to be still more persuasive; the identity of those who are making those arguments gives them a kind of credential or boost. If identity is shared, social influences will have even greater force. People do not like their reputations to suffer in the eyes of those who seem most like them. And if you think that group members are in some relevant sense different from you, their arguments are less likely to be persuasive, and social influences may not operate as much or at all. If "people like you" support your initial inclination, you will become more confident. But if "people not like you" support that inclination, you might become less confident and start to rethink your position. If your political opponents—those whom you think most confused and destructive—think that your position is right, you might end up thinking that it is wrong.

GROUP POLARIZATION ONLINE

Group polarization is unquestionably occurring online. From the evidence discussed so far, it seems plain that the Internet is serving, for many, as a breeding ground for extremism, precisely because like-minded people are connecting with greater ease and frequency with one another, and often without hearing contrary views. Repeated exposure to an extreme position, with the suggestion that many people hold it, will predictably move those exposed, and likely predisposed, to believe in it.

One consequence can be a high degree of fragmentation, as diverse people, not originally fixed in their views and perhaps not so far apart, end up in extremely different places simply because of what they are reading and viewing. (Recall the Colorado experiment.) Another consequence can be a high degree of error and confusion. YouTube is a lot of fun, and in a way it is a genuine democratizing force, but there is a risk that isolated clips, taken out of context, will lead like-minded people to end up with a distorted understanding of some issue, person, or practice.

Call this the "Jon Stewart strategy." Stewart, once a nightly television show host, is immensely talented and even a kind of genius. As a comedian, one of his most successful approaches has been to display some brief clip in which the speaker seems evil, ugly, foolish, or (most often) idiotic. If everyone is laughing together (at, say, a famous politician), the clip will seem to capture the person; it will show his essence. That might be fair—but it usually isn't (except perhaps on a comedy show). In some contexts, it's completely unfair—a kind of violation.

If you follow any human being on video for a lengthy period of time, you will almost certainly be able to uncover a clip in which he appears to be evil, ugly, foolish, or idiotic—all the more so if the clip is played over and over again. Repetition can make anyone seem ridiculous. That's a terrific comic strategy, but it can be used for political purposes as well—and it certainly is. If you want to get people to dislike or ridicule a political opponent, here's a clue: use the Jon Stewart strategy. But if you do, you should not be proud of yourself.

A number of studies have shown group polarization in online settings or those that mimic them. An especially interesting experiment finds particularly high levels of polarization when group members meet relatively anonymously and group identity is emphasized.[18] From this experiment, it is reasonable to conclude that polarization is highly likely to occur, and to be extreme, under circumstances in which group membership is made salient and people have a high degree of anonymity. These are, of course, frequent features of online deliberation.[19]

Consider in this regard a revealing study not of extremism but of serious errors within working groups, both face-to-face and online.[20] The purpose of the study was to see how groups might collaborate to make personnel decisions. Résumés for three candidates applying for a marketing manager position were placed before several groups. The experimenters rigged attributes of the candidates so that one applicant was clearly best matched for the job described. Packets of information, each containing only a subset of information from the résumés, were given to the subjects, so that each group member had only part of the relevant information. The groups consisted of three people, some operating face-to-face, and others operating online.

Two results were especially striking. First, group polarization was common, in the sense that groups ended up in a more extreme position in line with members' predeliberation views. Second, almost none of the deliberating groups made what was conspicuously the right choice!

The reason is that they failed to share information in a way that would permit the group to make the correct decision. In online groups, the level of mistakes was especially high, for the simple reason that members tended to share positive information about the emerging winning candidate and negative information about the losers, while also suppressing negative information about the emerging winner and positive information about the emerging losers. These contributions served to "reinforce the march toward group consensus rather than add complications and fuel debate."[21] In fact, this tendency was *twice* as large within the online groups. There is a warning here about the consequences of the Internet for democratic deliberation.

It is true that many people go online and use social media to learn about alternative positions, not merely to reinforce their existing tendencies. It is certainly possible for more information and less polarization to result from the increase in available sources. This happens every day. But the study just described offers a clear warning. When people deliberate together, they often give disproportionate weight to "common knowledge"—information that they all share in advance. By contrast, they frequently give too little weight to unshared information—information that is held by one or only a few people. There is every reason to think that the same asymmetry is occurring online.

HASHTAG NATION AND HASHTAG ENTREPRENEURS

Consider #Syria, #BlackLivesMatter, #BobDylan, #ObamaIsA Muslim, #StarWars, and #Republic. All those are convenient sorting mechanisms. Do hashtags contribute to polarization?

The history here is illuminating. Hashtags were originally used in the Internet Relay Chats of the early 1990s, as a way to organize groups within chats. Twitter was the first social media site to use them. In 2007, just a year after the service launched, hashtags were proposed by Chris Messina, an open-source advocate, as an ad hoc strategy for sorting through conversations. He expanded on the proposal in a blog post a few days later, clarifying that hashtags should not be used for creating groups on Twitter ("I'm not at all convinced that groups . . . are ultimately a good idea or a good fit for Twitter") but instead for "improving *contextualization*, *content filtering* and *exploratory serendipity* within Twitter."[22] The mechanism proved both popular and useful, and it has been incorporated into many other social media platforms, including Instagram, Tumblr, and Vine. It is also used in e-mail. It is instructive that Messina referred at once to two potentially contradictory ideas— content filtering and exploratory serendipity—though it is not exactly clear what he meant by the latter.[23]

For my purposes, the question is whether hashtags produce one or the other, or instead both. Thus far, content filtering clearly seems to be the dominant effect. Hashtags typically signal subject matter, and they may also signal a point of view. If a hashtag says #DemocratsAreCommunists or #RepublicansAreFascists, people know the kind of thing that they will find. But if a hashtag says #AffirmativeAction, #Polygamy, or #TurkeyCoup, you know the topic, but you cannot be sure what perspective you will discover. When serendipity occurs, it is typically because a hashtag leads users to perspectives and points of view that they did not expect. The empirical literature is constantly expanding. Consider here a few representative examples.

In a 2016 study, Deen Freelon and his colleagues gathered 40.8 million tweets that included #BlackLivesMatter and related terms and hashtags (generally consisting of the full and hashtagged names of twenty African Americans killed by police over the relevant one-year period).[24] One of their central findings is that activists used hashtags, above all #BlackLivesMatter, for the purposes of both education and amplification, usually seeking to draw attention to what they saw as a form of structural racism. As one activist put it, "Getting something on Twitter means that people are talking, they are conscious. And that consciousness can lead to action."[25] Freelon and his coauthors found that social media posts played a large role in spreading identifiable narratives and accounts of killings by the police. The Black Lives Matter movement had a significant impact on both opinion and action in many cities as well as at the national level. #BlackLivesMatter mattered.

Similar polarization can be seen with the use of #AllLivesMatter, a hashtag whose purpose was to offer a competing narrative to that reflected in #BlackLivesMatter, to the effect that it is partisan or parochial, or even racist, to single out "black lives" for special emphasis. The use of #AllLivesMatter is for identifiable purposes (usually conservative), and it appeals to people with identifiable views, critical of #BlackLivesMatter.[26] Research has found that on social media, "the only other lives that were significantly discussed within #AllLivesMatter are the lives of law enforcement officers, particularly during times in which there is heavy protesting."[27] It is clear that the #AllLivesMatter hashtag arose to create an ideologically defined narrative, clearly showing polarization.

An influential study by Sarida Yardi and dana boyd explored thirty thousand tweets about the 2009 shooting of George Tiller, a late-term abortion doctor, and the subsequent conversations among antiabortion and prochoice advocates. They found that many users adopted hashtags that signaled a specific view about the debate. Importantly, users with the same ideologies were most likely to interact with each other, but not with those with competing views. Moreover, and consistent with my concerns here, Yardi and boyd demonstrated that "replies between like-minded individuals strengthen group identity whereas replies between different-minded individuals reinforce ingroup and outgroup affiliation."[28]

Nonetheless, serendipitous encounters did happen, in the sense that those searching through various hashtags were likely to come across a diverse set of viewpoints. But meaningful discussion across ideological lines remained extremely rare; people with differing points of view were more likely to talk over or past each other than to engage in substantive conversation. In light of the character limit on Twitter, that is not exactly surprising.

An especially interesting line of research explores how members of Congress are using hashtags, often framing issues in their preferred ways and promoting echo chambers that serve their interests.[29] A central finding is that while Democrats and Republicans discuss overlapping issues, they use notably different hashtags. Among Democrats, the most popular issues in the relevant period include health care (#ACA, for the Affordable Care Act), student loans (#DontDoubleMyRate), and employment (#JOBS). The Republicans' top issues are not so different: employment (#4jobs), themselves (#tcot), and health care (#Obamacare). But the two parties do use radically different frames. The term #ACA, preferred by Democrats, has a positive or neutral valence about the Affordable Care Act, whereas #Obamacare and #Fullrepeal, favored by Republicans, are clearly meant to be negative.

Like political activists, members of Congress can be seen as hashtag entrepreneurs. They choose a particular frame: #AllLives Matter, #TheSystemIsRigged, or #CorruptHillary. They hope that it will attract widespread interest, helping to construct both emotions and beliefs. Hashtag entrepreneurship is increasingly central to modern political life.

There is no question that we will learn much more over time. But two conclusions seem plain. First, hashtags work as engines for group polarization (and also cybercascades; see chapter 4). Second, hashtags create communities of interest around identifiable subjects, and those communities can include diverse views. Both of these effects involve a high degree of sorting and filtering, but the second need not produce polarization, and it might result in encounters with widely diverse points of view.

A GLANCE AT POLITICIANS, INCLUDING DONALD TRUMP

All over the world, politicians have been using social media, often to create the conditions for polarization effects. A full discussion would require a book all its own, so consider just two prominent examples.

In the United States, Barack Obama was the first president to use social media to promote his campaign. The numbers from the 2008 general election tell the tale: on every social media platform, Obama did far better than his rival, John McCain. Obama had more than 2 million Facebook supporters, compared to 600,000 for McCain. Obama counted 112,000 active Twitter followers, as opposed 4,600 for McCain. On YouTube, Obama had more videos, subscribers, and video views than did McCain by about four to one.[30] In developing his social media campaign, Obama hired tech entrepreneurs, including Chris Hughes, a cofounder of Facebook.[31] At the height of his campaign, Obama employed 100 staff members devoted to social media.[32] With the help of social media, podcasting, and mobile messaging, Obama managed to capture 70 percent of the group of eighteen- to twenty-five-year-old voters—the highest margin since exit polling started in 1976.[33] Of course we cannot say that his success is attributable to his use of social media. But the Obama campaign used Facebook and Twitter in a way that undoubtedly spurred a high degree of group polarization (with greater enthusiasm among his supporters).

In the 2012 campaign, Obama mobilized social media resources against Mitt Romney. Again, he outperformed his rival by wide margins. He spent ten times more on his digital campaign spending ($47 million versus $4.7 million), garnered twice as many Facebook "likes," and had twenty times more retweets.[34] True, none of that is the best measure of popularity, but it does show far better use of social media.

In the 2016 election, Donald Trump took a unique path. Perhaps because of his background in entertainment, he was able to use social media to excellent effect, with his own preferred hashtags, above all #MakeAmericaGreatAgain but also #CrookedHillary. Even before the Republican convention, Trump had about ten million likes on Facebook, and his YouTube channel had over six million views and forty thousand subscribers.[35] Trump maintained a presence on Vine, Periscope, and Instagram, but his use of Twitter was a defining feature of his campaign, including insults that went viral ("Little Marco," "Lyin' Ted," and again, "Crooked Hillary"). He live-tweeted himself, and in a relatively short period, he came to have more than eleven million followers. That number understates the impact of his tweets, many of which received attention in the national media and hence were greatly amplified. There is no doubt that his activity on Twitter put him at the center of what was, for many, an engine for group polarization—and helped vault him to the presidency.

FRAGMENTATION, POLARIZATION, RADIO, AND TELEVISION

An understanding of group polarization casts light not only on online behavior but also on the potential effects of contemporary radio and television, at least if stations are numerous and many take a well-defined point of view. Recall that mere exposure to the positions of others creates group polarization. It follows that this effect will be at work for nondeliberating groups, in the form of collections of individuals whose communications choices go in the same direction, and who do not expose themselves to alternative positions. The same process is likely to occur for newspaper choices. If some people are reading the liberal newspaper, and others are reading the conservative one, polarization is inevitable. When they are working well, general-interest intermediaries have a distinctive role here by virtue of their effort to present a wide range of topics and views. Polarization is far less likely to happen when such intermediaries dominate the scene. A similar observation can be made about the public forum doctrine. When diverse speakers have access to a heterogeneous public, individuals and groups are less likely to be able to insulate themselves from competing positions and concerns. Fragmentation is correspondingly less likely.

Group polarization also raises more general issues about communications policy. Consider the "fairness doctrine," now largely abandoned, but once requiring radio and television broadcasters to devote time to public issues and allow an opportunity for opposing views to speak. The latter prong of the doctrine was designed to ensure that listeners would not be exposed to any single view. If one view was covered, the opposing position would have to be allowed a right of access.

When the Federal Communications Commission abandoned the fairness doctrine, it did so on the ground that much of the time, this second prong led broadcasters to avoid controversial issues entirely and to present views in a way that suggested a bland uniformity. Subsequent research has indicated that the commission was right. The elimination of the fairness doctrine has indeed produced a flowering of controversial substantive programming, sometimes involving extreme views of one kind or another; consider talk radio.[36]

Typically this is regarded as a story of wonderfully successful deregulation, and in general that is correct. The effects of eliminating the fairness doctrine were precisely what was sought and intended. Those effects are indeed good, and they should be celebrated. But if we attend to the problem of group polarization, the evaluation is a bit more complicated. On the good side, the existence of diverse pockets of opinion enriches society's total argument pool, potentially to the benefit of all of us. At the same time, the growth of a wide variety of issue-oriented programming—expressing strong, often extreme perspectives, and appealing to dramatically different groups of listeners and viewers—undoubtedly creates group polarization. All too many people are now exposed mostly to louder echoes of their own voices, resulting, on too many occasions, in misunderstanding and enmity. On one view, it is better for people to hear fewer controversial positions than for them to hear a single such view, stated over and over again.

I do not suggest or believe that the fairness doctrine should be restored. Law professor Heather Gerken has rightly drawn attention to "second-order diversity"—the kind of diversity that comes when society consists of many institutions and groups, some of which have little in the way of internal diversity.[37] As Gerken has shown, we all benefit from a decentralized system in which different groups have different predispositions and sometimes go to different extremes. Instead of seeking diversity *within* each group, we might want diverse groups, even if many or most demonstrate little internal diversity.

The same goes for communications outlets (and social media as well). If some radio shows press quite conservative arguments, and others press quite liberal ones, we might all be able to benefit from what emerges. It's a strong argument. But at the very least, there is a risk in the current situation that too many people will choose to insulate themselves from exposure to views that are more moderate, extreme in another direction, or in any case different from their own.

IS GROUP POLARIZATION BAD? OF ENCLAVE DELIBERATION

Notwithstanding the tenor of the discussion thus far, we cannot always say, from the mere fact of group polarization, that there has been a movement in the *wrong* direction. In some cases, the more extreme tendency is better rather than worse. It might even be much better. Indeed, group polarization has helped fuel many movements of great value—including, for example, the civil rights movement, the antislavery movement, the disability rights movement, the movement for equality between men and women, and the movement for same-sex marriage. All these movements were extreme in their time, and within-group discussion certainly bred greater extremism, but extremism need not be a word of opprobrium. If greater communications choices produce greater extremism, society may be better off as a result.

One reason is that when many different groups are deliberating with one another, society will hear a far wider range of views; recall the idea of second-order diversity. Even if the "information diet" of many individuals is homogeneous or insufficiently diverse, society as a whole might have a richer and fuller set of ideas. This is another side of the general picture of social fragmentation. It suggests some large benefits from pluralism and diversity—benefits even if individuals customize and cluster in groups. Another benefit of clustering is that it can counteract "epistemic injustice," in which people lack a sufficient ability to interpret their experiences, and in which they cannot obtain a hearing for those experiences.[38] Social media can counteract that injustice. In fact, they do that every day.

We might define *enclave deliberation* as that form of deliberation that occurs within more or less insulated groups, in which like-minded people speak mostly to one another. The Internet, including social media, makes it much easier (and less costly) to engage in enclave deliberation. Your Facebook page might itself allow for a form of such deliberation. It is obvious that enclave deliberation can be extremely important in a heterogeneous society, not least because members of some groups tend to be especially quiet when participating in broader deliberative bodies.

In this light, a special advantage of enclave deliberation is that it promotes the development of understanding, knowledge, and positions that would otherwise be invisible, silenced, or squelched in general debate. The efforts of marginalized groups to exclude out-siders, and even of political parties to limit their primaries to party members, might be justified in similar terms. Even if group polar-ization is at work—perhaps *because* group polarization is at work—enclaves, emphatically including those produced by social media, can provide a wide range of social benefits, not least because they greatly enrich the social "argument pool." There is no question that Twitter in particular is doing exactly that.

A central empirical point here is that in deliberating bodies, high-status members tend to speak more than others, and their ideas are more influential—partly because low-status members sometimes lack confidence in their own abilities, and partly be-cause they fear retribution.[39] For example, women's ideas are often less influential and sometimes are "suppressed altogether in mixed-gender groups."[40] In many circumstances, cultural minorities have disproportionately little influence on decisions by culturally mixed groups. In light of the inevitable existence of some status-based hierarchies, it makes sense to be receptive to deliberating enclaves in which members of multiple groups may speak with one another and develop their views. Online communication is especially valu-able insofar as it makes this easier.

But there is also a serious danger in such enclaves. The danger is that members will move to positions that lack merit but are pre-dictable consequences of the particular circumstances of enclave deliberation. In extreme cases, enclave deliberation may even put social stability at risk. And it is impossible to say, in the abstract, that those who sort themselves into enclaves will generally move in a direction that is desirable for society at large or even its own members.

It is easy to think of illustrations to the contrary—as, for in-stance, in the rise of Nazism, hate groups, terrorism, and cults of various sorts. If we take the idea of cults broadly enough, we can find them all over social media, such as people who believe that Barack Obama was not born in the United States, Israel was re-sponsible for the attacks of 9/11, vaccines cause autism, or Elvis

Presley is still alive. And of course terrorist organizations present special challenges on this count—a point to which I will return.

ENCLAVES AND A PUBLIC SPHERE

Whenever group discussion tends to lead people to more strongly held versions of the same view with which they began, there is legitimate reason for concern. Certainly this does not mean that the discussions can or should be regulated. But it does raise questions about the idea that "more speech" is necessarily an adequate remedy for bad speech—especially if many people are inclined and increasingly able to wall themselves off from competing views. In democratic societies, a possible response is suggested by the public forum doctrine, whose most fundamental goal is to increase the likelihood that at certain points, there is an exchange of views between enclave members and those who disagree with them. It is total or near-total self-insulation, rather than group deliberation as such, that carries with it the most serious dangers, often in the highly unfortunate (and sometimes literally deadly) combination of extremism with marginalization.

To explore some of the advantages of heterogeneity, let us engage in a thought experiment. Imagine a deliberating body consisting not of a subset of like-minded people but instead all citizens in the relevant group; this may mean all citizens in a community, a state, a nation, or even the world. Imagine that through the magic of the computer, everyone can talk to everyone else. By hypothesis, the argument pool would be enormous. It would be limited only to the extent that the set of citizen views was similarly limited.

Of course, reputational influences would remain. If you are one of a small minority of people who deny that global warming is a serious problem, you might decide to join the crowd. But when deliberation revealed to people that their private position was different in relation to the group from what they thought it was, any shift would be in response to an accurate understanding of all relevant citizens, and not a product of a skewed sample. And in fact, we can think of some online efforts as attempting to approximate this thought experiment. Wikipedia, for example, allows anyone to be an editor (within limits), and the theory is that countless people can contribute their dispersed information to produce a resource offering an immense amount of human knowledge. This largely successful effort, resulting in a single product to which all can contribute, might be compared with deliberating enclaves of like-minded people.

The thought experiment, or the Wikipedia example, does not suggest that a fragmented or balkanized speech market is always bad, or that the hypothesized, all-inclusive deliberating body would be ideal. It would be foolish to suggest that all discussion should occur, even as an ideal, with all others. The great benefit of deliberating enclaves is that positions may emerge that otherwise would not, and they deserve to play a larger role within both the enclave and the heterogeneous public. Properly understood, the case for deliberating enclaves is that they will improve social deliberation, democratic and otherwise, precisely because enclave deliberation is often required for incubating new ideas and perspectives that will add a great deal to public debate. Social media, including Facebook, Twitter, Instagram, and Snapchat, can be exemplary here.

But for these improvements to take place, members must not insulate themselves from competing positions. At the very least, any such attempt at insulation must not be a prolonged affair. The phenomenon of group polarization suggests that with respect to communications, consumer sovereignty might well produce serious problems for individuals and society at large—and these problems will occur by a kind of iron logic of social interaction.

NO POLARIZATION AND DEPOLARIZATION

It is not exactly news that political candidates and their supporters are using the Internet, including social media, to their advantage. What is perhaps more interesting is that candidates for public office and their supporters have also been using the Internet, including social media, in a way that shows an intuitive understanding of group polarization. Their sites operate as forums in which like-minded people congregate and adopt shared positions about policies, adversaries, and their candidates. Candidates try to produce echo chambers—their own online version of the Colorado experiment in which social interactions produce more consensus and enthusiasm—eventually yielding both time and money. The mechanisms discussed here may or may not cause harm, but those who are aware of them can certainly use them strategically. In the 2016 campaign for the presidency, Donald Trump showed a keen working knowledge of social influences and group polarization, constantly emphasizing how popular he was, and pointing constantly to the polls as evidence.

In certain circumstances, however, polarization can be decreased or even eliminated. No shift should be expected from people who are quite confident about what they think, and who are simply not going to be moved by what they hear from other people. If you are entirely sure of your position with respect to nuclear power—if you are confident not only of your precise view but of the degree of confidence with which you ought to hold it too—the positions of other people will not affect you. People of this sort will not shift by virtue of any changes in the communications market.

I have mentioned that federal judges are prone to polarization: Republican appointees show especially conservative voting patterns when sitting with fellow Republican appointees, and Democratic appointees show especially liberal voting patterns when sitting with fellow Democratic appointees. But on two issues, federal judges appear to be uninfluenced by their peers: abortion and capital punishment.[41] On these issues, federal judges show essentially the same voting patterns regardless of whether they are sitting with zero, one, or two judges appointed by a president of the same political party as the president who appointed them. Apparently there is no polarization on abortion and capital punishment simply because judges' views are deeply held and entrenched. We can easily imagine other issues about which ordinary people are similarly unlikely to be affected by group members. In the political domain, polarization finds its limits here, whatever candidates attempt to do.

With artful design of deliberating groups, moreover, it is possible to produce *depolarization*—shifts toward the middle, away from the extremes. Suppose, for example, that a group of twelve people is constructed so as to include six people who have one view and six people who think the opposite—say, half the group's members believe that air pollution from particulate matter is a serious problem, while the other half think that it is not. If most of the members do not have entirely fixed positions, there is likely to be real movement toward the middle. The persuasive arguments view helps explain why this is so. By hypothesis, the "argument pool" includes an equal number of claims both ways. If people are willing to dismiss those who disagree with them, depolarization might not occur. A group consisting of three Israelis and three members of Hamas might not depolarize; group members might simply dismiss the views of those who disagree. But for many questions, people are likely to listen to one another and hence depolarization is possible.

Of course mixed groups are no panacea. Typically group members end up at a more extreme point in line with the predeliberation tendency. No less than like-minded groups, mixed groups can polarize.[42] More generally, confronting opposing positions can dampen political participation, in part because people who become more ambivalent and more uncertain about their own views might simply stand to one side.[43]

But mixed groups have been shown to have two desirable effects. First, exposure to competing positions generally increases political tolerance.[44] After hearing a variety of views, including those that diverge from their own, many people are more respectful of alternative positions, and more willing to consider them to be plausible or legitimate. An important result of seeing a political conflict as legitimate is a "greater willingness to extend civil liberties to even those groups whose political views one dislikes a great deal."[45]

Second, mixing increases the likelihood that people will be aware of competing rationales and see that their own arguments might be met with plausible counterarguments.[46] This effect is especially pronounced for those who start with a "civil orientation toward conflict," in the sense that they are committed to a degree of social harmony and are willing to acknowledge in advance that dissenting views should be expressed.[47] These desirable effects of deliberation within mixed groups will not be realized in any deliberative process in which people are sorted or sort themselves into politically homogeneous groups.

There is a valuable lesson about possible uses of communications technologies to produce convergence and possibly even learning among people who disagree with one another. If people hear a wide range of arguments, they are more likely to be moved in the direction of those who disagree with them, at least if the arguments are reasonable, and if those who disagree cannot easily be dismissed as untrustworthy or unreliable.

BALANCED PRESENTATIONS, UNBALANCED VIEWS

Unfortunately, a diverse collection of studies also establishes that when people are exposed to balanced information, movements toward the middle might not occur. For over three decades, it has been well known that such information might not produce consensus, even if it appears directly to address the concerns that led in the first place to divided views. The underlying phenomenon is typically described as *biased assimilation*.[48] The basic idea is that people assimilate information in a way that is skewed in the direction of support for their prior beliefs.[49]

The initial studies involved capital punishment.[50] People were asked to read several studies arguing both in favor of and against the view that capital punishment deterred crime. A key finding was that both supporters and opponents of the death penalty were far more convinced by the studies supporting their own beliefs than by those challenging them. After reading the opposing studies, both sides reported that their beliefs had shifted toward a stronger commitment to what they originally thought.

One consequence is that the two sides were more polarized than they were before they began to read. That looks a lot like group polarization—but it happened in response to balanced presentations, not echo chambers.

Similar findings have been made in many contexts.[51] For example, experiments provided people with competing views on the questions whether sexual orientation has a genetic component and whether same-sex couples are likely to be good parents. After receiving information on both sides of those issues, people's preexisting beliefs were *strengthened*—and there was greater, not less, polarization on the issue of same-sex relationships.[52] In studies of this kind, people are provided with "pro" and "con" arguments, and at least under certain conditions, provision of such arguments leads to an increase in polarization.

All this complicates the story I am telling here, and it has clear implications for social media: if people online encounter a wide range of views, they might not depolarize at all—at least if they listen to people with whom they are inclined to agree and dismiss everybody else.

WHEN CORRECTIONS BACKFIRE

Suppose that a society is divided on some proposition. The first group believes A, and the second group believes not-A. Suppose that the first group is entirely correct, and that the second group is full of nonsense. Finally, suppose that truthful information is provided, not from members of the first group, but from some independent source, in support of A. It would be reasonable—you might think—to suppose that the second group would come to believe A.

But in important settings, the opposite happens. The second group continues to believe not-A, and even more firmly than before. The result of the correction is to increase polarization.

In one experiment, people were exposed to a mock news article in which President George W. Bush defended the Iraq War, in part by suggesting (as he in fact did) that there "was a risk, a real risk, that Saddam Hussein would pass weapons or materials or information to terrorist networks."[53] After reading this article, people in the experiment read about the Duelfer Report, which documented the lack of weapons of mass destruction in Iraq. People were then asked to state their agreement, on a five-point scale (from "strongly agree" to "strongly disagree"), with the statement that Iraq "had an active weapons of mass destruction program, the ability to produce these weapons, and large stockpiles of WMD."

The effect of the correction greatly varied by political ideology. For very liberal subjects, there was a modest shift in favor of disagreement with this statement; the shift was not significant, because these subjects already tended to disagree with it. But for those who characterized themselves as conservative, there was a statistically significant shift in the direction of *agreeing* with the statement. "In other words, the correction backfired— conservatives who received a correction telling them that Iraq did not have WMD were more likely to believe that Iraq had WMD than those in the control condition."[54] It follows that the correction had a polarizing effect; it divided people more sharply, on the issue at hand, than they had been divided before.

An independent study confirmed the more general effect. People were asked to evaluate the proposition that cutting taxes is so effective in stimulating economic growth that it actually increases government revenue. They were then asked to read a correction from either the *New York Times* or foxnews.com. The correction turned out to increase people's commitments to the proposition in question: "Conservatives presented with evidence that tax cuts do not increase government revenues ended up believing this claim more fervently than those who did not receive a correction."[55]

Liberals are hardly immune to this effect.[56] In 2005, many liberals believed, wrongly, that President Bush imposed a ban on stem cell research. Presented with a correction from the *New York Times* or foxnews.com, liberals continued to believe what they did before. By contrast, conservatives accepted the correction. Hence the correction produced an increase in polarization.

Importantly but not surprisingly, it mattered, in terms of the basic effect, whether the correction came from the *New York Times* or Fox News: conservatives distrusted the former more, and liberals distrusted the latter more.

Think in this light about social media. If your Twitter feed is insisting that a particular scandal happened, or that some public official was reckless or worse, how likely is it that a correction will move you? How likely is it that people will see through fake news?

UNFAMILIAR ISSUES

What if the underlying issue is not familiar? In that event, will balanced information produce polarization or consensus? A measure of agreement might well be expected, if only because people do not begin with strong prior convictions. Online, we often encounter issues that we know nothing about. Maybe the balance of arguments will determine our answers? A study of nanotechnology casts light on that question.[57]

A large set of Americans was divided into two groups. In the "no-information" condition, people were simply told that nanotechnology is a process for producing and manipulating small particles. In that condition, people did not divide along ideological lines about the costs and benefits of using nanotechnology. There were no evident splits between conservatives and liberals, or Republicans or Democrats. Apparently the issue seemed highly technical, and the mere name and description did not split people along any relevant lines.

In the "information-exposed" condition, people were given factual material on the potential risks and benefits of nanotechnology. Notably, exposure to information had essentially no effect on people's views about those risks and benefits. But such exposure did split people in accordance with their preexisting political orientations. Those who tended to like free markets and distrust government interference ended up more favorably disposed toward the use of nanotechnology. Those who tended to favor social equality and trust government to promote social goals ended up less favorably disposed toward that use.

In the no-information condition, there was essentially no division between the two groups in their belief that the benefits of nanotechnology outweighed the risks. By a small majority (61 percent), both groups tended to accept that belief. But after exposure to balanced information, the split grew from 0 to 68 percent, with 86 percent of free market enthusiasts believing that the benefits outweighed the costs, and only 23 percent of egalitarians so believing.

For the idea of online learning, that's a definite problem.

MAKING SENSE

Here's a way to understand some of these studies. When people start with strong convictions and really know what they think, they're a lot less likely to be moved by contrary arguments. One reason is that they can just dismiss them, given what they already know. If you believe that the Holocaust happened, you won't be much affected by some report suggesting that the whole idea is a concoction of Jewish historians.

Suppose that contrary arguments have no effect on you, but that supportive arguments and new information in line with what you already think strengthen your convictions. That's certainly been known to happen. Sure enough, balanced presentations should end up fortifying those convictions. And if such presentations involve an unfamiliar subject, such as nanotechnology, something similar should happen, at least if the presentations end up triggering your long-standing concerns.

A second factor involves emotions, not knowledge. If you are strongly committed to a certain belief—say, that climate change is a serious problem—a contrary argument might do little to inform you. It might just make you mad. And if you're mad, you might more strongly hold the views with which you began. It is for this reason, in part, that corrections might not move you. And you might also wonder, Why would they issue that correction, if the underlying claim weren't true? Aren't they hiding something?

These points suggest that the findings of the various studies are important, but only in certain settings, and they do not capture how most people deal with most of what they see in print or online. True, if people begin with strong commitments, they aren't easy to move, and contrary arguments might backfire—at least if they do not come from a reliable source. That clarifies why the phenomenon of group polarization is paralleled by that of biased assimilation, which in turn means that if people get diverse sources of information online, they might polarize too. But for many issues, people aren't all that sure what they think. They start with a degree of open-mindedness. They're searching. They don't begin with intensely held convictions, and even if they tend to know what they think, they're willing to listen.

It follows that on a wide assortment of issues, it's a good thing if people do not sort themselves into communities of like-minded types. Let's not be too optimistic—but it's even possible that the truth will emerge.

CYBERCASCADES

Any discussion of social fragmentation and online behavior requires an understanding of social cascades—above all because they become more likely when information, including false information, can be spread to hundreds, thousands, or even millions by the simple press of a button. Cascades are often hard or even impossible to predict, but they are all around us, and they organize our culture and even our lives. Increasingly, cascades are a product of social media. They occur within isolated communities, which develop a commitment to certain products, films, books, or ideas. Terrorists, rebels, and revolutionaries attempt to create and use them. Frequently cascades take hold far more generally, helping to produce (for example) a right to same-sex marriage, a rebellion against an authoritarian government, a nation's exit from the European Union, a new president, or a massively popular new cell phone.

It is obvious that many social groups, both large and small, move rapidly and dramatically in the direction of one or another set of beliefs or actions.[1] These sorts of cascades typically involve the spread of information; in fact, they are usually *driven* by information. Almost all of us lack direct or entirely reliable information about many matters of importance—whether George Washington actually lived, whether the earth goes around the sun, whether matter contains molecules, whether dinosaurs existed, whether there is a risk of war in India, whether the Islamic State of Iraq and the Levant (ISIL) is dangerous, whether a lot of sugar is actually bad for you, or whether Mars is real. For the vast majority of your beliefs, you really don't have direct information. You rely on the statements or actions of trusted others.

TWO KINDS OF CASCADES

To understand the social dynamics here, we need to distinguish between two kinds of cascades: informational and reputational.

Informational cascades. In an informational cascade, people cease relying at a certain point on their private information or opinions. They decide instead on the basis of the signals conveyed by others. It follows that the behavior of the first few people, or even one, can in theory produce similar behavior from countless followers.

To use a stylized example, suppose that Joan is unsure whether climate change is a serious problem. She may be moved to think that it is if her friend Mary thinks and says that climate change is a serious problem. If Joan and Mary are both favorably alarmed about climate change, their friend Carl may end up agreeing with them, at least if he lacks reliable independent information to the contrary. If Joan, Mary, and Carl believe that climate change is a serious problem, their friend Don will need to have a good deal of confidence to reject their shared conclusion. And if Joan, Mary, Carl, and Don present a united front on the issue, their other friends and even acquaintances may well go along. Something like this happens online every day.

It is important to emphasize a wrinkle here, which is that if one person sees that five, ten, a hundred, or a thousand people are inclined to say or do something, there is a tendency to think that each and every individual has made an independent decision to say or do it. The reality may well be that only a small fraction of the group made an independent decision. The rest are following the crowd, thus amplifying the very signal to which they were themselves subject. That signal may be extremely loud and seem quite impressive even though it incorporates the judgments of remarkably few people.

Environmental issues provide examples of how information travels, and can become quite widespread and entrenched, whether or not it is right. A disturbing illustration is the widespread popular belief that abandoned hazardous waste dumps rank among the most serious environmental problems; science does not support that belief, which seems to have spread via cascade.[2] Another environmental example is the widespread and false belief that foods containing GMOs are hazardous to people's health; the scientific consensus is that they are not. Many cascades are widespread but local; consider the view, which had real currency in some African American communities in the 1980s, that white doctors are responsible for the spread of AIDS among African Americans. Or consider the notion, apparently widely held among American conservatives, that President Obama was not born in the United States—and the opinion, held by many parents and apparently defended at one point by Donald Trump, that vaccinations cause autism. One group may end up believing something, and another the exact opposite, and the reason is the rapid transmission of information within one group but not the other.

Even among specialists and indeed doctors, cascades are common. "Most doctors are not at the cutting edge of research; their inevitable reliance upon what colleagues have done and are doing leads to numerous surgical fads and treatment-caused illnesses."[3] Thus an article in the influential *New England Journal of Medicine* explores "bandwagon diseases" in which doctors act like "lemmings, episodically and with a blind infectious enthusiasm pushing certain diseases and treatments primarily because everyone else is doing the same."[4] It should be easy to see how cascades might develop among groups of citizens. And when informational cascades are operating, there is a serious social problem: people who are in the cascade do not disclose to their successors and the public the information (or reservations) that they privately hold.

Reputational cascades. We can also imagine the possibility of reputational cascades, parallel to their informational siblings.[5] In a reputational cascade, people think that they know what is right, or what is likely to be right, but they nonetheless go along with the crowd in order to maintain the good opinion of others. Even the most confident people sometimes fall prey to this pressure, silencing themselves in the process. Fearing the wrath of others, people might not publicly contest practices and values that they privately abhor.

The social practice of sexual harassment long predated the legal notion of "sexual harassment," and the innumerable women who were subject to harassment did not like it. But mostly they were silent, simply because they feared the consequences of public complaint. It is interesting to wonder how many current practices fall in the same general category—they produce harm, and are known to produce harm, but they persist because most of those who are harmed believe that they will suffer if they object in public. Whole governments can fall once reputational cascades start growing, as they often do when people learn that their disaffection is widely shared.

To see how a reputational cascade might work, suppose that Albert suggests vaccinations can cause autism, and Barbara concurs with Albert, not because she actually thinks that Albert is right, but because she does not wish to seem, to Albert, to be ignorant or indifferent to a serious risk faced by children. If Albert and Barbara seem to agree that vaccinations can cause autism, Cynthia might not contradict them publicly and might even appear to share their judgment, not because she believes that judgment to be correct, but because she does not want to face their hostility or lose their good opinion.

It is easy to see how this process might generate a reputational cascade. Once Albert, Barbara, and Cynthia offer a united front on the issue, their friend David might be most reluctant to contradict them even if he thinks that they are wrong. The apparent views of Albert, Barbara, and Cynthia carry information; that apparent view might be right. But even if David thinks that they are wrong and has information supporting that conclusion, he might be most reluctant to take them on publicly. Reputational cascades impose increasing pressure as larger numbers of people join the cascade. A position that was once highly unpopular, leading people to silence themselves, may come to seem widely held, so much so that people risk their reputations if they oppose it.

INFORMATION AS WILDFIRE AND TIPPING POINTS

The Internet greatly increases the likelihood of diverse but inconsistent cascades. Cybercascades occur every day. On Twitter and Facebook, you can find them in an instant. They might involve politics, miraculous products, deadly diseases, conspiracies, unsafe food, supposed events in Moscow or Berlin, or anything else.

Here is some fun and illuminating evidence of how online cascades can happen, from the domain of music.[6] A team of experimenters, led by Matthew Salganik, Peter Dodds, and Duncan Watts, created an artificial music lab, including 14,341 participants. The participants were given a list of dozens of previously unknown songs from unknown bands; they were asked to listen to a brief selection of any songs of interest to them, decide what songs (if any) to download, and assign a rating to the songs they chose. About half the participants were asked to make their decisions independently, based on the names of the bands and the songs and their own judgment about the quality of the music. About half the participants could see how many times each song had been downloaded by other participants. These participants were also randomly assigned to one or another of eight possible "worlds," or subgroups, with each evolving on its own; those in any particular world could see only the downloads in their own world. A key question was whether people would be affected by the choices of others—and whether different music would become popular in the different "worlds."

Did social influences matter? Did cascades develop? There is not the slightest doubt. In all eight worlds, individuals were more likely to download songs that had been previously downloaded in significant numbers, and less likely to download those that had not been so popular. Most strikingly, the success of songs turned out to be almost entirely unpredictable! Almost all the songs could become popular or unpopular, with everything depending on the choices of the first downloaders. The identical song could be a hit or a failure—simply because other people, at the start, were seen to choose to download it or not. (Think for a moment about how rumors spread or fail to spread on social media.)

To be sure, there is some relationship between quality and success. "In general, the 'best' songs never do very badly, and the 'worst' songs never do extremely well, but almost any other result is possible."[7] But even for the best and worst songs, there's a high degree of unpredictability in terms of ultimate market shares, depending on whether they benefit from early popularity—and for the vast majority of songs, everything turns on social influences.

Salganik, Dodds, and Watts acknowledge that in many ways, the real world is different from this experiment. They in fact controlled numerous variables, ensuring that their results are weaker than what happens in actual markets, where unpredictability is even greater, and where cascades are inevitable. Media attention, marketing efforts, critical reviews, and other pressures inflate the role of social influences. When experts fail to predict success, it is "because when individual decisions are subject to social influence, markets do not simply aggregate pre-existing individual preferences."[8] Note here that marketers often try hard to create early online "buzz" by suggesting that a certain cultural product is already popular; indeed, some marketing efforts actually involve artificial efforts to overstate the demand for the product, through purchases not by ordinary people, but by those allied with the artist.

Social media are full of such efforts. An acquaintance of mine, the author of an excellent book in the general domain of behavioral science, has tweeted on numerous occasions something like, "My book is doing great and well above expectations! Thanks for the support!" Actually the book isn't doing so great, but the author knows well that if people think that other people are buying it, they'll be more likely to buy it themselves.

Consider in this regard the 2013 Oscar winner for best documentary, *Searching for Sugar Man*, a stunning film about an unsuccessful Detroit singer-songwriter named Sixto Rodriguez, who released two long-forgotten albums in the early 1970s. Almost no one bought his albums, and his label dropped him. Rodriguez stopped making records and worked as a demolition man. What Rodriguez didn't know, while working in demolition, was that he had become a spectacular success in South Africa—a giant, a legend, comparable to the Beatles and the Rolling Stones. Describing him as "the soundtrack to our lives," South Africans bought hundreds of thousands of copies of his albums, starting in the 1970s. *Searching for Sugar Man* is about the contrast between the failed career of Detroit's obscure demolition man and the renown of South Africa's mysterious rock icon.

The film is easily taken as a real-world fairy tale, barely believable—a story so extraordinary that it gives new meaning to "you couldn't make it up." But as the music lab experiment shows, it is a bit less extraordinary than it seems, and it offers a profound lesson not only for music and culture markets but for business and politics as well.

We like to think that intrinsic quality produces success, and that quality will ultimately prevail in free markets. To be sure, quality is usually necessary, but it's not enough. Social dynamics—who is conveying enthusiasm to whom, and how loudly, and where, and exactly when—can separate the rock icon from the demolition man, and mark the line between stunning success and crashing failure.

And if this is true for online music, it is likely to be so for many other things as well, including movies, books, political candidates, and even ideas. ("Everyone is flocking to candidate X," or "idea Y is really catching on.") Candidates and ideas may enjoy stunning success (or failure) simply because social dynamics give them an early boost (or not). Here we can see a large effect from collaborative filtering, which may help move or entrench, and not merely reflect, individual preferences.

POLITICAL CASCADES AND TURBULENCE

These points suggest a hypothesis: political life is a lot like the music lab. In fact, it is a kind of real-world politics lab. Bill Clinton, George W. Bush, Obama, and Trump succeeded not only because of their evident talents but also because they received the equivalent of many early downloads. There are many talented politicians who never succeeded, and the reason isn't that they were not quite talented enough. It is that they failed to attract the right level of attention, either early or at some crucial time. The same is true for policy reforms.

It is not simple to test this hypothesis, but Helen Margetts, Peter John, Scott Hale, and Taha Yasseri have made significant strides in their book, *Political Turbulence*.[9] Their subtitle is *How Social Media Shape Collective Action*, but their thesis is far more specific and striking. They argue that there is a great deal of unpredictability in modern political life, that the level of predictability is significantly increased by social media, and that social influences heighten unpredictability. Explicitly referring to the music lab experiment, they claim that in the age of social media, political movements are likely to be highly turbulent.

With respect to social influences, some of their best evidence comes from petitions. Both the United Kingdom and the United States have created online petition platforms. Most petitions fail—and fail quickly. No one pays them the slightest attention. As it turns out, the first day that a petition becomes public is critical. Early popularity makes all the difference, because political momentum builds on itself. In the United Kingdom, five hundred signatures are required to obtain an official response, and a large percentage of successful petitions get there within two days. It is reasonable to think that a certain (small) number of petitions spur and benefit from early cascade effects; they are a lot like Rodriguez in South Africa. But the vast majority of petitions fail to do that; they are just like Rodriguez in the United States.

That is indeed a reasonable thought, but it is not the only reading of the data. It is possible that some petitions receive large numbers of independent signatories, and that social influences do not much matter. But Margetts and her colleagues offer strong reasons to think otherwise. For one thing, social media have a large effect. The number of signatures and the number of tweets are closely correlated; the more tweets, the more signatures. The authors' analysis of both timing and content suggests that tweets are driving signatures, rather than the other way around.

But the strongest evidence of the power of social influences comes from the fact that in April 2012, the UK Cabinet Office introduced "trending petitions" information on its web page so that everyone could see which petitions were succeeding and how many other people had signed. Margetts and her colleagues explore the effects of that information. Somewhat surprisingly, it had no effect on the overall level of petition signing. But it greatly affected the distribution of signatures. Using a method akin to that in the music lab study, the researchers find that *after the trending information was introduced, signatures were much more concentrated on a small number of petitions*. That is important evidence that "the information-rich get richer, and the information-poor get poorer."[10] Note that we are speaking here of what kinds of petitions receive attention from high levels of government. On that question, what is observed mirrors the music lab experiment.

As one might expect, Margetts and her colleagues find that small design changes can have large and unintended consequences. The United Kingdom lists the top six petitions (measured by number of signatures) in order on its website, and it also provides visitors with the option to click to see six more. Margetts and her colleagues tested whether and how the trending information affected people's signatures. The details of the test need not detain us, but the central finding is major: the first-ranked positions received more concentrated attention—and signatures—as a result of that information. The upshot is that "the addition of the trending petitions facility causes the most popular trending petitions to receive more signatures, and that these signatures come at the expense of signatures to other petitions on the site."[11] We can undoubtedly reach broadly similar conclusions about how social media might promote or undermine political candidates. One result is unpredictability and turbulence, as modest differences in initial popularity map onto long-term variations.

As a further test of social influences, the researchers enlisted a website, WriteToThem, designed to help visitors write to public officials. The site reduces the costs of citizen engagement. In an experiment, people were randomly assigned to one of two groups. The first was the control, in which visitors to the site saw no social information. The second was the treatment, in which visitors could see how many others had written to a particular representative. Overall, 39 percent of those visitors who went to the page for their own representative ended up sending a letter. But there was a substantial difference between the two groups: 32.6 percent in the control, and 49.1 percent in the treatment.

Surprisingly, it did not matter, in the treatment group, whether the social information showed low, medium, or high levels of writing from previous visitors. What mattered was the information as such. One reason may be that people did not have the comparative information right before them; without a little work, they would not see that some representatives had higher percentages than others. Another reason may be that the differences between low (around 47 percent) and high (around 53 percent) were quite modest. With a wider range, we might expect something more like the music lab experiment and the petition data, where variations in numbers really did matter (and were visible).

This expectation is strongly supported by another experiment by the same researchers, testing people's willingness to sign petitions and pledge small donations on an assortment of political issues, such as climate change, protection of humpback whales, protection of the people of Darfur, negotiation of new trade rules to combat poverty, and protection of human rights in China. In the control group, people saw the petitions in random order. In the treatment groups, people did so as well, but they were also given social information, stating whether there were already large numbers of signatories (over one million), small numbers (less than a hundred), or medium numbers (ranging from a hundred to one million).

Overall, people in the control group signed 61.5 percent of the petitions. As compared to the control, small and medium numbers had no significant effect on whether people signed. But for those who saw large numbers, there was a real impact; that treatment group signed 66.7 percent of the time. True, that is not the level of effect that is observed in the music lab experiment (or the petition study). But it makes sense to think that the participants in this experiment were already inclined to sign, as reflected by the 61.5 percent overall signature rate, so that a massive difference among treatment conditions should not be expected. What matters is that high numbers had a consistent and statistically significant impact on the likelihood of signing—consistent in the sense that it cut across every one of the tested issues, notwithstanding varying levels of initial support.

Emphasizing that people with different personality traits show different propensities to engage, that it matters whether engagement is visible, and that people show different levels of susceptibility to social influences, Margetts and her colleagues conclude that "tiny acts," made possible by social media, are "a growing form of political participation, which in some countries and contexts is overtaking voting as the political act that people are most likely to undertake."[12]

Their most striking finding involves the nature of the underlying social dynamics. According to the researchers, "extroversion" predicts a willingness to participate at an early stage; if there is a significant number of extroverts, people with higher thresholds for participation might be moved—and once they are moved, those with lower thresholds will join, eventually encompassing large numbers of people. Because the costs of participating are so low (if only via a "like," a retweet, or a signature), millions of people can form a movement in this way. And indeed, processes of this general kind seemed to have played a role in the collapse of authoritarian nations in North Africa—and in the fullness of time, they are likely to have large effects elsewhere as well.[13]

RUMORS AND TIPPING

On the Internet, rumors often spread rapidly, and cascades are frequently involved. Many of us have been deluged with e-mails about the need to contact our representatives about some bill or other—only to learn that the bill did not exist, and the whole problem was a joke or a fraud. Even more of us have been earnestly warned about the need to take precautions against viruses that do not exist. In the 1990s, many thousands of hours of Internet time were spent on elaborating paranoid claims about alleged nefarious activities, including murder, on the part of President Clinton. Numerous sites, discussion groups, and social media posts spread rumors and conspiracy theories of various sorts. An old one: "Electrified by the Internet, suspicions about the crash of TWA Flight 800 were almost instantly transmuted into convictions that it was the result of friendly fire. . . . It was all linked to Whitewater. . . . Ideas become E-mail to be duplicated and duplicated again."[14] In 2000, an e-mail rumor specifically targeted at African Americans alleged that "No Fear" bumper stickers bearing the logo of the sportswear company of the same name really promote a racist organization headed by former Ku Klux Klan grand wizard David Duke.

Both terrorism and voting behavior have been prime areas for false rumors, fake news, and cascade effects. In 2002, a widely circulated e-mail said that a Boeing aircraft had not in fact hit the Pentagon on September 11. In 2004, many people were duly informed that electronic voting machines had been hacked, producing massive fraud. (If you're interested in more examples, you might consult www.snopes.com, a website dedicated to widely disseminated falsehoods, many of them spread via the Internet.)

During the Obama presidency, countless e-mails were widely circulated about the alleged misconduct, incompetence, lying, disloyalty, and weirdness of President Obama and those who worked for him. The idea that Obama was born in Kenya (propagated by Donald Trump, among many others) is just one prominent example; another is that he is a Muslim. From 2009 to 2012, I had the honor of working in the Obama administration, and I was stunned to see the spread of false rumors about my own conduct and beliefs. (Some people said that I wanted to "steal people's organs"; others said that I was behind Wikileaks.) What is especially interesting is that those who believe such rumors need not be irrational. They are simply reacting to what other people seem to believe.

Most of these examples are innocuous, because no real harm is done, and because many cascades can be corrected. But as a disturbingly harmful illustration, consider widespread doubts in South Africa in the 1980s about the connection between HIV and AIDS. Because the AIDS virus infected a significant percentage of the adult population, any such doubts were especially troublesome. South African president Thabo Mbeki was a well-known Internet surfer, and he learned the views of the "denialists" after stumbling across one of their websites. The views of the denialists were and are not scientifically respectable—but to a nonspecialist, many of the claims on their (many) sites seemed plausible. At least for a period, President Mbeki both fell victim to a cybercascade and, through his public statements, helped to accelerate one—to the point where many South Africans at serious risk were not convinced of an association between HIV and AIDS. It is highly likely that this cascade effect produced a number of unnecessary infections and deaths. It literally killed people.

Recall the existence of cascade effects among those who believe that childhood vaccinations are harmful and can in particular cause autism. If apparently reliable reports suggest that vaccinations cause autism, many parents will refuse them. That's hardly innocuous. It can result in illness and death. In fact, the Internet is a breeding ground for false information about health and risk avoidance. It also provides reams of truth and makes it available to all. But every day, damaging falsehoods spread through informational cascades; consider the problem of fake news.

With respect to information in general, there is even a tipping point phenomenon, creating a potential for dramatic shifts in opinion. After being presented with new information, people typically have different "thresholds" for choosing to believe or do something new or different. As the more likely believers—that is, people with low thresholds—come to a certain belief or action, people with somewhat higher thresholds then join them, soon producing a significant group in favor of the view in question. At that point, those with still higher thresholds may join, possibly to a point where a critical mass is reached, making large groups, societies, or even nations "tip."[15] The result of this process can be to produce cascade effects, as large groups of people end up believing something—whether or not that something is true or false—simply because other people in the relevant community seem to believe that it is true.

There is a great deal of experimental evidence of informational cascades, which are easy to induce in the laboratory; real-world phenomena also have a great deal to do with cascade effects.[16] Consider, for example, going to college, smoking, participating in political protests, voting for third-party candidates, striking, recycling, filing lawsuits, using birth control, rioting, or even leaving bad dinner parties.[17] In all these cases, people are greatly influenced by what others do. Often a tipping point will be reached. Sometimes we give an aura of inevitability to social developments, with the thought that deep cultural forces have led to (for instance) an increase in smoking, protesting, or a candidate's success, when in fact social influences have produced an outcome that could easily have been avoided. Social media provide an obvious breeding ground for cascades, and as a result, thousands or even millions of people who consult sources of a particular kind will move in one or another direction, or even believe something that is quite false.

The good news is that the Internet, including social media, is easily enlisted to debunk false rumors as well as start them. Online, people can correct those rumors in a hurry. For this reason, most such rumors do no harm. But it remains true that the opportunity to spread apparently credible information to so many people can induce fear, error, and confusion in a way that threatens many social goals, including democratic ones. As we have seen, this danger takes on a particular form in a balkanized speech market as local cascades lead people in dramatically different directions. When this happens, correctives, even via the Internet, may work too slowly or not at all, simply because people are not listening to one another. Recall the (terrible) problem of the backfiring correction.

UP AND DOWN VOTES

We continue to learn more about how social influences work online. Lev Muchnik, a professor at the Hebrew University of Jerusalem, and his colleagues carried out an ingenious experiment on a particular website—one that displays a diverse array of stories and allows people to post comments, which can in turn be voted "up" or "down."[18] With respect to the posted comments, the website compiles an aggregate score, which comes from subtracting the number of down votes from the number of up votes. To study the effects of social influences, the researchers explored three conditions: "up-treated," in which a comment, when it appeared, was automatically and artificially given an immediate up vote; "down-treated," in which a comment, when it appeared, was automatically and artificially given an immediate down vote; and "control," in which comments did not receive any artificial initial signal. Millions of site visitors were randomly assigned to one of the three conditions. The question was simple: What would be the ultimate effect of an initial up or down vote?

You might well think that after so many visitors (and hundreds of thousands of ratings), a single initial vote could not possibly matter. Some comments are good, and some comments are bad, and in the end, quality will win out. It's a sensible idea, but if you thought it, you would be wrong. After seeing an initial up vote (and recall that it was entirely artificial), the next viewer became 32 percent more likely to give an up vote too. What's more, this effect persisted over time. After a period of five months, a single positive initial vote artificially increased the mean rating of comments by a whopping 25 percent! It also significantly increased "turnout" (the total number of ratings).

With respect to negative votes, the picture was not at all symmetrical—an intriguing finding. True, the initial down vote did increase the likelihood that the first viewer would also give a down vote. But that effect was rapidly corrected. After a period of five months, the artificial down vote had zero effect on median ratings (although it did increase turnout). Muchnik and his colleagues conclude that "whereas positive social influence accumulates, creating a tendency toward ratings bubbles, negative social influence is neutralized by crowd correction."[19] They think that their findings have implications for product recommendations, stock market predictions, and electoral polling. Maybe an initial positive reaction, or just a few such reactions, can have major effects on ultimate outcomes—a conclusion very much in line with Salganik, Dodds, and Watts's evidence. But maybe negative reactions will get corrected pretty quickly.

It's an interesting thought, but we should be careful before drawing large lessons from a single study, particularly when participants had no money on the line. It's possible that negative reactions can have long-term effects on products, people, movements, and ideas. But there is no question that when groups move in the direction of one or more of these, it may not be because of their intrinsic merits but instead because of the functional equivalent of early up votes. (Politicians, including Barack Obama and Donald Trump, often succeed as a result.) There are lessons here about the extraordinary unpredictability of groups—and their frequent lack of wisdom. Of course Muchnik and his colleagues' own study involved large groups. But the same thing can happen in small ones, sometimes even more dramatically, because an initial up vote—in favor of some plan, product, or verdict—has a large effect on others.

HOW MANY MURDERS?

Here's a clean test of group wisdom and social influences. The median estimate of a large group is often amazingly accurate. But what happens if people in the group know what one another are saying? You might think that knowledge of this kind will help, but the picture is a lot more complicated.

Jan Lorenz, a researcher in Zurich, worked with several colleagues to learn what happens when people are asked to estimate certain values, such as the number of assaults, rapes, and murders in Switzerland.[20] They found that when people were informed about the estimates of others, there was a significant reduction in the diversity of opinions, which tended to make the crowd less wise.[21]

There's another problem with the crowd, which is that because people hear about other estimates, they also become more confident. Notably, people in the study received monetary payments for getting the right answer, so their mistakes were really mistakes—not an effort to curry favor with others. The authors conclude that for decision makers, the advice given by a group "may be thoroughly misleading, because closely related, seemingly independent advice may pretend certainty despite substantial deviations from the correct solution."[22] There's a lesson there for the wisdom of crowds in online settings. Because people are interacting with one another, they might not be so wise.

SEGREGATION, MIGRATION, AND INTEGRATION

The Daily Me is not a lived reality, at least for most of us. Facebook, Twitter, Instagram, and Snapchat accounts can certainly spread diverse points of view, and many people use them in exactly that way. Facts and opinions on liberal sites often migrate to conservative sites, and vice versa. We have seen that even if opinions are clustering, society can benefit from the wide range of arguments that ultimately make their way to the general public. And for many of us, voluntary choices do not produce clustering.

But there is also evidence of an echo chamber effect, at least for some of us. For example, a 2009 study finds modest but clear evidence of such an effect.[23] Examining the behavior of 727 people over a six-week period, R. Kelly Garrett found that people are significantly more likely to click on information that reinforces their views, and somewhat less likely to expose themselves to information that contradicts those views. In her account, people seek support for their own positions, and they do so consistently. It follows that people "are more likely to be interested in reading a story that they expect to support their opinion, and they spend more time reading it. They are also marginally less likely to be interested in stories containing opinion-challenging information, but they do not systematically avoid them."[24] The fact that people spend more time with stories that support their views is worth underlining.

The echo chamber effect here is not large: while people prefer information that supports their convictions, they do not run from information that undermines them. In Garrett's words, "People's desire for opinion reinforcement is stronger than their aversion to opinion challenges." Her conclusion is that people "do not seek to completely exclude other perspectives from their political universe, and there is little evidence that they will use the Internet to create echo chambers, devoid of other viewpoints, no matter how much control over their political information environment they are given."[25] In short, her study finds an inclination to find like-minded sources, but importantly, they are hardly sealed.

At the same time, Garrett offers an ominous projection: "Polarized news outlets serving niche audiences, which are more economically feasible online where production costs are lower, are another threat. Faced with a choice between a news source that is almost exclusively supportive of their opinions and another that almost exclusively challenges those same opinions, news consumers seem likely to choose the former."[26] Garrett has done a great deal of work on these issues, and it is broadly consistent with her central findings here and also signals the existence of that threat.[27]

One of the most systematic treatments of these issues comes from economists Matthew Gentzkow and Jesse M. Shapiro, who compare ideological segregation online and offline.[28] To measure ideological segregation, they use an "isolation index," which, in their words, is

> equal to the average conservative exposure of conservatives minus the average conservative exposure of liberals. If conservatives visit only foxnews.com and liberals only visit nytimes.com, for example, the isolation index will be equal to 100 percentage points. But if both conservatives and liberals get all their news from cnn.com, the two groups will

have the same kind of exposures, and the isolation index will be equal to 0.[29]

That's a useful measure of segregation. Using data sources from 2004 to 2009, Gentzkow and Shapiro find a clear difference between what conservatives and liberals see online. On the Internet, the average conservative's exposure to conservative news is 60.6 percent, while the average liberal's is 53.1 percent, producing an isolation index for the Internet of 7.5 percentage points. That's significant, but again, it's not huge. You could easily see it as modest. Gentzkow and Shapiro find that most people are not using the Internet to live in echo chambers. For example, a consumer who received news exclusively from foxnews.com would have a more conservative news diet than 99 percent of Internet news users, which suggests that the vast majority of people are clicking on sites that do not fit a narrow political profile.

For four reasons, however, their data should be taken with some grains of salt, at least as applied to my concerns here. First, Gentzkow and Shapiro also find that isolation for the Internet is higher than for broadcast television news (1.8 percentage points), cable television news (3.3), magazines (4.7), and local newspapers (4.8)—though lower than that of national newspapers (10.4). The fact that it is higher than four standard sources of information is hardly comforting. Second, they are speaking of aggregate behavior, and the aggregate masks the extent to which significant subpopulations are creating echo chambers. Third, their findings are now dated; it is possible that the degree of isolation on the Internet is increasing. Fourth, more recent work finds that the echo chamber effect is dramatically higher on social media.

An intriguing qualification of the Gentzkow and Shapiro findings focuses directly on the question of subpopulations. Andrew Guess studied individual-level media consumption data to explore online behavior.[30] Looking at both surveys and browsing history, he finds that the percentage of visits that involve news and information about politics is actually quite low—about 6.9 percent of all visits. Most of the time, people do not go online to explore politics. More relevantly for present purposes, both Democrats and Republicans do not sort themselves into echo chambers but instead tend to cluster around sites that can be counted as centrist, such as MSN.com and AOL.com. In general, Democrats and Republicans do not look radically different in their online behavior. The most important qualification is that Republicans also visit conservative sites (Townhall, the Drudge Report, and Breitbart) that Democrats entirely ignore. Democrats also show a greater interest than do Republicans in certain liberal sites (the Huffington Post and the Daily Kos). But overall, Guess finds "a remarkable degree of balance in respondents' overall media diets regardless of partisan affiliation," because most people's choices "cluster around the center of the ideological spectrum."[31]

It follows that most people do not consume news in a partisan way. But some people definitely do, including a set of left-leaning Democrats and (more pronounced in Guess's data) a subgroup of Republicans who visit conservative sites but not liberal ones. It follows that a small group of people is driving traffic to the most partisan outlets. Consistent with this finding, Guess also finds that in the aftermath of disclosures in 2015 about Hillary Clinton's use of a private e-mail server, Republicans suddenly flocked to increased consumption of news and information from identifiably conservative sources. Guess concludes that "a scandal that naturally maps onto the political divide involving a well-known figure can immediately drive traffic to more partisan sources."[32] A reasonable conclusion is that while most people do not live in echo chambers, those who do may have disproportionate influence, because they are so engaged in politics.[33]

HOMOPHILY ON TWITTER

I have been discussing online behavior in general. What about social media? It is tempting to offer these hypotheses about Twitter in particular, consistent with my general concerns here: *people's Twitter feeds consist largely of like-minded types. When people retweet, it is generally because they agree with what they are retweeting. Because people generate their own feeds, they create echo chambers.* To be sure, some people are at pains to say that a retweet "is not an endorsement," but most of the time you retweet something because you like it and because you want your followers to see it as well. It is true that you might follow people with whom you do not agree, because you want to learn from them or you're interested in knowing what the other side is thinking. But in general, we might hypothesize that Twitter is creating many thousands of information cocoons.

We can go a bit further. In business and government as well as the nonprofit sector, people are aware of the power of social media, and they use Twitter to their advantage. They try hard to create networks that will foster the preferred information environment. They tweet to produce positive impressions of their ideas and products—magazines, movies, television shows, books, candidates, and ideologies—and they have an intuitive awareness of group polarization and cascade effects. They create echo chambers by design.

Is that true? Though the full story is complicated and continues to emerge, there is considerable evidence that it is.[34] On Twitter, research finds a great deal of homophily. An important overview from 2001 finds homophily in all sorts of social networks, involving race, ethnicity, age, religion, and education, and constituting "niches" of identifiable kinds.[35] Eight years later, Gueorgi Kossinets of Google and Duncan Watts of Yahoo! Research (and now at Microsoft) explored the *origins* of homophily, with particular emphasis on the role of individual choices and structures. Investigating actual behavior, they find that over many "generations," a seemingly small and modest preference for similar others can "produce striking patterns of observed homophily."[36]

Building on the basic concept, Itai Himelboim and his coauthors find a great deal of homophily on Twitter. Studying Twitter networks involving ten controversial political topics, they find that

"Twitter users are unlikely to be exposed to cross-ideological content from the clusters of users they followed, as these were usually politically homogeneous."[37] To be sure, people create social ties on Twitter on the basis of many common interests, not merely politics. In the political domain, interest in content is largely confined to like-minded users. There is little cross-ideological communication, at least of a meaningful kind.

Similarly, M. D. Conover and his coauthors investigated networks of political communication on Twitter, including more than 250,000 tweets from more than 45,000 users during the six weeks in advance of the 2010 US congressional midterm elections. Studying retweets, they find a massive degree of ideological segregation, with "extremely limited connectivity between left- and right-leaning users." The "retweet network," as the authors call it, separates users into two homogeneous communities, corresponding to the political right and left.[38] The sheer level of clustering is quite remarkable, suggesting two different communications universes.

At the same time, there is a puzzle—a finding that cuts in the other direction. If you look at "mentions" as opposed to retweets ("mentions" are tweets that contain another Twitter user's @username), you will find far less in the way of political segregation. On Twitter, conservatives do mention tweets from people with liberal views, and liberals do mention tweets from people with conservative views. The authors speculate that hashtags might be a big reason. If someone issues a tweet that says #SecondAmendment, a lot of people might be interested in it, especially if it is seen as having a neutral or mixed valence.

But the authors ultimately conclude that the interactions they find "are almost certainly not a panacea for the problem of political polarization." The problem is that despite the large number of mentions, ideologically opposed users "very rarely share information from across the divide with other members of their community." Hence "political segregation, as manifested in the topology of the retweet network, persists in spite of substantial cross-ideological interaction."[39]

A study of Twitter data from the 2012 election cuts in the same direction.[40] On November 5 of that year—the day before the election—economists Yosh Haberstam and Brian Knight downloaded information from 2.2 million Twitter users who had followed the Twitter handles of candidates for the House of Representatives. The researchers coded Twitter users as liberal or conservative "voters" based on the party affiliation of the candidates they followed (for example, those who followed more Republican candidates were considered conservative), and then confirmed those ideologies based on the type of news outlets the voters followed (for instance, liberals were much more likely to follow *Hardball* with Chris Matthews). From these politically engaged Twitter "voters," Haberstam and Knight analyzed 90 million links to other Twitter users as well as 500,000 candidate retweets and mentions of candidates.

The researchers found that people were disproportionately exposed to like-minded tweets. Specifically, the researchers discovered that conservative exposure among conservatives was 77.6 percent, but just 37.2 percent among liberals, yielding an isolation index of 40.3 percentage points on Twitter. That's far higher than the 7.5 percent found by Gentzkow and Shapiro for ideological segregation on the Internet. How could that be?

To reconcile their study with Gentzkow and Shapiro's findings, the researchers focused on two factors: people who follow politicians might strongly prefer to link to like-minded individuals, and news consumption on Twitter in particular might affect ideological segregation. The researchers found that the isolation index was indeed significantly lower (21.7 percent) for Twitter users who followed candidates from more than one party (so-called moderates).[41] It was also significantly lower (24.1 percent) for media consumption—that is, among users who followed media outlets (think Fox News or *New York Times*), the level of ideological segregation was still significant but less pronounced than it was for those who do not follow such outlets. In Haberstam and Knight's words, "[The] same Twitter users experience[d] lower segregation when consuming news from media outlets than when using Twitter as a social network" by linking to other voters.[42] If these two factors are put together, the isolation index turns out to be just 6.7 percent, close to Gentzkow and Shapiro's finding.

It follows that if you use Twitter to follow both media outlets and candidates from more than one party—that is, if you're a "moderate"—then your ideological exposure will be slightly skewed, but not by much, and it will be comparable to ideological segregation on the Internet in general. But if you use Twitter primarily to follow candidates from just one political party (which many people do), and if you do not follow media outlets, then you'll be exposed to dramatically different and far more limited viewpoints.

What does all this mean? For many users, Twitter is more ideologically segregated than radio, newspapers, and the Internet. Indeed, the researchers found that among the House candidate tweets that liberal voters saw, 90 percent came, on average, from Democrats; similarly, 90 percent of the candidate tweets that conservative voters saw came, on average, from Republicans.[43] (If the exposure had been random, these Twitter voters would have seen about half Democratic and half Republican tweets.) All this means that Twitter makes it easy for people inclined to hear like-minded viewpoints to do exactly that—and many people are following their inclinations.

Studying Republicans and Democrats in the United States, Elanor Colleoni and her coauthors find a great deal of political homophily, but with some intriguing differences between Democrats and Republicans.[44] In brief, Democrats in general show significantly higher levels of political homophily, but Republicans who follow official Republican accounts show higher levels of homophily than do Democrats.

A great deal remains to be learned about the differences between Democrats and Republicans, and how these change over time. In some years, one or another party will be more inclined to isolate itself on social media, and these inclinations probably shift from one period to another. Among both Democrats and Republicans, there are almost certainly differences between moderates and extremists. It is reasonable to speculate that those who consider themselves on the left wing of the Democratic Party are more inclined to homophily than those who consider themselves to be merely somewhat left of center, and something similar might be true of right-wing members of the Republican Party as compared to those who are merely somewhat right of center. It would also be intriguing and perhaps important to learn about the role of demographic characteristics. In Twitter, how does homophily differ between men and women, young and old, well educated and poorly educated, rich and poor?

In the fullness of time, an entire book should be written on this topic. It will undoubtedly complicate and qualify the intuitive hypotheses with which this section began. But the complications and qualifications are highly likely to be consistent with the claim that homophily is commonplace on Twitter, and that when millions of people use it to find news and opinions, birds of a feather are flocking together.

FRIENDS AND FACEBOOK

In general. What about Facebook? A study by its own employees strongly suggests that to some extent, Facebook's users are indeed creating political echo chambers.[45] Investigating how 10.1 million Facebook users interacted with news, the study explored the effects of Facebook's own (earlier) algorithm, which does a degree of filtering, and also users' own choices. One of the signal virtues of this study is that it cleanly separates the consequences of the Facebook algorithm from those of people's decisions whether or not to click. The authors' own emphasis is on the effects of the latter, with the suggestion that "the power to expose oneself to perspectives from the other side in social media lies first and foremost with individuals."[46] That suggestion is not inconsistent with their actual findings, but the full story is more interesting.

Facebook's algorithm matters. As the authors' evidence shows, the algorithm suppresses exposure to diverse content by 8 percent for self-identified liberals and 5 percent for self-identified conservatives. That means that the algorithm will filter out one in thirteen crosscutting stories that a liberal might see, and one in twenty such stories that a conservative might see. True, those numbers are not huge, but they do mean that people are seeing (modestly) fewer news items that they would disagree with, solely because of the effects of the algorithm. And it shows Facebook's potential power to alter our news consumption: if people are getting a lot of their news from Facebook, the algorithm will create a skew.

With respect to individual choices, there is an additional and larger effect: clicking behavior results in exposure to 6 percent less diverse content for liberals and 17 percent less diverse content for conservatives. In this respect, the authors find clear evidence of *confirmation bias*, a product of motivated reasoning: people are more likely to click on material that confirms their beliefs and avoid material that undermines them. The best way to understand the study is to take the algorithm and individual choices together. In the aggregate, there is a great deal of self-sorting on Facebook, resulting in a situation in which people are likely to be seeing items with which they agree.

It is also true that as Facebook's researchers note, "Individuals do not encounter information at random in offline environments nor on the Internet."[47] And it is not so easy to measure how much less ideologically diverse information people are seeing on Facebook compared to face-to-face interactions or without Facebook's algorithm. Still, the figures do raise questions about what Facebook and other social media companies can or should do to promote ideological diversity. As we have seen, Facebook decided in 2016 to change its algorithm to prioritize posts by friends and family members over those of news publishers like the *Wall Street Journal* or *Huffington Post*.[48] That means that what you see on Facebook will depend more on who your friends are, what they share, and what you click on. The change is highly likely to increase the echo chamber effect.

"Spend time viewing." Facebook itself has a distinctive view about how to think about this situation. As Mark Zuckerberg, cofounder, chair, and chief executive officer of Facebook, once remarked, "A squirrel dying in front of your house may be more relevant to your interests than people dying in Africa."[49] A clear example of the company's commitment to consumer sovereignty is an upbeat blog post written by two people at the company in 2016. Revealingly, the post is titled "More Articles You Want to Spend Time Viewing." The authors announce, "We are adding another factor to News Feed ranking so that we will now predict how long you spend looking at an article in the Facebook mobile browser or an Instant Article after you have clicked through from News Feed." Cheerfully, they suggest that "with this change, we can better understand which articles might be interesting to you based on how long you and others read them, so you'll be more likely to see stories you're interested in reading."[50]

Without the slightest trace of self-consciousness, they add that the most recent changes to Facebook's algorithm are intended to provide users "more articles [they] want to spend time viewing"—instead of the broad array of stories that users might not have otherwise considered (and on which they might not spend a whole lot of time). As algorithms become more accurate in the future, the company's capacity to prescreen posts for what users want to read will inevitably improve. In a way, that's great—but in a way, it really isn't.

Science and conspiracies. A series of studies of Facebook users provides strong evidence that at least in certain domains, echo chambers exist on Facebook, and they are created by confirmation bias.[51] One of those studies, led by Michela Del Vicario of Italy's Laboratory of Computational Social Science, explores the behavior of Facebook users from 2010 to 2014.[52] A central goal of the study was to test whether users create the virtual equivalent of gated communities.

Del Vicario and her coauthors examined how Facebook users spread conspiracy theories (using thirty-two public web pages), science news (using thirty-five such pages), and "trolls," which intentionally spread false information (using two web pages). Their data set is massive; it covers all Facebook posts during the five-year period. The researchers looked at which Facebook users linked to one or more of the sixty-nine web pages, and whether they learned about those links from their Facebook friends.

In sum, the researchers find communities of like-minded people. Conspiracy theories, even if they are baseless, spread rapidly within such communities. On these issues, Facebook users tend to choose and share stories containing messages they accept—and neglect those they reject. If a story fits with what people already believe, they are far more likely to be interested in it and thus spread it. As Del Vicario and her coauthors put it, "Users mostly tend to select and share content according to a specific narrative and to ignore the rest." On Facebook, the result is the formation of a lot of "homogeneous, polarized clusters."[53] Within those clusters, new information moves quickly among friends (often in just a few hours).

The consequence is the "proliferation of biased narratives fomented by unsubstantiated rumors, mistrust, and paranoia."[54] In that sense, confirmation bias is self-reinforcing, producing a vicious spiral. If people begin with a certain belief and find information that confirms it, they will intensify their commitment to that belief, strengthening their bias. Strong support for this conclusion comes from research from the same academic team, which finds that on Facebook, efforts to debunk false beliefs are typically ignored—and when people pay attention to them, they often strengthen their commitment to the debunked beliefs. The United States saw a lot of this during the 2016 presidential campaign.

Or consider how people respond to *intentionally* false claims. The researchers studied clearly unrealistic and satirical claims—for example, a post declaring that chemical analysis revealed that chemtrails contain sildenafil citratum (the active ingredient in

ViagraTM).[55] The central finding is that many people liked and commented favorably on such claims. Even when information is deliberately false and framed with a satirical purpose, its conformity with the conspiracy narrative transformed it into suitable (and welcome) content for the relevant groups. To be sure, conspiracy theories, and those who like and spread them, are not exactly typical fare. We might expect to see an especially large echo chamber effect for such theories. But there is good reason to think that less extreme versions of the same general patterns of self-sorting can be found on Facebook.

Findings of this kind are important because people increasingly rely on social media for news. According to public opinion polls by the Pew Research Center, as of 2016, six out of ten US adults (62 percent) get news from social media, and 18 percent do so frequently. The polls also show that a majority of Twitter (59 percent) and Facebook users (66 percent) receive news on those platforms (both up significantly from 2013, when only about half these users got news there). Polls also demonstrate that while the percentage of the population that uses Twitter is relatively low (16 percent), Facebook is widely used (67 percent)—which means that some 44 percent of all US adults receive news from Facebook.[56]

For people born after 1980, often called millennials, Facebook is by far the most common source of news about politics and government. In 2016, six out of ten millennials (61 percent) reported getting political news from Facebook, whereas only about four in ten (44 percent) said CNN, the next most popular source.[57] Facebook accounts for more than 40 percent of the referral traffic to news sites.[58] For better or worse, social media and Facebook in particular have a large effect in determining what people learn about political issues.

FACTS, VALUES, AND GOOD NEWS

To paraphrase an observation attributed to the late senator Daniel P. Moynihan, people are entitled to their own opinions, not to their own facts. But on some of the most politically charged issues, people's ideological commitments settle their judgments about questions of fact. This point helps illuminate the effects of a fragmented media market; it contributes to polarization.

While many of the issues that divide people boil down to ideology and preference, there is at least one on which hard science should have a strong say—climate change. But do numbers and figures change people's opinions? In an experiment in 2016, my colleagues Sebastian Bobadilla-Suarez, Stephanie Lazzaro, Tali Sharot, and I asked more than three hundred Americans several climate-related questions, such as whether they believed that man-made climate change was occurring and whether the United States was right to support the recent Paris agreement to reduce greenhouse gas emissions.[59] On the basis of their answers, we divided participants into three groups: strong believers in man-made climate change, moderate believers, and weak believers.

Next we informed participants that many scientists have said that by the year 2100, the average temperature in the United States will rise at least 6 degrees Fahrenheit, and asked them for their own estimates of likely temperature rise by 2100. The overall average was 5.6 degrees Fahrenheit. As expected, there were significant differences among the three groups: 6.3 degrees for strong believers in man-made climate change, 5.9 degrees for moderate believers, and 3.6 degrees for weak believers.

Then came the important part of the experiment. Participants were randomly assigned to one of two conditions. Half of them received information that was more encouraging than what they originally received (good news for the planet and humanity); half of them received information that was less encouraging (bad news for the planet and humanity). In the good news condition, they were told to assume that in recent weeks, prominent scientists had reassessed the science and concluded the situation was far better than previously thought, suggesting a likely temperature increase of only 1 to 5 degrees. In the bad news condition, participants were told to assume that in recent weeks, prominent scientists had reassessed the science and concluded the situation was far worse than previously thought, suggesting a likely temperature increase of 7 to 11 degrees. All participants were then asked to provide their personal estimates. Note that our experiment fits nicely with what happens online and in social media. All the time, people receive news, with respect to climate change, that suggests that the problem will be much better or much worse than previously thought.

Here's what we found. Weak believers in man-made climate change were moved by the good news; their average estimate fell by about 1 degree. But their belief was entirely unchanged by the bad news; their average estimate stayed essentially constant. By contrast, strong believers in man-made climate change were far more moved by the bad news (their average estimate jumped by nearly 2 degrees), whereas with good news, it fell by less than half of that (0.9 degrees). Moderate climate change believers were equally moved in both cases (they changed their estimates by approximately 1.5 degrees in each case).

The clear implication is that for weak believers in man-made climate change, comforting news will have a big impact, and alarming news won't. Strong believers will show the opposite pattern. As the media, including social media, expose people to new and competing claims about the latest scientific evidence, these opposing tendencies will predictably create political polarization, and it will grow over time.

There is a more general psychological finding in the background here. In the case of information about ourselves (about how attractive others perceive us to be, or how likely we are to get sick or to succeed), people normally alter their beliefs more in response to good news than in response to bad news. If you hear that you are better looking than you think, you will probably learn from that nice information. If you hear that you are not quite so good looking, you might well dismiss that unpleasant news. In certain circumstances, something similar will be true for political issues, as in the case of weak climate change believers, who are most likely to credit information suggesting that things will not be so bad. But at times, good political news can threaten our deepest commitments, and we will be inclined give it less weight. Above all, we might want those commitments to be affirmed. Those who are most alarmed about climate change might prefer to learn that humanity really is at very serious risk than to learn that the climate change problem is probably not so bad. For them, bad news for humanity and the planet is, in a sense, good news (because it is affirming), and good news for humanity and the planet is, in an important sense, taken as bad news.

These findings help explain polarization on many issues, and the role of social media in increasing it. With respect to the Affordable Care Act, for example, people encounter good news, to the effect that it has helped millions of people obtain health insurance, and also bad news, to the effect that health care costs and insurance premiums continue to increase. For the act's supporters, the good news will have far more impact than the bad; for the opponents, the opposite is true. As the sheer volume of information increases, polarization will be heightened as well. Essentially the same tale can be told with respect to immigration, terrorism, and increases in the minimum wage. Which kind of news will have a large impact will depend partly on people's motivations and initial convictions.

But there's an important qualification. In our experiment, a strong majority showed movement; few people were impervious to new information. Most people were willing to change their views, at least to some extent. For those who believe in learning, and the possibility of democratic self-government, that's some good news.

IDENTITY AND CULTURE

A revealing body of research, coming largely from Yale Law School professor Dan Kahan, finds that "cultural cognition" shapes our reactions to science—and that our values affect our assessment of purely factual claims, even in highly technical areas.[60] As a result, Americans predictably polarize on factual questions involving, for example, gun control, climate change, nuclear waste disposal, and nanotechnology. Kahan's striking claim is that people's judgments stem, in large part, from their sense of identity—of what kind of person they consider themselves to be. As a result, seemingly disparate views cluster. Among conservatives, for instance, gun control is a bad idea, and so is affirmative action; climate change is not a big problem; the Supreme Court should not have recognized same-sex marriage; and the minimum wage should not be increased.

In principle, it might be possible to identify specific values that link these apparently diverse conclusions. But Kahan's claim is that the real source of people's views, at least on certain controversial questions, is their understanding of their identity, and their effort to protect it. And while Kahan does not focus on online behavior and social media, there is no question that online interactions contribute to the phenomena he is describing.

Consider current debates over GMOs and climate change. The strong majority of scientists accept two propositions. First, GMOs generally do not pose serious threats to human health or the environment. Second, greenhouse gases are producing climate change, which does pose serious threats to human health and the environment.

With respect to GMOs, Democrats are far more likely than Republicans to reject the prevailing scientific judgment. With regard to climate change, Republicans are far more likely than Democrats to reject the prevailing scientific judgment. The partisan divide is easy to demonstrate. Among national leaders, many Democrats are concerned about GMOs; relatively few Republican leaders share that concern. Among ordinary citizens, a strong majority of Democratic voters believes that GMOs are unsafe. Republican voters are evenly divided on the safety question—a higher level of concern than that of their elected representatives, but much lower than that of Democratic voters.

In Congress, it is not exactly news that Democrats are far more likely than Republicans to support action to reduce greenhouse gas emissions. Take just one example: in a 2013 Senate vote on a nonbinding resolution calling for a "fee on carbon pollution," Republicans were in unanimous opposition, while most Democrats were supportive. In recent years, about 75 percent of Democratic voters have said that they worry "a great deal" or "a fair amount" about climate change. For Republican voters, the percentage has ranged from 30 to 40 percent. As Kahan shows, Republicans who doubt climate change, and do not worry about it, do *not* display lower levels of scientific literacy.[61] They are fully aware of what most scientists think. They are hardly ignorant. Their judgments appear to be a product of their values or sense of identity.

What is the best explanation for the fact that Republicans are more inclined to follow scientific opinion for GMOs, while Democrats are more inclined to do so for greenhouse gases? There are three contributing factors. Interest groups are the first. On the Democratic side, the concerns are of course sincerely held, but well-organized groups have been lobbying hard against GMOs, and they have been able to intensify public objections. These groups, which include the organic food industry and Whole Foods Market, have influence and credibility within the Democratic Party, and have stood to gain from mandatory labeling (which would harm their competitors). With respect to climate change, by contrast, the most powerful economic interests (such as the coal industry) have far greater influence within the Republican Party. Environmental groups, pressing for control of greenhouse gases, carry weight mostly with Democrats.

A second explanation points to my principal concern here: the effects of echo chambers, including social media. With respect to GMOs, some Democrats listen largely to one another, and their fears have become amplified as a result of internal discussion, even if science is not on their side. For greenhouse gases, the same phenomenon is occurring among Republicans. Here as elsewhere, discussions among like-minded people increase confidence, extremism, and polarization.

A third explanation builds on Kahan's research. It points to the crucial role of preexisting ideological commitments, which on particular issues can crowd out the effects of scientific findings. Many Republicans are opposed, in principle, to government interference with free markets. They are inclined to be suspicious of scientific evidence that purports to justify that interference, especially in the environmental domain. By contrast, many Democrats are willing to indulge the assumption that corporate efforts to interfere with nature are potentially dangerous, especially if those efforts involve chemicals, new technologies, or pollution. Among Democrats, scientific claims about the risks associated with GMOs and greenhouse gases fall on receptive ears. In both cases, it is a matter of values first and scientific judgments second. And of course, a fragmented media market fortifies the relevant values.

To be sure, values do not always crowd out science. Some scientific questions do not trigger a sense of political identity; consider the question whether cigarettes cause lung cancer, or texting while driving increases the likelihood of accidents. Some scientific questions *migrate*: what was once a technical issue becomes politically inflamed, and what was once politically inflamed becomes technical.

As an example of the latter phenomenon, consider the depletion of the ozone layer, where the scientific evidence has long been overwhelming. That evidence led to bipartisan support for the Montreal Protocol, signed by President Ronald Reagan in 1988. Even so, there is no question that preexisting values help to account for political polarization with respect to GMOs and greenhouse gases. Taken together with the activities of interest groups and the echo chamber effect, those values help explain why the leaders of our two major political parties are strongly inclined to accept the dominant view within the scientific community in one case—and reject it in another.

The most unfortunate part is that interest groups, echo chambers, and conceptions of identity reinforce each other, creating a new kind of iron triangle. Interest groups use social media to promote their preferred view of the world as well as create or fortify conceptions of identity. The echo chambers increase the authority of those groups at the same time that they entrench those conceptions.

A CONTRAST: THE DELIBERATIVE OPINION POLL

By way of contrast to polarization and cybercascades, consider some work by James Fishkin, a creative political scientist at Stanford University who has pioneered a genuine social innovation: the deliberative opinion poll.[62] The basic idea is to ensure that polls are not mere "snapshots" of public opinion. People's views instead are recorded only after diverse citizens, with different points of view, have actually been brought together in order to discuss topics with one another.

Deliberative opinion polls have now been conducted in many nations, including the United States, England, and Australia. It is easy for deliberative opinion polls to be conducted on the Internet, and Fishkin has initiated illuminating experiments in this direction.

In deliberative opinion polls, Fishkin finds some noteworthy shifts in individual views. But he does not find a systematic tendency toward polarization.[63] In England, for example, deliberation led to a reduced interest in using imprisonment as a tool for combating crime.[64] The percentage believing that "sending more offenders to prison" is an effective way to prevent crime fell from 57 to 38 percent; the percentage believing that fewer people should be sent to prison increased from 29 to 44 percent; and belief in the effectiveness of "stiffer sentences" decreased from 78 to 65 percent.[65] Similar shifts were shown in the direction of greater enthusiasm for the procedural rights of defendants and increased willingness to explore alternatives to prison.

In other experiments with the deliberative opinion poll, shifts included a mixture of findings, with deliberation leading larger percentages of people to conclude that legal pressures should be increased on fathers for child support (from 70 to 85 percent), and that welfare and health care should be turned over to the states (from 56 to 66 percent).[66] These findings are broadly consistent with the prediction of group polarization, and to be sure, the effect of deliberation was sometimes to create an increase in the intensity with which people held their preexisting convictions.[67] But this was hardly a uniform pattern. On some questions, deliberation shifted a minority position to a majority position (with, for example, a jump from 36 to 57 percent of people favoring policies making divorce "harder to get"), and it follows that sometimes majorities became minorities.[68]

Fishkin's experiments have some distinctive features. They involve not like-minded people but instead diverse groups of citizens engaged in discussion after being presented with various sides of social issues by appointed moderators. Fishkin's deliberators do not seek to obtain a group consensus; they listen and exchange ideas without being asked to come into agreement. In many ways these discussions provide a model for civic deliberation, complete with reason giving.

It can be expensive, of course, to transport diverse people to the same place. But communications technologies make widespread uses of deliberative opinion polls as well as reasoned discussion among heterogeneous people far more feasible—even if private individuals, in their private capacity, would rarely choose to create deliberating institutions on their own. I have noted that Fishkin has created deliberative opinion polls on the Internet; there are many efforts and experiments in this general vein.[69] The social media can easily be enlisted for those purposes.

Here we can find considerable promise for the future in the form of discussions among diverse people who exchange reasons, and who would not, without current technologies, be able to talk with one another at all. If we are guided by the notion of consumer sovereignty, and if we celebrate unlimited filtering, we will be unable to see why the discussions in the deliberative opinion poll are a great improvement over much of what is now happening online. In short, aspirations for deliberative democracy sharply diverge from the ideal of consumer sovereignty—that is, a future in which, in Gates's words, "you'll be able to just say what you're interested in, and have the screen help you pick out a video that you care about."

But let's offer a cautionary note: for many political questions, what matters is getting the facts straight, and for that, you need experts, not deliberative opinion polls. Suppose that the question is whether current levels of particulate matter (an air pollutant) cause two deaths annually or two hundred, or instead two thousand. Or suppose the question is whether a requirement for greater fuel economy in trucks would produce less safe vehicles. On such questions, expertise is crucial. True, we might want the experts to deliberate. But a deliberative opinion poll might lead us in the wrong direction, even if people get pretty well informed.

Nonetheless, deliberative opinion polls are a lot better than nondeliberative ones. An enduring question is what sort of ideals we want to animate our choices, and what kinds of attitudes and regulations we want in light of that judgment. And here it is important to emphasize that current technologies, including social media, are in themselves hardly biased in favor of homogeneity and deliberation among like-minded people. Everything depends on what people seek to do with the new opportunities that they have. Consider the reflections of one Internet entrepreneur: "I've been in chat rooms where I've observed, for the first time in my life, African-Americans and white supremacists talking to each other. . . . [I]f you go through the threads of the conversation, by the end you'll find there's less animosity than there was at the beginning. It's not pretty sometimes . . . [b]ut here they are online, actually talking to each other."[70] The problem is that this is far from a universal practice.

OF DANGERS AND SOLUTIONS

I hope that I have shown enough to demonstrate that for citizens of a heterogeneous democracy, a fragmented communications market creates a considerable number of dangers. There are dangers for each of us as individuals; constant exposure to one set of views is likely to lead to errors and confusions, sometimes as a result of cybercascades. And to the extent that the process entrenches existing views, spreads falsehood, promotes extremism, and makes people less able to work cooperatively on shared problems, there are dangers for society as a whole.

To emphasize these dangers, it is unnecessary to claim that people do or will receive all their information online. There are many sources of information, and some of them will undoubtedly counteract the risks I have discussed. Nor is it necessary to predict that most people are speaking only with those who are like-minded. Of course many people seek out or otherwise encounter competing views. But when technology makes it easy for people to wall themselves off from others, there are serious risks for the people involved and society as a whole.

SOCIAL GLUE AND

SPREADING INFORMATION

Some people believe that freedom of speech is a luxury. In their view, poor nations, or nations struggling with social and economic problems, should be trying not to promote democracy but instead to ensure material well-being—economic growth, and a chance for everyone to have food, clothing, and shelter. This view is badly misconceived. If we understand what is wrong with it, we will have a much better sense of the social role of communications.

For many countries, the most devastating problem of all consists of famines, defined as the widespread denial of access to food and, as a result, mass starvation. In China's famine of the late 1950s, for example, about thirty million people died. Is free speech a luxury for nations concerned about famine prevention? Would it be better for such nations to give a high priority not to democracy and free speech but instead to economic development? Actually these are foolish questions. Consider the remarkable finding by the economist Amartya Sen that in the history of the world, there has *never* been a famine in a system with a democratic press and free elections.[1] Sen's starting point, which he also demonstrates empirically, is that famines are a social product, not an inevitable product of scarcity of food. Whether there will be a famine as opposed to a mere shortage depends on people's "entitlements"—that is, what they are able to get. Even when food is limited, entitlements can be allocated in such a way as to ensure that no one will starve.

But when will a government take the necessary steps to prevent starvation? The answer depends on that government's own incentives. When there is a democratic system with free speech and a free press, the government faces a great deal of pressure to ensure that people generally have access to food. And when officials are thus pressured, they respond. But a system without a democratic press or free elections is likely to enable government to escape public accountability and hence not to respond to famines. Government officials will not be exposed, nor will they be at risk of losing their jobs.

Here, then, is a large lesson about the relationship between a well-functioning system of free expression and citizens' well-being. Free speech and free press are not mere luxuries, or tastes of the most educated classes; they increase the likelihood that government will actually serve people's interests. This lesson suggests some of the virtues not only for liberty but also economic development of having freedom of speech.[2] And this lesson indicates the immense importance for liberty and well-being of the Internet itself, which is making it possible for countless people to learn about social and economic problems, and ask their governments to respond to what they have learned.

It is no accident that tyrannical governments have tried to control access to the Internet, partly in order to wall citizens off from knowledge of other systems, and partly to insulate their leaders from scrutiny and criticism, and potentially rebellion. Knowledge is the great ally of both freedom and welfare.

On this count, social media are particularly important. If public officials are engaging in repression in a local city, you can use Facebook, Twitter, or Instagram to get the news out immediately. Individual citizens can serve as reporters. They can expose misconduct, corruption, or suffering—and increase the likelihood that something will be done about it. During the Arab Spring, one Egyptian protester tweeted, "We use Facebook to schedule the protests, Twitter to coordinate, and YouTube to tell the world."[3] Social media publicize developments in real time, and they let the world know what is happening. Sometimes Facebook and Twitter are the best places to look if you want to know about some disaster, discovery, or coup.

But what may be most interesting for present purposes is the fact that once some people have the relevant knowledge (for instance, that a famine is actually on the horizon), they confer benefits (in the famine case, massive benefits) on others who entirely lack that knowledge. Here cascades can be extremely desirable, and in a well-functioning democracy, the factual reports that actually "stick" turn out to be true. There can be no doubt that many of the people who, as a result of this process, are protected from starvation and death, do not themselves choose in advance to learn about famines and related government policies.

An example from China may be useful here. In 2011, two high-speed trains crashed. The government apparently tried to cover up the accident, including by burying one of the cars on-site. An outpouring of posts on Weibo (China's version of Twitter) criticized the government for the attempted cover-up, pressured the government to unearth the train and send it for analysis, and by posting Prime Minister Wen Jiabao's official activities, disputed his claim that he did not visit the site because he was sick. The posts also prompted a surge in blood donations for the 40 people killed and 191 people injured.[4]

Many of the beneficiaries of democracy take little, if any, direct advantage of social media or even democratic elections. (A lot of people do not vote.) But it is not necessary that they do so in order for the system to work. When some people know about coming problems, they can speak out. In world history, one consequence is that famines are averted. And what is true for famines is true for many other problems; natural disasters, including hurricanes and earthquakes, can be far less devastating if freedom is genuinely protected, simply because freedom can increase accountability. In the United States, the massive harm done in New Orleans by Hurricane Katrina in 2005 was, in part, a failure of the democratic system, and it is profoundly to be hoped that democratic accountability will make such failures less likely in the future.

SHARED EXPERIENCES

Thus far I have focused on the social problems that would result from a fragmented communications universe. Let us now turn to two different points. The first involves the social benefits of a situation in which many people in a heterogeneous nation have a number of common experiences. The second involves the fact that once one person has information, it tends to spread and hence benefit others. A well-functioning system of free expression is difficult to understand without reference to these points.

Many private and public benefits come from shared experiences and knowledge as well as a sense of shared tasks. People are well aware of this, and they act accordingly. People may watch what they watch or do what they do largely because other people are watching or doing the same thing. (The immense popularity of the Harry Potter books and the *Star Wars* movies has a lot to do with that fact.) But when the number of communications options grows dramatically, people will naturally make increasingly diverse choices, and their shared experiences, plentiful in a time of general-interest intermediaries, will decrease accordingly. This can erode the kind of social glue that is provided by shared experiences, knowledge, and tasks.

Consider in this regard an instructive discussion of Israel's one-channel policy—ensuring, for a long period of time, that television "controlled by the Broadcasting Authority was the only show in town."[5] From the standpoint of democracy, any such policy obviously seems troublesome and indeed unacceptable. A free society certainly does not have a one-channel policy. But what is less obvious and more interesting are some unintended consequences of that policy: within two years of its inauguration, "almost everybody watched almost everything on the one monopolistic channel. . . . Moreover, the shared experience of viewing often made for conversation across ideological lines. . . . [T]he shared central space of television news and public affairs constituted a virtual town meeting."[6]

One lesson is that a democracy "may be enhanced, rather than impeded, by gathering its citizens in a single public space set aside for receiving and discussing reliable reports on the issues of the day."[7] It is not necessary to think that a one-channel policy is good or even tolerable in order to recognize that shared viewing, supplying common experiences for most or all people, can be extremely valuable from the democratic point of view. The central reason is that it promotes democratic discussion and might well promote better solutions from public officials.

There is a connected point. Information has a special property: when any one of us learns something, other people, and perhaps many other people, might end up benefiting from what we have learned. If you find out about crime in the neighborhood or risks associated with certain foods, others will gain from that knowledge. In a system with general-interest intermediaries, many of us come across information from which we may not substantially benefit as individuals, but that we nevertheless spread to others. Society as a whole is much better off as a result. As we have seen, a system in which individuals can design their own communications universe threatens to undermine this salutary process, not only because of the risk of spreading false information via cybercascades, but also because the situation of fragmentation prevents true (and valuable) information from spreading as much as it should.

SOLIDARITY GOODS

Most people understand the importance of common experiences, and many of our practices reflect a firm sense of the point. National holidays help constitute a nation by encouraging citizens to think, all at once, about events of shared significance. And they do much more than this. They enable people, in all their diversity, to have some common memories and concerns.

At least this is true in nations where national holidays have a vivid and concrete meaning, as they do, for example, in younger democracies such as South Africa, India, and Israel. In the United

States, many national holidays have become mere days-off-from-work, and the precipitating occasion for the day off—President's Day, Memorial Day, or Labor Day—has lost its salience; we seem to have forgotten our history, along with the struggles and celebrations that gave rise to the holidays themselves. This is a serious loss.

With the partial exception of the Fourth of July, Martin Luther King Jr. Day is probably the closest thing to a genuinely substantive national holiday in the United States, largely because that celebration involves not-ancient events that can be treated as concrete and meaningful. In other words, the holiday is *about* something. A shared celebration of a holiday with a clear meaning helps to constitute a nation and bring diverse citizens together. September 11 is a day of mourning, and hardly a holiday, but it is a time for national remembrance and reflection, and that is immensely important.

Nor need such events be limited to nations. One of the great values of the Olympics is its international quality, allowing people from different countries to form bonds of commonality, both directly through participation by athletes, and indirectly through shared viewing and interest. Of course the Olympics is also a vehicle for crude forms of nationalism. But at its best, the governing ethos is cosmopolitan in spirit.

Communications and the media are exceptionally important here. Sometimes millions of people follow an election, a sporting event, a release of a movie, or the coronation of a new monarch, and many of them do so because of the simultaneous actions of others. In this sense, some of the experiences made possible by modern technologies are *solidarity goods*—their value goes up when and because many other people are enjoying or consuming them. As Edna Ullmann-Margalit has shown, people often enjoy "solidarity in consumption."[8] The point very much bears on the historic role of both public forums and general-interest intermediaries. Street corners and public parks were and remain places where diverse people can congregate and see one another. General-interest intermediaries, if they are operating properly, give many people, all at once, a clear sense of social problems and tasks.

Why might these shared experiences be so desirable or important? There are three principal reasons.

1. Simple enjoyment may not be the most important thing, but it is far from irrelevant. Often people *like* many experiences—including experiences associated with television, radio, and the Internet—simply because those experiences are being shared. Consider a new *Star Wars* movie, the Super Bowl, or a presidential debate. For some of us, these are goods that are worth less, and possibly worthless, if many others are not enjoying or purchasing them too. Hence for many people, a presidential debate may be worthy of individual attention in part because so many other people consider it worthy of individual attention.

2. Sometimes shared experiences help to promote and ease social interactions, permitting people to recognize and speak with one another, and congregate around a common topic, issue, task, or concern, whether or not they have much in common. In this sense shared experiences provide a form of *social glue*. They help make it possible for diverse people to believe—to know—that they live in the same culture. Indeed, they help constitute that shared culture simply by creating common memories and experiences and a sense of a common enterprise. Most of the time, this benefit is relatively modest. But it can also help to connect people in difficult times, as when the economy is in terrible condition or the nation faces a threat to its security.

3. A fortunate consequence of shared experiences—and in particular, many of those produced by general-interest intermediaries—is that people who would otherwise see one another as quite unfamiliar, in extreme cases as nearly belonging to a different species, can come instead to regard one another as fellow citizens with shared hopes, goals, and concerns. This is a subjective good—felt and perceived as a

good—for those directly involved. But it can be an objective good as well, especially if it leads to cooperative projects of various kinds. When people learn about a disaster faced by fellow citizens, for example, they may respond with financial and other help. In the aftermath of the attacks of 9/11, Americans did exactly that, and saw one another, to a greater and deeper extent, as involved in a common enterprise. The point applies internationally as well as domestically; massive relief efforts are frequently made possible by virtue of the fact that millions of people learn, all at once, about the relevant need.

Any well-functioning society depends on relationships of trust and reciprocity, in which people see their fellow citizens as potential allies, willing to help and deserving of help when help is needed. The level, or stock, of these relationships sometimes goes by the name of "social capital."[9] We might generalize the points made thus far by suggesting that shared experiences, emphatically including those made possible by the system of communications, contribute to desirable relationships among citizens, even strangers. A society without such experiences will inevitably suffer a decline in those relationships.

FEWER SHARED EXPERIENCES

Even in a nation of unlimited communications options, some events, such as a serious terrorist attack, will inevitably attract widespread attention. On the Internet itself, some sites, such as newyorktimes .com and wallstreetjournal.com, play an especially prominent role; a degree of centralization remains. But simply as a matter of numbers, an increasingly diverse communications universe will reduce the level of shared experiences. When there were only three television networks, much of what appeared on television would have the quality of a genuinely common experience. The lead story on the evening news would provide the same reference point for many millions of people. This is decreasingly true. In recent decades, the three major networks have lost tens of millions of viewers. As a result of increased options, the most highly rated show on current network television has far fewer viewers than the fifteenth most highly rated show in a typical year in the 1970s.

To the extent that choices and filtering proliferate, it is inevitable that diverse individuals and groups will share fewer reference points. Events that are highly salient to some people will barely register on others' viewscreens. And it is possible that some views and perspectives that seem obvious for many people will be barely intelligible for others.

One more time: This is far from an unambiguously bad thing. On balance, it is almost certainly good. When people are able to make specific choices, they are likely to enjoy what they are seeing or doing. Of course a degree of diversity, with respect to both topics and points of view, is highly desirable. No one suggests that everyone should, or should be required to, watch the same thing. The question does not involve requirements at all. My only claim is that a common set of frameworks and experiences is valuable for a heterogeneous society, and that a system with limitless options, making for diverse choices, will compromise some important social values.

If we think, with Supreme Court Justice Brandeis, that a great menace to freedom is an "inert people," and if we believe that a set of common experiences promotes active citizenship and mutual self-understanding, we will be concerned by any developments that greatly reduce those experiences. The ideal of consumer sovereignty makes it hard even to understand this concern. But from the standpoint of republican ideals, the concern should lie at the center of any evaluation of a system of communications.

CONSUMERS AND PRODUCERS

None of this means that shared experiences are disappearing. Of course people know that such experiences are desirable, and often they cooperate with one another so as to ensure that they will have such experiences. Because the barriers to communication are far lower online, interested people can decide, at once, to do or watch the same thing. Collaborative filtering can be effective here. If you know that most "people like you" are going to go see a new movie about World War II, you might be more likely to go see that movie. Consumers themselves can band together, across geographic lines, to ensure that they do or watch the same thing.

In this way, current communications technologies can promote shared experiences, even among people who do not know each other or who would not otherwise think of one another as group members. With Facebook, millions or even hundreds of millions of people are able to have shared experiences. But even so, it can be less likely for large numbers of people to coordinate around a single option, simply because the array of options is so dazzlingly large. This point is enough to suggest the basis for my general concern.

It is true that producers of information have strong incentives to get people to coordinate around a shared experience. They might themselves emphasize, for instance, that most people, or most people like you, will be watching a television show dealing with crime in the area or the difficulty of raising children in an urban environment. Or advertisers might stress the importance for diverse people of examining a certain website, in general or at a specific time. In fact, an extremely effective way of getting people to engage in certain conduct is to say that most people, or most people like you, are doing exactly that. In this way, ordinary market forces are likely to diminish the problem.

But they will not eliminate it. To the degree that options are limitless, it is inevitable that producers will have some difficulty in getting people to watch something together, even if people would benefit from this activity. It is more likely that diverse groups, defined in demographic, political, or other terms, will occasionally coordinate on agreed-on alternatives, and this will introduce the various problems associated with fragmentation and group polarization.

INFORMATION AS A PUBLIC GOOD

Thus far I have dealt with the purposes served by ensuring common experiences, many of them made available via the media. There is a related and equally important point. Information is a "public good" in a technical sense used by economists: when one person knows something, others are likely to be benefited as well. If you learn that a heat wave is coming or there is a high risk of criminal assault three blocks away, other people are highly likely to learn these things too. In the terminology of economics, those of us who learn things do not fully "internalize" the benefits of that learning; the benefits amount to "positive externalities" for other people.

In this respect, information has properties in common with environmental protection and national defense. When one person is helped by a program for cleaner air or by a strong military, other people will necessarily benefit as well. It is standard to say that in circumstances of this kind—when public goods are involved—it is hazardous to rely entirely on individual choices. Acting on their own, those who litter or otherwise pollute are unlikely to consider the harms they impose on others. Acting on their own, people are unlikely to contribute to national defense, hoping that others will pick up the slack.

What is true for pollution and national defense is true as well for information. Made solely with reference to the concerns of the individuals involved, private choices will produce too much pollution and too little in the way of national defense or information. When you learn, or do not learn, about the pattern of crime in your city or whether employers are discriminating on the basis of sex, you are usually not thinking about the consequences of your learning, or failure to learn, for other people (except perhaps your immediate family). An implication is that an individual's rational choices, made only with reference to individual self-interest, will produce too little knowledge of public affairs. These are the most conventional cases of market failure—which in the context of pollution and national defense, are addressed through government programs designed to overcome the predictable problems that would come from relying entirely on individual choices. With the decline of general-interest intermediaries, we may need to think similarly about how to address market failures in our communications system.

No one ever planned this, but when they work well, general-interest intermediaries provide an excellent corrective. When individuals do not design their communications universe on their own, they will be exposed to a great deal of material from which they may not much benefit as individuals, but from which they will be able to help many others. Perhaps you would not ordinarily seek out material about new asthma treatments for children, but once you learn a little bit about them, you might tell your friend whose son has asthma. Perhaps you are not much interested in traffic safety risks, but once you learn about the hazards associated with texting while driving, you might be reinforced in your desire not to text while driving, and you might tell people you know about the underlying problems, trying to convince them. Every day, in fact, millions of people are beneficiaries of information that they receive only because someone else who has not sought out that information in advance happens to learn it.

I am certainly not arguing that from the point of view of dissemination of information, it would be better to abolish the Internet and rely on a system dominated by a few general-interest intermediaries. Nothing could be further from the truth. As we have seen, current technologies dramatically accelerate the spreading of information, true as well as false.

General-interest intermediaries have interests and biases of their own, and for sheer practical reasons, they cannot provide exposure to all topics and viewpoints. On balance, the increase in options is likely to produce more and better information. Social media are a terrific boon on that count. My only suggestion is that insofar as there is a perfect ability to filter, people will sometimes fail to learn things from which they might have ended up benefiting others. Even if an increase in communications options is, with respect to information, a significant gain, this remains a serious loss.

FAMINE AS METAPHOR, AND A CLARIFICATION

Let's now return to Sen's finding that famines do not occur in nations with free elections and a democratic press. We should take all this not as an isolated or exotic example limited to poor countries at risk of famine but instead as a metaphor for countless situations in which a democratic government averts social problems precisely because political pressure forces it to do so. The underlying problems often involve crime, pollution, natural disasters, employment opportunities, health risks, medical advances, political candidates, or even corruption.

This point shows that there are serious problems if information is seen as an ordinary consumer product. The simple reason is that in a system in which individuals make choices among innumerable options based only on their private interest, they will fail to learn about topics and views from which they may not much benefit, but from which others would gain a great deal.

Current technologies have great potential on these counts as well. If the press is free and the Internet is available, information about a potential or actual famine, or any other problem, can be spread to an entire nation and even the entire world. Facebook, Twitter, Instagram, and Snapchat can easily be used for that purpose. Fragmentation might even help here, at least if relevant information spreads across the fragmented groups; the problem arises if such spreading does not occur. What I am offering is simply an account of the frequently overlooked importance, for a system of free expression, of shared experiences and the provision of information to people who would not have chosen it in advance.

OF NICHES AND LONG TAILS

In an illuminating and instructive book, Chris Anderson celebrates niches and niche marketing, seeing them as an extraordinary development made possible by the Internet.[10] To simplify his story, Anderson argues that companies can and do make increasing amounts of money by catering to niche markets through a large volume of products (books a la Amazon.com or movies a la Netflix). Few people buy many of these products. At a bookstore, little money can be made by the poor sellers, which are at the end of the long tail of the distribution system. At Amazon.com, by contrast, the immense stock of books and the large customer base can ensure that significant aggregate sales come from the long tail.

Anderson sees this as an important and wonderful trend. With the aid of the Internet and other modern technologies, it is often nearly costless to sell not just the blockbusters but also goods that cater to small markets. Indeed, the total profits from doing so may be high. "Niche" is a key word in Anderson's argument.

Anderson makes a valuable point. He is right to emphasize that the Internet can greatly increase niche marketing in a way that offers extraordinary economic opportunities from the long tail. He is also right to suggest that communities can form around highly specialized tastes. But it is also important to see what might be wrong with a world of niches. The power to choose the particular good that each particular person particularly wants is not an unambiguous good; there is more to do than to notice and celebrate this process. Anderson's analysis appears implicitly premised on the idea that freedom and the good life are promoted by, and maybe even captured in, the opportunity to choose what is specifically sought on either the large head or the long tail. Of course it is appropriate to celebrate the increase in available options, but from the standpoint of democracy, the assessment is not so simple.

The reluctance to raise questions about the proliferation of niches is characteristic of a great deal of thinking about the Internet and social media, even among their most creative and sharpest analysts. Indeed, we might go further. Many of those who know most about the underlying technology and what is becoming possible often display a kind of visceral, unreflective libertarianism—a belief that all that matters is that people are allowed to see what they want and choose what they like. The commitments to free markets and perfecting them are no less intense than what can be found in the ideas of the Chicago school of economics, most famously captured in the work of Milton Friedman. As a longtime professor at the University of Chicago, where I taught from 1981 until 2007, I confess a great deal of fondness for the Chicago school; in my view, it is mostly right, and certainly more right than wrong. For consumer goods—such as sneakers, cars, soaps, and candy—it provides the right foundation for analysis. But when we are speaking of politics and the democratic domain, it misses a great deal.

The risk is that the proliferation of niches will harm aspects of our shared culture and also promote fragmentation, especially along political lines. It is not enough to rest content with general observations about how a good many people are curious, and how niches include and even create shared cultures of different kinds.

OF BIASES AND ELITES

It is an understatement to say that many people deplore the mass media. Some insist that television networks and large newspapers are biased in one direction or another. Perhaps they reflect some kind of left-of-center consensus. Perhaps they refuse to take on the status quo. Perhaps they pander to ratings and the bottom line at the expense of real news. Perhaps they simply reflect a pale, watered-down version of the dense reality of what people actually think (the "lamestream media"). Perhaps the mass media are simply not in touch with people's struggles and concerns.

Many people think that the mass media are hopelessly superficial, even sensationalistic, obsessed with reporting on who said the latest mean or cruel thing, who's fighting with whom, or crimes and celebrities and sound bites. (In the 2016 presidential campaign, of course, Trump's insults were inevitably big news.) Still others think that general-interest intermediaries are inevitably few in number, and hence that they produce a stifling degree of homogeneity. "Let millions or even billions speak in their own authentic voice," they say. Or, "Here comes everybody." For any of these people, a world with the Internet is infinitely better than a world in which general-interest intermediaries dominate the scene. In this light, any effort to celebrate those intermediaries and emphasize the risks of social fragmentation might seem positively quaint at best. Isn't it elitist, or confused, to wish for a world in which people cannot read what they want and are subjected to filters by a self-appointed media elite?

It would hardly be desirable for a few newspapers and broadcasters to dominate the scene. With the Internet, the situation is definitely better, not worse. The social media are a great boon, not least because people can both receive so much information and get a lot of it out there. Nor do I claim that newspapers and broadcasters generally do an excellent or even good job. Those who think that newspapers and weekly magazines are biased or otherwise inadequate should have no quarrel with the suggestion that unchosen encounters and shared experiences, of one or another sort, are important for democracy.

We have seen that some of the most popular Internet sites work in a similar fashion to general-interest intermediaries. Indeed, they *are* general-interest intermediaries, performing the same functions online that they do on television or paper; consider ABC, CBS, NBC, Fox News, the *New York Times*, the *Washington Post*, the *Los Angeles Times*, the *Wall Street Journal*, and many more. In any case, many popular sites contain links, advertising, and multiple news stories. To the extent that important Internet sites continue to serve the social role of intermediaries, there is less to worry about.

There is nonetheless a difference between an evening program or newspaper, which puts numerous stories before your eyes with at least a modicum of detail, and an Internet site, which may contain a visible headline or quick link to new topics, but that does not expose people in nearly the same way to diverse topics and points of view. I have a good friend (actually, it's my wife) who insists on reading the daily newspaper in hard copy rather than online. The reason is exactly this: she wants to see, in front of her eyes, the full spread of stories on the various pages. She doesn't want a situation in which she merely sees a menu of options and is authorized to click on what interests her. The opening paragraphs matter, and sometimes they grab her, and she wants them right in front of her eyes.

It is true and important that the most popular sites contain links, advertising, and multiple news stories. But concerns about self-insulation remain. And with personalization—by choosers or those who choose for them—the problem is compounded.

THE NETWORKED PUBLIC SPHERE

The idea of the Daily Me points to the risk of social fragmentation. But precisely because time is limited, it has been possible to think that the Internet will not make all that much of a difference to how we get our information—that a few providers will pretty much dominate the Internet no less than they do television and radio. Online, attention is a highly scarce commodity, and it is inevitable that many people will congregate around a few major sites, perhaps the sites of those that constitute the mass media in any case. The *New York Times* and the *Washington Post* have large circulations, and millions of people visit their sites; the *New York Review of Books* and the *National Review* have significant but much smaller circulations, and they are read online in similar proportions. If we stress these points, continuing concentration, and not echo chambers, might seem to be the wave of the future. The basic tale is less one of change than of continuity, with differences of degree rather than kind.

What do we actually know about use of the Internet? A picture is already emerging, and I will be offering many more details. But let's begin with a careful and illuminating analysis, now dated but still unsurpassed, in which law professor Yochai Benkler describes and celebrates the "networked public sphere."[11]

Benkler shows that the prediction of continuity is essentially inconsistent with the current reality. To be sure, some sites are exceedingly popular, and others are seen by very few people. At the same time, the new model is different from that of the old mass media. In the networked public sphere, there are numerous voices, and what is seen or heard depends on how things emerge in relevant networks. A small voice can become a large one. In Benkler's words, "Clusters of moderately read sites provide platforms for vastly greater numbers of speakers than were heard in the mass-media environment."[12] Even if your site or blog has few readers, one of those readers might draw your words to the attention of someone with more readers. If that happens, a still more popular site might pick up your words, and eventually you might have a real influence. We might even see a cascade. That's altogether different from anything that happened before.

Something of this kind happens online every day, and it works for those who run smaller websites as well. It works even more clearly with Facebook and Twitter. A tweet might get retweeted by one person with five thousand followers, and then by someone with twenty thousand followers, and then by someone with eight hundred thousand followers. To be sure, the real Internet does not operate as a system in which "everyone [is] a pamphleteer."[13] But it is genuinely new, simply because it has so many more voices, so much more information, and such broad participation, with overlapping and unpredictable networks, leading to cascade effects, and suddenly visible bits of information whose popularity no one could have foreseen.

Of course what emerges may be a perspective or formulation, rather than information as such; consider what makes things go viral on Twitter (for example, #BlackLivesMatter). Benkler wrote before the emergence of anything like the social media in their current form, but his argument works at least as well for the contemporary situation.

Like many others, Benkler insists that the networked public sphere is essentially immune from the risks of fragmentation and polarization—that a common discourse remains, in the form of a public sphere that generates shared concerns and public knowledge. Benkler's interpretation has considerable truth, but we have seen strong reasons to question it, and we will see more. Indeed, his own evidence much complicates his conclusion. As he suggests, we now know that "sites cluster—in particular, topically and interest-related sites link much more heavily to each other than to other sites."[14] This has been precisely my concern here. Many people segregate themselves along lines of both topics and points of view. In Benkler's own words, individuals "cluster around topical, organizational, or other common features," and like-minded people "read each other and quote each other much more than . . . the other side," if only to sort out their internal disagreements.[15]

With social media, that is exactly what is happening. We have seen that on Twitter and Facebook, people definitely cluster, at least on some issues; they tend to circulate stories with which they agree. As we have also seen, an evident reason is confirmation bias: people are biased to like and to publicize opinions and information (real or apparent) that support what they think. Falsehoods spread rapidly, and to the extent that people are reading and speaking to like-minded others, group polarization is inevitable. It is a fact of life in the networked public sphere.[16]

In sum, the public sphere is definitely networked, and ideas in a tweet or blog post often bubble up to a larger group. But there is a lot of fragmentation, and for self-government, that can be a problem.

SPREADING INFORMATION

A heterogeneous society benefits from shared experiences, many of them produced by the media. These shared experiences provide a kind of social glue, facilitating efforts to solve shared problems, encouraging people to view one another as fellow citizens, and sometimes helping to ensure responsiveness to genuine problems and needs, and even helping to identify them as such. A special virtue of unsought exposures to information is that even if individuals frequently do not gain much from that information, they will tell other people about it, and it is here that the information will prove beneficial.

To the extent that the communications market becomes more personalized, it reduces the range of widely shared experiences and at the same time fails to confer some of the benefits that come when individuals receive information, often more helpful to others than to themselves, that they would not have chosen in advance. If the role of public forums and general-interest intermediaries is diminished, and if good substitutes do not develop, those benefits will be diminished as well, with harmful results for democratic ideals.

CITIZENS

The authors of the US Constitution met behind closed doors in Philadelphia during summer 1787. When they completed their labors, the American public was, naturally enough, exceedingly curious about what they had done. A large crowd gathered around what is now known as Convention Hall. One of its members asked Benjamin Franklin, as he emerged from the building, "What have you given us?" Franklin's answer was hopeful, or perhaps a challenge: "A republic, if you can keep it." In fact, we should see Franklin's remark as a reminder of a continuing obligation. The text of any founding document is likely to be far less important in maintaining a republic than the actions and commitments of the nation's citizenry over time.

This suggestion raises questions of its own. What is the relationship between our choices and our freedom? Between citizens and consumers? And how do the answers relate to the questions of whether and how government should deal with people's emerging power to filter speech content?

In this chapter, my basic claim is that we should evaluate communications technologies and social media by asking how they affect us as citizens, not only by asking how they affect us as consumers. A central question is whether emerging social practices, including consumption patterns, are promoting or compromising our own highest aspirations. More particularly I make two suggestions, designed to undermine from a new direction the idea that consumer sovereignty is the appropriate goal for communications policy.

The first is that people's preferences do not come from nature or the sky. They are a product, at least in part, of social circumstances, including existing institutions, available options, social influences, and past choices. Prominent among the circumstances that create preferences are markets themselves. "Free marketeers have little to cheer about if all they can claim is that the market is efficient at filling desires that the market itself creates."[1] Unrestricted consumer choices are important—sometimes very important. They are a large part of freedom. But they do not exhaust that idea, and they should not be entirely equated with it.

The second point has to do with the fact that in their capacity as citizens, people sometimes seek policies and embrace goals that diverge from the choices they make in their capacity as consumers. If citizens seek to do this, there is no legitimate objection from the standpoint of freedom—at least if citizens are not disfavoring any particular point of view or otherwise violating rights. Often citizens attempt to promote their highest aspirations through democratic institutions. If the result is to produce a communications market that is different from what individual consumers would seek—if as citizens we produce a market, for example, that promotes exposure to serious issues and a range of shared experiences—freedom will be promoted, not undermined.

The two points are best taken together. Citizens are often aware that their private choices under a system of limitless options may lead in unfortunate directions, both for them as individuals and society at large. They might believe that their own choices with respect to television and the Internet do not entirely promote their own well-being, or that of society as a whole. They might attempt to restructure alternatives and institutions so as to improve the situation.

At the same time, I will suggest that even insofar as we are consumers, new purchasing opportunities, made ever more available through the Internet, are far less wonderful than we like to think. The reason is that these opportunities are accelerating the "consumption treadmill," in which we buy more and better goods, not because they make us happier or better off, but because they help us keep up with others. As citizens, we might well seek to slow down this treadmill, so as to ensure that social resources are devoted not to keeping up with one another but instead to goods and services that really improve our lives.

CHOICES AND CIRCUMSTANCES, AND CHINA

Many people seem to think that freedom consists of respect for consumption choices, whatever their origins and content. Indeed, this thought appears to underlie enthusiasm for the principle of consumer sovereignty itself. On this view, the central goal of a well-functioning system of free expression is to ensure unrestricted choice. A similar conception of freedom lies behind many of the celebrations of emerging communications markets.

It is obvious that a free society is generally respectful of people's choices. But freedom requires certain preconditions, ensuring not just respect for choices and the satisfaction of preferences, whatever they happen to be, but also the free formation of desires and beliefs. Most preferences and beliefs do not preexist social institutions; they are formed and shaped by existing arrangements. Much of the time, people develop tastes for what they are used to seeing and experiencing. If you are used to seeing stories about the local sports team, your interest in the local sports team is likely to increase. If news programs deal with a certain topic—say, welfare reform, immigration, refugees, environmental protection, or a current threat of war—your taste for that topic is likely to be strengthened.

If you learn that most people like a certain movie, book, political candidate, or idea, you will be more likely to like them too, and this effect is increased if the relevant people are "like you." (Donald Trump used this phenomenon to excellent effect in the 2016 campaign for the presidency.) Recall the experiment with music downloads, in which the success or failure of songs was largely a product of people's perceptions of what other people had done.

When people are deprived of opportunities, they are likely to adapt, and develop preferences and tastes for what little they have. We are entitled to say that the deprivation of opportunities is a deprivation of freedom—even if people have adapted to it and do not much want anything more. Similar points hold for the world of communications. If people are deprived of access to competing views on public issues, and if as a result they lack a taste for those views, they lack freedom, whatever the nature of their preferences and choices. The problem is most serious, of course, in authoritarian societies, which engage in the defining evil of censorship. But it can arise also in a world with a sea of choices.

Consider in this regard the behavior of the Chinese government on social media. In his great classic of behavioral science, *How to Win Friends and Influence People*, first published in 1936, Dale Carnegie contended that you can't really win an argument, so you shouldn't even try. "Nine times out of ten, an argument ends with each of the contestants more firmly convinced than ever that he is absolutely right."[2] In important respects, the Chinese government is taking Carnegie's advice to heart.

It has long been widely believed that China has been paying civilians a small fee (about 50¢ per post) to go online using pseudonyms to rebut the claims of those who are critical of the government and its policies. That kind of "reverse censorship," undertaken by a supposed "50c Party," has been thought to be one of the government's favorite strategies for combating dissent.

Using a complex and ingenious empirical strategy, Harvard's Gary King and his colleagues find otherwise.[3] They begin by analyzing in depth a large archive of e-mails leaked from the Internet Propaganda Office of Zhanggong, a district of Ganzhou City in Jiangxi Province. Extrapolating to the rest of China, and checking their numbers through multiple routes, they estimate that the government fabricates an astonishing number of social media posts per year: 448 million. But there is no 50c Party of ordinary citizens. The fabrications come mostly from government employees, contributing part time outside their regular jobs.

More important, the contents of those posts are not at all what people think (or what King and his colleagues themselves expected). The fabricated posts hardly ever engage in arguments with the government's critics. On the contrary, they ignore them. For the most part, they focus instead on the wonderful things that the government is supposedly doing. King and his colleagues call this "cheerleading," and it includes "expressions of patriotism, encouragement and motivation, inspirational slogans or quotes, gratefulness, discussions of aspirational figures, cultural references, or celebrations."[4]

The government's goal, then, is not to meet criticism on the merits but instead to distract people by redirecting their attention in its preferred direction. It follows a passive principle: *do not engage at all on controversial issues*. Hence the government makes no effort to confront social media posts that contain general grievances about the regime or its leaders. Nor does it censor such posts, at least as a general rule.

How come? King and his coauthors contend that China's government has no reason to respond or censor, because "numerous grievances of a population ruled autocratically by non-elected leaders are obvious and omnipresent."[5] If citizens learn about one more grievance, officials have little reason for concern. But one class of social media posts does alarm the Chinese government: discussions that, in its view, have real potential to give rise to collective action. Such discussions include information about imminent protest activity or specific plans to initiate some kind of uprising.

Because the government sees these discussions as threatening, it responds in two ways. First, it engages in censorship. Second, it coordinates identifiable and timely "bursts" of cheerleading, designed to focus people on what's going well. In view of this pervasive pattern, King and his coauthors conclude that officials in the Chinese regime think that the main threat "is not military attacks from foreign enemies but rather uprisings from their own people."[6]

The behavior of the Chinese government is consistent with two general insights in modern social science. The first is that if you want to win friends and influence people, you would do better to change the subject than to pick an argument. We have seen that in the political domain, substantive arguments can intensify people's commitment to their original beliefs. One reason is that those arguments focus people on the issues that most concern them. A lesson for politicians, employers, and spouses alike is that it is often smarter to change the subject.

The second insight is that information about current protest activities and collective action designed to spur rebellion can turn into sparks, ultimately creating big fires.[7] When members of the public are widely dissatisfied, a seemingly small protest movement can sound a general alarm, informing citizens that others are dissatisfied too—and prepared to do something about it. And once people hear that alarm, things can spiral out of control. In the Arab Spring, that's exactly what happened.[8] And that's exactly what Chinese officials want to avoid.

The Chinese government certainly has had many extraordinary achievements over the past decades, above all in terms of economic growth. But every nondemocratic system has a degree of fragility. The government's surprising behavior on social media attests to its keen awareness of that fact—and its evident belief that at least in the domain of politics, Carnegie had it right.

PREFERENCE FORMATION

These points about online attention and distraction—sometimes through cheerleading—have much broader implications, because they tell us something about how preferences are formed (or deformed). If people are exposed mostly to sensationalistic coverage of the lives of movie stars, only to sports, or only to left-of-center views and never to international issues, their preferences will develop accordingly. If people are mostly watching a conservative station—say, Fox News—or if their Twitter feed consists of conservative views, they will inevitably be affected by what they see. If people are mostly exposed to material that celebrates the current government— whether it is China, Cuba, France, or the United States—their preferences might well be changed as a result. Whatever one's political views, there is, in an important respect, a problem from the standpoint of freedom itself. This is so even if people are voluntarily choosing the limited fare.

The general idea here—that preferences and beliefs are a product of existing institutions and practices, and that the result can be a form of unfreedom, one of the most serious of all—is hardly new. It is a long-standing theme in political and legal thought. Thus Alexis de Tocqueville wrote of the effects of the institution of slavery on the desires of many slaves themselves that "plunged in this abyss of wretchedness, the Negro hardly notices his ill fortune; he was reduced to slavery by violence, and the habit of servitude has given him the thoughts and ambitions of a slave; he admires his tyrants even more than he hates them and finds his joy and pride in servile imitation of his oppressors."[9]

In the same vein, Dewey wrote that "social conditions may restrict, distort, and almost prevent the development of individuality." He insisted that we should therefore "take an active interest in the working of social institutions that have a bearing, positive or negative, upon the growth of individuals." For Dewey, a just society "is as much interested in the positive construction of favorable institutions, legal, political, and economic, as it is in the work of removing abuses and overt oppressions."[10] Robert Frank and Philip Cook have urged that in the communications market, existing "financial incentives strongly favor sensational, lurid and formulaic offerings," and that the resulting structure of rewards "is especially troubling in light of evidence that, beginning in infancy and continuing through life, the things we see and read profoundly alter the kinds of people we become."[11]

On social media, something very much like this happens every day. You may or may not be what you eat, but you can turn into what you read. If you read snark, you might well become snark. At least some people who read materials that promote terrorism will become terrorists. If you join an echo chamber, or turn your Facebook page into one, you might well end up changing your own values and even your own character.

Every tyrant knows that it is important and sometimes possible not only to constrain people's actions but also to manipulate their desires, partly by making people fearful, partly by putting certain options in an unfavorable light, and partly by limiting information. And nontyrannical governments are hardly neutral with respect to preferences and desires. They hope to have citizens who are active rather than passive, curious rather than indifferent, engaged rather than inert. Indeed, the basic institutions of private property and freedom of contract—fundamental to free societies and freedom of speech—have significant effects on the development of preferences themselves.

Thus both private property and freedom of contract have long been defended not on the ground that they are neutral with respect to preferences but instead because they help to form good preferences—by producing an entrepreneurial spirit and encouraging people to see one another, not as potential enemies or members of different ethnic groups, but as potential trading partners.[12] The right to free speech is itself best seen as part of the project of helping to produce an engaged, self-governing citizenry.

LIMITED OPTIONS: OF FOXES AND SOUR GRAPES

Whenever government imposes restrictions on people's opportunities and information, it is likely to undermine freedom by affecting not merely their choices but also their preferences and desires. Of course, this is what concerned Tocqueville and Dewey, and in unfree nations, we can find numerous examples in the area of communications and media policy, as official censorship prevents people from learning about a variety of ideas and possibilities.

This was common practice in Communist nations in the Soviet bloc, and some nations have sought to reduce general access to the Internet, partly in an effort to shape both preferences and beliefs. When information is unavailable, and when opportunities are shut off and known to be shut off, people may end up not wanting them at all. To be sure, the opposite might happen: people might want things precisely *because* they are unavailable. But human beings are adaptive, and they don't like to be miserable, and when things are unavailable, many people will lose interest or just not want them.

The social theorist Jon Elster illustrates the point through the old tale of the fox and the sour grapes.[13] The fox does not want the grapes because he believes them to be sour, but the fox believes them to be sour *because* they are unavailable, and he adjusts his attitude toward the grapes in a way that responds to the fact of their unavailability. The fox cannot have the grapes, and so he concludes that they are sour and that he doesn't want them. Elster says, quite rightly, that the unavailability of the grapes cannot be justified by reference to the preferences of the fox, when the unavailability of the grapes is the very *reason* for the preferences of the fox.

Elster's broader suggestion is that citizens who have been deprived of options may not want the things of which they have been deprived, and the deprivation cannot be justified by reference to the fact that citizens are not asking for these things, when they are not asking *because* they have been deprived of them. People's preferences and even their values may be a result of what they have not been able to obtain. That is a deep objection to any effort to defend a status quo by pointing to what people currently "want."

We can specify a problem with authoritarian systems in this light. Imagine that an authoritarian government ensures a system of few or dramatically limited options—including, for example, an official government news program and nothing else. Imagine that such a government restricts access to social media. It is predictable that many citizens will despise that system, at least when they speak privately. But even if there is little or no public demand for more options, the system cannot reasonably be defended on the ground that most people do not object to it. The absence of the demand is likely to be a product of the deprivation. It does not justify the deprivation. This point holds with respect to television, radio stations, and social media as with everything else.

Thus far I have been making arguments for a range of opportunities, even in societies in which people, lacking such opportunities, are not asking for more. Of course the issue is very different in the communications universe that is the main topic of this book—one in which people have countless possibilities from which to choose. But here too social circumstances, including markets, affect preferences, not only the other way around. From the standpoint of citizenship and freedom, problems can emerge when people are voluntarily choosing alternatives that sharply limit their own horizons.

Preferences are a product not only of the number of options but also of what markets accentuate, social influences (especially in one's peer group), and one's own past choices, which can impose constraints of their own. Suppose, for instance, that one person's choices have been limited to sports and lead her to learn little about political issues; that another person focuses only on national issues because she has no interest in what happens outside US borders; and that still another restricts herself to material that reaffirms her own political convictions. In different ways, each of these person's choices constrains both citizenship and freedom, simply because it dramatically narrows their field of interests and concerns.

This is hardly a claim that people should be required to see things that do not interest them. It is a more mundane point about how any existing market and our own choices can limit or expand our freedom. Indeed, people are often aware of this fact, and make choices so as to promote wider understanding and better formation of their own preferences. Sometimes we select radio and television programs, websites, and items on our Twitter feed from which we will learn something, even if what we choose is more challenging and less fun than the alternatives. And we may even lament the very choices that we make on the ground that what we have done, as consumers, does not serve our long-term interests. Whether or not people actually lament their choices, they sometimes have good reason to do so, and they know this without admitting it. These points underlie some of the most important functions of public forums and general-interest intermediaries.

Both of these produce unanticipated exposures that help promote the free formation of preferences, even in a world of numerous options. In this sense, they are continuous with the educational system. They provide a kind of continuing education for adults—something that a free society cannot do without. It does not matter whether the government is directly responsible for the institutions that perform this role. What matters is that they exist.

DEMOCRATIC INSTITUTIONS AND CONSUMER SOVEREIGNTY

None of these points means that some abstraction called "government" should feel free to move preferences and beliefs in what it considers to be desirable directions. The central question is whether citizens in a democratic system, aware of the points made thus far, might want to make choices that diverge from those that they make in their capacity as private consumers. Sometimes this does appear to be their desire. The public's effort to counteract the adverse effects of consumer choices should not be disparaged as a form of government meddling or unacceptable paternalism, at least if the government is democratic and reacting to the reflective judgments of the citizenry.

What we think and what we want often depend on the social role in which we find ourselves, and the role of citizen is quite different from that of consumer. Citizens do not think and act as consumers. Most citizens have no difficulty in distinguishing between the two roles. Frequently a nation's political choices could not be understood if viewed only as a process of implementing people's desires in their capacity as consumers. For example, some people seek stringent laws protecting the environment or endangered species even though they do not use the public parks or derive material benefits from protection of such species; they approve of laws calling for social security and welfare even though they do not save or give to the poor; they support antidiscrimination laws even though their own behavior is hardly race or gender neutral. The choices people make as political participants can be systematically different from those they make as consumers.

Why is this? Is it a puzzle or paradox? The most basic answer is that people's behavior as citizens reflects a variety of distinctive influences. In their role as citizens, people might seek to implement their highest aspirations when they do not do so in private consumption. So too, they might aspire to a communications system of a particular kind—one that promotes democratic goals—and they might try to promote that aspiration through law. Acting in the fashion of Ulysses anticipating the sirens, people might "precommit" themselves in democratic processes to a course of action that they consider to be in the general interest. And in their capacity as citizens, they might attempt to satisfy altruistic or other-regarding desires, which diverge from the self-interested preferences often characteristic of the behavior of consumers in markets. In fact, social and cultural norms can incline people to express aspirational or altruistic goals more frequently in political behavior than in markets.

It is certainly true that selfish behavior is common in politics. The whole field of public choice theory sees political action as a product of the efforts of self-interested individuals and institutions to move government in their preferred directions. There is considerable truth in that account—though my own experience in the executive branch of the US government during the Obama administration suggests that public choice theorists wildly exaggerate the reality. At least within the executive branch, public officials usually try to do the right thing; they are hardly the tools of self-interested advocates.

No one should doubt that social norms sometimes press people, in their capacity as citizens, in the direction of a concern for others or the public interest. Acting together as citizens, people can solve collective-action problems that prove intractable for consumers. For each of us, acting individually, it is nearly impossible to make any substantial contribution to the problem of air pollution or the assistance of those who are suffering from the effects of a natural disaster. (Social media can be a real help here, of course.) If we are able to act collectively—perhaps through private institutions, perhaps through government—we might be able to do a great deal. As citizens, people might well attempt to promote democratic goals—by, say, calling for free airtime for candidates in the late stages of campaigns—even if they do little to promote those goals in their purely individual capacities.

The deliberative aspects of politics, bringing additional information and perspectives to bear, often affects people's judgments as these are expressed through governmental processes. A principal function of a democratic system is to ensure that through representative or participatory processes, new or submerged voices, or novel depictions of where interests lie and what they in fact are, are heard and understood. If representatives or citizens are able to participate in a collective discussion of broadcasting or the appropriate uses of the Internet, they can generate a far fuller and richer picture of the central social goals, and how they might be served, than can be supplied through individual decisions as registered in the market. It should hardly be surprising if preferences, values, and perceptions of what matters, to individuals and societies, are changed as a result of that process.

Of course it cannot be denied that government officials have their own interests and biases, and that participants in politics might invoke public goals in order to serve their own private agendas. In the area of communications, not excluding the Internet, parochial pressures have often helped to dictate public policy. In the end, it is indispensable to preserve free markets against those pressures. But if citizens are attempting to promote their own aspirations, they might well be able to make those markets work better; and it is certainly important to listen to what they have to say.

UNANIMITY AND MAJORITY RULE

Arguments based on citizens' shared desires are irresistible if no one's rights are invaded and the measure at issue is adopted unanimously—if all citizens are for it. But more serious difficulties are produced if (as is usual) the law imposes on a minority what it regards as a burden rather than a benefit. Suppose, for example, that a majority wants to require free television time for candidates or to have three hours of educational programming for children each week—but that a minority objects, contending that it is indifferent to speech by candidates, and that it does not care if there is more educational programming for children. It might be thought that those who perceive a need to bind themselves to some obligation or some course of action should not be permitted to do so if the consequence is to bind others who perceive no such need.

Any interference with the preferences of the minority is unfortunate, and in the end it might be a decisive objection, certainly if people's rights are being invaded. But if not, why should the minority have veto power? By hypothesis, the status quo does not have majority support; indeed, the majority rejects it. Why is the status quo sacrosanct, such that it can be changed only if support for change is unanimous, whereas even majority support for a change is not enough? Far too often, the status quo seems to have a kind of magnetic appeal, giving undue weight to minorities who like it.

Of course we need to investigate the context. But in general, it is difficult to see what argument there might be for an across-the-board rule against modest democratic efforts to improve the communications market. If the majority is prohibited from promoting its aspirations or vindicating its considered judgments through legislation, people will be less able to engage in democratic self-government. The choice is between the considered judgments of the majority and the preferences of the minority. I am not suggesting, of course, that the minority should be foreclosed where its rights are genuinely at risk.

THE CONSUMPTION TREADMILL

Throughout the discussion here, I have assumed that insofar as people are acting as consumers, modern communications technologies are an unambiguous boon. This is a widespread assumption, and it is easy to see why. If you want to buy anything at all, it has become much easier to do so. If you'd like a Toyota Camry, a Honda Accord, or an SUV, many sites are available for the purpose; wallets, watches, and wristbands are easily found online; and shirts, sweaters, and cell phones can be purchased in seconds. Nor is convenience the only point. As a result of the Internet, ordinary people have a much greater range of choices, and competitive pressures are, in a sense, far more intense for producers. Recall Anderson's celebration of "the long tail"; people with unusual tastes are now able to find what they want, overcoming the barriers of space that limit the options in bookstores, movie theaters, and much more.

To be sure, the growth of options for consumers has been a prime engine behind the growth of the Internet. Consider a little history. In the early years, .edu domains dominated the list of the most popular sites. As late as 1996, no .com sites ranked among the top 15 sites. By 1999—only three years later—the picture had fundamentally changed, to the point that the top-ranked .edu site (the University of Michigan) ranked number 92. Only 3 of the 15 top-ranked sites from January 1996 remained in the top rank three years later (AOL, Netscape, and Yahoo!). And by that time, commercial enterprises had a substantial presence on the list. They grew rapidly, to the point where there were nearly 25 million .com sites as early as 2000, as compared to 6 million .edu sites, and under 1 million .gov sites. The increase, in sheer numbers and proportions, has been remarkable since that time. As of April 2016, there were close to 125 million .com sites, and .edu sites were not even in the top 10 types of domains.[14] The Internet is dominated by .com sites.

Insofar as the number of .coms is constantly growing, it might seem clear that consumers, as consumers, are far better off as a result. On balance, they certainly are. But there is a qualification: extensive evidence shows that *our experience of many goods and services is largely a product of what other people have, and when there is a general improvement in everyone's consumer goods, people's well-being is increased little or not at all.*[15] Notwithstanding the impressive evidence on its behalf, this might seem to be a positively weird suggestion. Isn't it obvious that better consumer goods are good for consumers? Isn't it obvious that it's better to have a computer that is faster or lighter?

Actually it isn't so obvious. The reason is that people evaluate many goods by seeing how they compare to goods generally. If consumer goods as a whole are (say) 20 percent better, people are not going to be 20 percent happier, and they may not be happier at all.

To see the point, imagine that your current car is the average vehicle, in your preferred category, from ten years ago. Chances are good that ten years ago, that car was entirely fine, for you as for most other people. Chances are also good that if there had been no advances in cars, and if each of us had the same car, in terms of quality, as we had ten years ago, it would not be so terrible. But in light of the improvements in cars in the last decade, it would undoubtedly be disappointing to continue to use one from ten years before. In fact you might hate it. Partly this is because the frame of reference has been set by much more advanced cars; those cars set the standard by which you evaluate what you own.

This point need not depend on a claim that people are envious of their neighbors (though sometimes they are), or that people care a great deal about their status and how they are doing in comparison with others (though status is important). For many goods, the most important point, developed by the economist Robert Frank, is that *the frame of reference is set socially, not individually.*[16] Our experience of what we have is determined by that frame of reference. What the Internet is doing is to alter the frame of reference, and by a large degree. This is not an unmixed blessing for consumers, even if it is a terrific development for many sellers.

To evaluate the Internet's effects on consumers, it is necessary only to see a simple point: when millions of consumers simultaneously find themselves with improved opportunities to find goods, they are certainly better off, but they are also likely to find themselves on a kind of "treadmill" in which each is continually trying to purchase more and better, simply in order to keep up with others and the ever-shifting frame of reference. Indeed, what is true for cars is all the more so for countless other goods, including most of the vast array of products available on the Internet, such as SUVs, tablets, and televisions.

Cars are evaluated socially, to be sure, but at least it can be said that safer, faster, and more fuel-efficient ones can genuinely improve our lives in many ways. But for many consumer goods, where the frame of reference is also provided socially, what really matters is how they compare to what other people have, and not how good they are in absolute terms. What would be a wonderful tablet or television in one time and place will seem ridiculously primitive in another.

In sum, the problem with the consumption treadmill, which is moving ever faster as a result of the Internet, is that despite growing expenditures and improved goods, the shift in the frame of reference means that consumers are unlikely to be much happier or better off. If the Internet is making it far easier for consumers to get better goods, or the same goods at a better price, they are certainly better off, perhaps even significantly so. But there is every reason to doubt that this is producing as much of an improvement in life, even for consumers, as we like to think.

This argument should not be misunderstood. Many goods actually do improve people's well-being, independently of shifts in the frame of reference. These goods tend to involve "inconspicuous consumption," from which people receive benefits apart from what other people have or do.[17] When people have more leisure time, when they have a chance to exercise and keep in shape, or when they are able to spend more time with family and friends, their lives are likely to be better, whatever other people are doing. But when what matters is the frame set for social comparison, a society focused on better consumer goods will face a serious problem: people will channel far too many resources into the consumption treadmill, and far too few resources into goods that are not subject to the treadmill effect or that would otherwise be far better for society (such as improved protection against crime, environmental pollution, or assistance for poor people).

It follows that the purchase of consumer goods and the opportunity to buy more and better do much less for people than they think—certainly not nothing, but much less. The emerging work on these topics raises many questions, and I do not attempt to answer them here. But insofar as consumers have an increasing range of purchasing options and can buy exactly what they want, it is far from clear that their lives are much better.

For present purposes, my conclusions are simple. The Internet unquestionably makes purchases easier and more convenient for consumers. We can get more and better goods, and we can get them in a hurry. To this extent, it is a genuine boon for most of us. But it is less of a boon than we usually think, particularly to the degree that it accelerates the consumption treadmill without making life much better for consumers of most goods. If citizens are reflective about their practices and lives, they are entirely aware of this fact. As citizens, we might well choose to slow down the treadmill, or ensure that resources that now keep it moving will be devoted to better uses. And insofar as citizens are attempting to accomplish that worthy goal, the idea of liberty should hardly stand in the way.

DEMOCRACY AND PREFERENCES

When people's preferences are a product of injustice or excessively limited options, there is a problem from the standpoint of freedom, and we do freedom a grave disservice by insisting on respect for preferences. When options are plentiful, things are much better. But from the standpoint of freedom, there is also a problem when people's past choices lead to the development of preferences that limit their own horizons and capacity for citizenship.

Consumers are not citizens, and it is a large error to conflate the two. One reason for the disparity is that the process of democratic choice often elicits people's aspirations. When we are thinking about what we as a nation should do—rather than what each of us as consumers should buy—we are frequently led to think of our larger, long-term goals. We may therefore hope to promote a high-quality communications market even if, as consumers, we seek "infotainment." Within the democratic process, we are also able to act as a group and are not limited to our options as individuals. Acting as a group, we are thus in a position to solve various obstacles to dealing properly with issues that we cannot, without great difficulty, solve on our own.

These points obviously bear on a number of questions outside the area of communications, such as environmental protection, income inequality, and antidiscrimination law. In many contexts, people acting in their capacity as citizens favor measures that diverge from the choices they make in their capacity as consumers. Of course it is important to impose constraints, usually in the form of rights, on what political majorities may do under this rationale. A system of limitless individual choices with respect to communications has countless advantages. But in some respects, it is not in the interest of citizenship and self-government, and efforts to reduce the resulting problems ought not to be rejected in freedom's name.

WHAT'S REGULATION? A PLEA

Well over a decade ago, my computer received an odd e-mail, titled "love letter for you." The e-mail contained an attachment. When I opened the e-mail, I learned that the attachment was a love letter. The sender of the e-mail was someone I'd never met—as it happens, an employee at Princeton University Press, the publisher of this very book. I thought I probably should look at this love letter, so I clicked once. But it occurred to me that this might not be a love letter at all, and so I didn't click twice.

I had been sent the ILOVEYOU virus. This was a particularly fiendish virus. If you opened it, you received not only a love note but also a special surprise: your computer would send the same love note to every address in your computer's address book. For many people, this was funny in a way, but also extremely awful and embarrassing—not least for a law professor, finding himself in the position, not exactly comfortable, of sending countless unwelcome love letters to both students and colleagues.

The ILOVEYOU virus was capable of many impressive feats. For example, it could delete files. It was apparently capable of mutating, so that many people found themselves not with love letters but instead with notes about Mother's Day—less intriguing and more innocuous perhaps than a love letter, but also capable of mischief, as when an employee at a random company finds himself sending dozens of Mother's Day notes to friends and colleagues, many of them near strangers (and not mothers). The ILOVEYOU virus was apparently capable of mutating into, or in any case was shortly followed by, its own apparent cure, with matching attachment:

"HOW TO PROTECT YOURSELF FROM THE ILOVEYOU BUG!" This attachment turned out to be a virus too.

The worldwide costs of the ILOVEYOU virus went well beyond embarrassment. In Belgium, ATMs were disabled. Throughout Europe, e-mail servers were shut down. Significant costs were imposed on the taxpayers as well—partly because affected computers included those of government, and partly because governments all over the world cooperated in enforcement efforts. In London, Parliament was forced to close down its servers, and e-mail systems were crippled in the US Congress. At the US Department of Defense, four classified e-mail systems were corrupted. The ultimate price tag has been estimated at over $10 billion. Ultimately, the Federal Bureau of Investigation (FBI) traced the origin of this virus to a young man in the Philippines.

A COMMON VIEW

My discussion thus far has involved the social foundations of a well-functioning system of free expression—what such a system requires if it is to work well. But it would be possible for a critic to respond that government and law have no legitimate role in responding to any problems that might emerge from individual choices. On this view, a free society respects those choices and avoids "regulation," even if what results from free choices is quite undesirable; that is what freedom is all about.

If the claim here is really about freedom, I have already attempted to show what is wrong with it. Freedom should not always be identified with "choices." Of course free societies usually respect free choices. But sometimes choices reflect and can in fact produce a lack of freedom.

Perhaps the argument is rooted in something else: a general hostility to any form of government regulation. This is, of course, a pervasive kind of hostility. A common argument is that legal interference with the communications market should be rejected simply because it is a form of government regulation, and be disfavored for exactly that reason. It is certainly easy to find that claim on Facebook and Twitter.

Many people make such an argument about radio and television. With the extraordinary number of channels, they contend, scarcity is no longer a reason for regulation. Shouldn't government simply leave the scene? Shouldn't it eliminate regulation altogether? The same argument is being made about the Internet, even more forcefully, with the suggestion that it should be taken as a kind of government-free zone. In 1996, free speech activist (and former Grateful Dead lyricist) John Perry Barlow produced an influential "Declaration of the Independence of Cyberspace," urging, among other things, "Governments of the Industrial World . . . I ask you of the past to leave us alone. You are not welcome among us. You have no sovereignty where we gather. . . . You have no moral right to rule us nor do you possess any methods of enforcement we have true reason to fear."[1] That sounds like 1960s' stuff, a kind of My Generation manifesto, opposing the we-who-gather to those of the past. But it resonated in the 1990s. It's still resonating.

AN INCOHERENT VIEW:
REGULATION AND LAW EVERYWHERE

With respect for Barlow's clarity and commitment, the story of the ILOVEYOU virus suggests that his argument is absurd. Could any sensible person support a system in which government is banned from helping to protect against computer viruses? From preventing efforts to hack into systems in such a way as to compromise personal privacy and national security? From cyberterrorism? But the story of the ILOVEYOU virus also suggests something subtler and more interesting. The real problem is that opposition to government regulation is incoherent.

There is no avoiding "regulation" of the communications market—of television, print media, and the Internet. The question is not whether we will have regulation; it is what kind of regulation we will have. Newspapers and magazines, radio and television stations, websites, and Facebook and Instagram accounts—all benefit from government regulation every day. Indeed, a system of regulation-free speech is barely imaginable. Those who complain most bitterly about proposed regulation are often those who most profit, usually financially, from the current regulation. They depend not only on themselves but also on government and law. What they are complaining about is not regulation as such—they need it—but instead a regulatory regime from which they would benefit less than they do under the present one.

To see the point, begin by considering the actual status of broadcast licensees in both television and radio for the last decades and more. Broadcasters do not have their licenses by nature or divine right. Their licenses are emphatically a product of government grants—legally conferred property rights, in the form of monopolies over frequencies, originally given out for free to ABC, CBS, NBC, and PBS. In the early 1990s, government went so far as to give existing owners a right to produce digital television— what Senator Robert Dole and many others called a "$70 billion giveaway." This gift from the public—the grant of property rights via government, and in this case, for free rather than through auction—is simply a highly publicized way in which government and law are responsible for the rights of those who own and operate radio and television stations.

But we don't need any gifts. Many economists think that rights to the spectrum should be allocated through an auction system. And indeed, the Federal Communications Commission has adopted this suggestion, at least to some extent. But even when auctions are involved, owners still benefit from property rights. If you get channel 770 through an auction, no one else can use channel 770 without your consent. The government will protect you. We don't need to speak of the traditional over-the-air broadcast stations, such as CBS and NBC. Showtime, HBO, and your local stations also benefit from property rights, protected and enforced by law. Sure, the operators of any station could hire the equivalent of an online police force, equipped to prevent any unwelcome intrusions. But that's not exactly easy. Without the law, access to radio and television stations would be a free-for-all, and the current owners would spend a lot more money and a lot more time defending what is theirs.

If you have a Facebook account, you didn't pay for it. But it's definitely yours. If someone commandeers your account and starts posting pictures of Stalin with accompanying text ("the greatest person who ever lived!"), your rights have been violated. You can probably get legal recourse. The same thing is true of your Twitter account. If someone sends out tweets under your name ("qcfgv-wav" or "Twitter is Satan's toolbox"), they have intruded on what is, in a legal sense, your property. For both Facebook and Twitter, that's important.

Though many people don't think of them this way, property rights, when conferred by law, are a quintessential form of government regulation. They create and limit power. They determine who owns what, and they say who may do what to whom. They allow some people to exclude others. That's regulation, in a nutshell.

In the case of radio and television broadcasters, property rights impose firm limits on others, who may not, under federal law, speak on CBS, NBC, or Fox unless CBS, NBC, or Fox allows them to do so. It makes no sense to decry government regulation of television broadcasters when it is government regulation that is responsible for the very system at issue. That system could not exist without a complex regulatory framework from which broadcasters benefit.

Nor is it merely the fact that government created the relevant property rights in the first instance. Government also protects these rights, at taxpayers' expense, via civil and criminal law, both of which prohibit people from gaining access to what broadcasters "own." If you try to get access to the public via CBS, to appear on its channels without its permission, you will have committed a crime, and the FBI itself is likely to become involved. There is considerable irony in the fact that for many years, broadcasters have complained about government regulation; such regulation is responsible for their rights in the first place. There is a particular irony in broadcasters' vociferous objections to the modest public interest requirements that have been imposed on them, in the form of (for instance) requirements for educational programming for children, attention to public issues, and an opportunity for diverse views to speak. They purport to object to regulation as such, but they really object to the particular regulations that they don't like. (True, they're hardly the first to do that, and they won't be the last either.)

Of course broadcasters may have some legitimate objections here, at least if they can show that meeting these requirements does little good. But what is not legitimate is for broadcasters to act as if public interest regulation imposes law and government where neither existed before. Broadcasters could not exist in their current form if not for the fact that law and government are emphatically present. It is law and government that make it possible for them to make money in the first place.

What is true for broadcasters is also true for newspapers and magazines, though here the point is less obvious. Newspapers and magazines benefit from government regulation too through the grant of property rights, again protected at taxpayers' expense. Suppose, for example, that you would like to publish something in the *Washington Post* or *Time* magazine. Perhaps you believe that one or the other has neglected an important perspective, and you would like to fill the gap. If you request publication and are refused, you are entirely out of luck. The most important reason is that the law has created a firm right of exclusion—a legal power to exclude others—and given this right to both newspapers and magazines. The law is fully prepared to back up that right of exclusion with both civil and criminal safeguards. No less than CBS and ABC, the *Washington Post* and *Time* magazine are beneficiaries of legal regulation, preventing people from saying what they want to say where they want to say it.

Now it may be possible to imagine a world of newspapers and magazines without legal protection of this kind. This would be a world without regulation. But what kind of world would this be?

Without the assistance of the law—to enforce contracts, protect property rights, and punish those who violate such rights—all sides would be left with a struggle to show superior force. In such a world, people would be able to publish where they wanted if, and only if, they had the power to insist. Newspapers and magazines would be able to exclude would-be authors so long as they had enough power to do so. Who can know who would win that struggle? (Perhaps you have a gun or small private army, and can force the *Washington Post* to publish you at gunpoint.) In our society, access to newspapers and magazines is determined not by power but instead by legal regulation, allocating and enforcing property rights, and doing all this at public expense.

THE CASE OF THE INTERNET: SOME HISTORICAL NOTES

Despite the widespread claim that the Internet is and should be free of government controls, things are similar online. Here too regulation and government support have been omnipresent. But there are some interesting wrinkles in this context, and they are worth rehearsing here, because they bear on the relationship between regulation and the Internet, and because they are noteworthy in their own right.

Consider history first. This supposedly government-free zone was a creation not of the private sector but instead of the national government. Indeed, the private sector was given several chances to move things along, but refused, and in a way that shows a remarkable lack of foresight. (Puzzling but entirely true.) We are used to hearing tales of the unintended bad consequences of government action. The Internet is an unintended good consequence of government action—by the Department of Defense no less.

Beginning in the 1960s, the US Defense Advanced Research Projects Agency created a new computer network, originally called the Arpanet, with the specific purpose of permitting computers to interact with one another, thus allowing defense researchers at various universities to share computing resources. In 1972, hundreds and then thousands of early users began to discover e-mail as a new basis for communication. In the early 1970s, the government sought to sell off the Arpanet to the private sector, contacting AT&T to see if it wanted to take over the system. The company declined, concluding that the Arpanet technology was incompatible with the AT&T network. (So much for the universal prescience of the private sector.)

Eventually the Arpanet—operating under the auspices of the federal government in the form of the National Science Foundation—expanded to multiple uses. By the late 1980s, a number of new networks emerged, some far more advanced than the Arpanet, and the term "Internet" came to be used for the federally subsidized network consisting of many linked networks running the same protocols. In 1989, the Arpanet was transferred to regional networks throughout the country. A key innovation came one year later, when researchers at the European Organization for Nuclear Research (CERN) near Geneva, Switzerland, created the World Wide Web, a multimedia branch of the Internet. CERN researchers attempted to interest private companies in building the World Wide Web, but they declined ("too complicated"), and Tim Berners-Lee, the lead researcher and web inventor, had to build it on his own.

Hard as it now is to believe, the Internet started to commercialize only in 1992, as a result of the enactment of new legislation removing restrictions on commercial activity. It was around that time that direct government funding was largely withdrawn, but indirect funding and support continues. In 1995, the backbone of the national network (the physical pipes on which data travels) was sold to a private consortium of corporations, and the government gave one company the exclusive right to register domain names (you can now buy names from a range of sellers). Originally created by the government, the Internet is now largely free of ongoing federal supervision—but with the important, background exceptions of guaranteed property rights and various restrictions on unlawful speech (such as conspiracy, bribery, and child pornography).

Perhaps all this seems abstract. But the basic point lies at the very heart of the most fundamental of current debates about Internet policy. Consider, for example, a revealing online exchange connected with an Internet symposium in the *American Prospect* magazine in 2000. Eric S. Raymond, a highly influential developer and theorist of open-source software, sharply opposed "government regulation," and endorsed "laissez faire" and "voluntary norms founded in enlightened self-interest." Internet specialist Lawrence Lessig, writing in much the same terms as those urged here, responded that "contract law, rightly limited property rights, antitrust law, [and] the breakup of AT&T" are also "regulations," made possible by "governmental policy."

Answering Lessig, Raymond was mostly aghast. He acknowledged that he had no disagreement if the term "regulation" is meant to include "not active coercive intervention but policies which I and hackers in general agree with him are *not* coercive, such as the enforcement of property law and contract rights." But to Raymond, who purports to speak for a large "community consensus," the use of the term "regulation" to include this kind of law reflects a deep confusion in Lessig's "model of the world." "Contract and property law contain no proper names; they formalize an equilibrium of power between equals before the law and are good things; regulation privileges one party designated by law to dictate outcomes by force and is at best a very questionable thing. The one is no more like the other than a handshake is like a fist in the face."

Raymond stated a widespread view, but the deep confusion is his, not Lessig's. Property law and contract rights are unquestionably "coercive" and entirely "active." These rights do not appear in nature, at least not in terms that are acceptable for human society. When would-be speakers are subject to a jail sentence for invading property rights, coercion is unquestionably involved. This is not true only for homeless people, whose very status as such is unquestionably a product of law. Even those who create open-source software rely heavily on property law—in fact, they depend on contract law (through licenses) and at least some form of copyright law to control what happens to their software. Anyone who is punished for violating the copyright law, or intruding on the "space" of CBS or a website owner, is coerced within any reasonable understanding of the term.

Nor do contract and property law merely "formalize an equilibrium of power." By conferring rights, they *create* an equilibrium of power—one that would and could not exist without "active" choices by government. In a genuine state of lawlessness, in which everything was left to forcible self-help, who knows what the equilibrium would look like with respect to software on the Internet or anywhere else? Contract and property laws are good, even wonderful things. But to many people much of the time, they are no mere handshake, but much more like "a fist in the face." (What does it mean to be homeless? Among other things, it means that if you try to get access to a home, you get a fist in the face, or something a lot like it.)

It's both true and important that the law of property and contract contains "no proper names." The law does not say that Jones can own property but that Smith cannot, or that Christians can own property but that Jews cannot. (At least the law does not say anything like that now, with narrow exceptions.) That's a massive social achievement. But how many (other kinds of) regulations contain proper names? Let's take some examples of unacceptable regulations—say, a ban on criticism of Congress or the Supreme Court, or a prohibition on objections to a current war effort. There are no proper names there. And when government does something that is regulatory and more acceptable—say, a ban on spreading viruses, or on bribes and extortion—it doesn't need to name names. It follows that both unacceptable and acceptable regulations do not name names, and so any such naming cannot produce a helpful dividing line. Recall Raymond's suggestion that contract and property law "formalize an equilibrium of power between equals before the law . . . ; regulation privileges one party designated by law to dictate outcomes by force." As a conceptual matter, it is just not possible to make sense of those claims.

I do not mean to deny that Raymond is onto something. There are differences between contract and property law, which help facilitate private ordering and usually leave a lot of flexibility, and more rigid regulatory commands, which tell people (for example) that they must recycle, follow specified emissions limits on their automobiles, or refrain from smoking in public buildings. In regulation itself, flexibility is often a good idea, because it increases freedom and reduces costs. We should refrain from praising contract and property law in the abstract, but in the abstract, they're good. Still, they're forms of regulation. If we deny that point, we'll confuse ourselves.

THE CASE OF THE INTERNET: REGULATION AGAIN

Simply because government creates and enforces property rights online, the Internet, no less than ordinary physical spaces, remains pervaded by government regulation. That's true of social media too. This does not mean that government should be permitted to do whatever it wants. But it does mean that the real question is what kind of regulation to have, not whether to have regulation.

As a result of the ILOVEYOU and other viruses, considerable attention has been given in recent years to the problem of cybersecurity and the risk and reality of "cyberterrorism"—not only through e-mail attachments, but also when "hackers" invade websites in order to disable them, steal information, or post messages of their own choosing. The problem is one of national security, and it is immensely important. Strong steps must be taken to combat that problem, for which many nations are not adequately prepared. Computer viruses may or may not endanger national security, but according to one (dated) estimate, they cost the United States $13 billion each year.[2] Speaking of cybercrime generally, the costs were estimated in 2016 at $575 billion annually.[3] Some of the costs are not easy to monetize; consider Russia's reported interference with the 2016 presidential election by hacking into the servers of the Democratic National Committee and releasing e-mails. Both private and public institutions are highly vulnerable. It would not be at all surprising if something quite terrible happens in the next ten or twenty years.

Despite the magnitude of the problem, serious disruptions do not occur as often as one might expect. Why not? Companies devote a lot of time and effort to avoiding them; they are helped by the fact that such disruptions are against the law. A complex framework of state, federal, and international law regulates behavior on the Internet, protecting against intrusions and giving site owners, including those who have accounts on the social media, an entitlement to be free from trespass. These entitlements are created publicly and enforced at public expense. Indeed, immense resources—billions of dollars, including massive efforts by the FBI—are devoted to the protection of these property rights. And when cyberterrorism does occur, everyone knows that the government is going to intervene to protect property rights, in part by ferreting out the relevant lawbreakers, and in part by prosecuting them.

If we want, we might decline to call this government "regulation." But why? That would be a matter of semantics, and it would not be helpful. When government creates and protects rights, and when it forbids people from doing what they want to do, it is regulating within any standard meaning of the term. The Internet is hardly a space of lawlessness, or regulation free. The reason is that governments stand ready to protect those whose property rights are at stake.

In this way the system of rights on the Internet is no different, in principle, from the system of rights elsewhere. But the Internet does present one complication. In ordinary space, it is usually not possible, realistically speaking, to conceive of a system of property rights without a large government presence. Such a system would mean that property holders would have to resort to self-help, as through the hiring of private police forces, and for most property owners, including broadcasters, newspapers, and magazines, this is not really feasible. To be sure, there are some complications here. Distinguished social scientists, including Nobel Prize winner Elinor Ostrom and Yale law professor Robert Ellickson, have illuminatingly explored the existence of "spontaneous orders," in which people succeed in creating stable societies without law.[4] But in most places on the planet, that is not going to happen. Paris, Berlin, Cape Town, Boston, Beijing, and Mexico City all require a strong legal presence.

It is not entirely crazy to think that the Internet might be more like what Ostrom and Ellickson identify. We might think, for example, that government *could simply step out of the picture and enable site owners to qualify as such only to the extent that they can use their technological capacities to exclude others.* In such a system, regulation would indeed be absent. Amazon.com would be run and operated by Amazon.com, but it would be free from intrusion by outsiders only to the degree that the owners of Amazon.com could use technology to maintain their property rights. Amazon.com, in sum, would have a kind of sovereignty as a result of technology rather than law, and perhaps it could ensure this sovereignty through technology alone. So too, you would have a Twitter account, but people could hack into it, unless you could work with Twitter or other private companies to eliminate that risk.

Because of current technological capacities, this is not an unimaginable state of affairs. Perhaps many people can protect themselves well enough from invaders, cyberterrorists, and others without needing the help of government. But in the end, that's far from adequate and even a bit wild, at least under currently imaginable conditions. It would not make much sense to force people to rely on technology alone in light of the immense value of civil and criminal law as an aid to the enjoyment of property rights. Happily, this imaginary world of self-help is not the one in which we live. The owners of websites and the users of social media benefit from government regulation, and without it, they would have a much less secure existence online.

REGULATION EVERYWHERE, THANK GOODNESS

None of these points should be taken as an argument against those forms of regulation that establish and guarantee property rights.

On the contrary, a well-functioning system of free expression *needs* property rights. Such a system is likely to be much better if the law creates and protects owners of newspapers, magazines, broadcasting stations, websites, and social media accounts. Property rights make these institutions far more secure and stable, and for precisely this reason, produce much more in the way of speech.

In the Communist nations of the Soviet era, communications outlets were publicly owned, and all holdings were subject to governmental reallocation; it is an understatement to say that free speech could not flourish in such an environment. Friedrich Hayek, the greatest critic of socialism in the twentieth century, emphasized the omnipresence of legal regulation every bit as much as I have here. Hayek is often depicted as an advocate of laissez-faire, but he was hardly that. "In no system that could be rationally defended would the state just do nothing," Hayek argued. "An effective competitive system needs an intelligently designed and continuously adjusted legal framework as much as any other."[5]

Nor does anything I have said suggest that it would be appropriate, or even legitimate, for government to control the content of what appears in newspapers and magazines (online or otherwise), by saying, for instance, that they must cover presidential elections, or offer dissenting opinions a right of reply. But any objection to such requirements must be based on something other than the suggestion that they would interfere with some law-free zone—that requirements of this sort would introduce a government presence where government had been absent before. Government has been there already, and it is still there, and we are much better off for that. If government is trying to do something new or different, one question is whether what it is trying to do would improve or impair democracy, or the system of freedom of speech. That question cannot be resolved by reference to complaints about government regulation in the abstract.

If government is attempting to regulate television or radio in their contemporary forms, websites or social media, or some future technology that combines or transcends them, it makes no sense to say that the attempt should fail because a free society opposes government regulation as such. No free society opposes that. Government regulation of speech, at least in the form of property rights that shut out would-be speakers, is a pervasive part of a system of freedom that respects and therefore creates rights of exclusion for owners of communications outlets.

Here, then, is my plea: when we are discussing possible approaches to the Internet or other new communications technologies—today, on the horizon, or not yet imagined—we should never suggest that one route involves government regulation and another route does not. Statements of this kind produce confusion about what we are now doing and about our real options. And the confusion is far from innocuous. It puts those who are asking how to improve the operation of the speech market at a serious disadvantage. A democratic public should be permitted to discuss the underlying questions openly and pragmatically, and without reference to self-serving myths invoked by those who benefit, every hour of every day, from the exercise of government power on their behalf.

FREEDOM OF SPEECH

Were those responsible for the ILOVEYOU virus protected by the free speech principle? It would be silly to say that they are. But if this form of speech may be regulated, what are the limits on the government's power?

Consider a case involving not e-mail but rather a website—a case that, in some ways, may turn out to be emblematic of the future. The site in question had a dramatic name: the Nuremberg Files. It began by stating, "A coalition of concerned citizens throughout the USA is cooperating in collecting dossiers on abortionists in anticipation that one day we may be able to hold them on trial for crimes against humanity." The site contained a long list of "Alleged Abortionists and Their Accomplices," with the explicit goal of recording "the name of every person working in the baby slaughter business in the United States of America." The list included the names, home addresses, and license plate numbers of many doctors who performed abortions, and also included the names of their spouses and children.

So far, so good—perhaps. But three of these doctors ended up being killed. Whenever a doctor was killed, the website showed a line drawn through his name. The site also included a set of "wanted posters," Old West style, with photographs of doctors with the word "Wanted" under each one. A group of doctors brought suit, contending the practices to which this site was a part amounted to "a hit list" with death threats and intimidation. The jury awarded them over $100 million in damages; the verdict was upheld on appeal, although the dollar award was reduced substantially (it remained in the millions).

Should the free speech principle have protected the Nuremberg Files? Maybe it should have. But if you think so, would you allow a website to post names and addresses of doctors who performed abortions, with explicit instructions about how and where to kill them? Would you allow a website to post bomb-making instructions? To post such instructions alongside advice about how and where to use the bombs? To show terrorists exactly where and how to strike?

There is nothing fanciful about these questions. Dozens of sites now contain instructions about how to make bombs—though to my knowledge, none of them tells people how and where to use them. If you have no problem with bomb-making instructions on websites, you might consider some other questions. Does your understanding of free speech allow people to work together at a site called pricefixing.com, through which competitors can agree to set prices and engage in other anticompetitive practices? (I made that one up.) Does your understanding of free speech allow people to make unauthorized copies of movies, music, and books, and give or sell those copies to dozens, thousands, or millions of others? (I didn't make that one up.) Does your understanding of free speech allow terrorists to recruit people to commit acts of murder? (As we will see, that's all too real.)

My basic argument here is that the free speech principle, properly understood, is not an absolute, and it allows government to undertake a wide range of restrictions on what people want to say on the Internet. However the hardest questions should be resolved, the government can regulate computer viruses, criminal conspiracy, and explicit incitement to engage in criminal acts, at least if the incitement is likely to be effective. As we will see, hard questions are raised by the use of the Internet to recruit people to commit terrorist acts; that issue takes us to the frontiers of the free speech principle.

This is not the place for a full discussion of constitutional doctrines relating to freedom of expression. But in the process of showing the democratic roots of the system of free expression, I attempt to provide an outline of the basic constitutional principles.

EMERGING WISDOM? (NOT)

An emerging view, with considerable support in the courts, is that the First Amendment to the Constitution requires government to respect an ideal of "consumer sovereignty," which means, very simply, that it must allow people to choose however they like. Indeed, courts and commentators sometimes treat the First Amendment as if it is based on the view that consumer choice is what the system of communications is all about. Although it is foreign to the original conception of the free speech principle, this view can be found in many places in current law.

For one thing, it helps to explain the constitutional protection given to commercial advertising. This protection is exceedingly recent. Until 1976, the consensus within the Supreme Court and the legal culture in general was that the First Amendment did not protect commercial speech at all.[1] Since that time, commercial speech has come to be treated more and more like ordinary speech, to the point where Justice Clarence Thomas has even doubted whether the law should distinguish at all between commercial and political speech.[2] To date, Justice Thomas has not prevailed on this count; the Court gives commercial speech somewhat less protection. (For example, false and deceptive advertising can be regulated.) But the Court's commercial speech decisions often end up striking down restrictions on advertising, and for that reason, those decisions are best seen as a way of connecting the idea of consumer sovereignty with the First Amendment itself.

Belonging in the same category is the Supreme Court's intense constitutional hostility to campaign finance regulation. After the Court's highly controversial decision in the *Citizens United* case, corporations are basically allowed to spend what they want on political campaigns.[3] By the slim margin of five to four, the Court has made it clear that financial expenditures on behalf of political candidates are generally protected by the free speech principle—and in what seems to me an act of considerable hubris, the Court has also held that it is illegitimate for government to try to promote political equality by imposing ceilings on permissible expenditures.[4] The inequality that comes from divergences in wealth is not, in the Court's view, a proper subject for democratic control.

According to the Court, campaign finance restrictions cannot be justified by reference to equality at all. It is for this reason that candidate expenditures from candidates' personal funds may not be regulated. It is also for this reason that restrictions on campaign *contributions* from one person to a candidate can be regulated only as a way of preventing the reality or appearance of corruption.

The constitutional debate over campaign finance regulation is complex and contested, and the members of the Supreme Court are badly divided.[5] Some of the justices would further reduce the government's existing authority to regulate campaign contributions on the theory that such contributions are at the heart of what the free speech principle protects. Here too an idea of consumer sovereignty seems to be at work. In many of the debates over campaign expenditures and contributions, the political process itself is being treated as a kind of market in which citizens are seen as consumers, expressing their will not only through votes and statements but also through money. I do not mean to suggest that the government should be able to impose whatever restrictions it wishes. I mean only to notice and reject the idea that the political domain should be seen as a market, and the influential claim, which has obtained majority support on the Court, that government is entirely disabled from responding to the translation of economic inequality into political equality.

Even more relevant for present purposes is the widespread suggestion, with strong support in current constitutional law, that the free speech principle forbids government from interfering with the communications market by, for instance, attempting to draw people's attention to serious issues or regulating the content of what appears on television.[6] To be sure, everyone agrees that the government is permitted to create and protect property rights, even if this means that speech will be regulated as a result. We have seen that the government may give property rights to websites and broadcasters; there is no constitutional problem with that.

Everyone also agrees that the government is permitted to control monopolistic behavior and thus enforce antitrust law, which is designed to ensure genuinely free markets in communications. Structural regulation, not involving direct control of speech but instead intended to make sure that the market works well, is usually unobjectionable. Hence government can create copyright law, and, at least within limits, forbid unauthorized copying. (There is, however, an extremely important and active debate about how to reconcile copyright law and the free speech principle.)[7] But if government attempts to require television broadcasters to cover public issues, provide free airtime for candidates, or ensure a certain level of high-quality programming for children, many people will claim that the First Amendment is being violated.

What lies beneath the surface of these debates?

TWO FREE SPEECH PRINCIPLES

We might distinguish here between the free speech principle as it operates in courts and the free speech principle as it operates in public debate. As far as courts are concerned, there is as yet no clear answer to many of the constitutional questions that would be raised by government efforts to make the speech market work better. For example, we do not really know, as a matter of constitutional law, whether government can now require educational and public affairs programming on television. The Supreme Court allowed such regulation when three or four television stations dominated the scene, but it has left open the question of whether such regulation would be legitimate today.[8] As a matter of prediction, the most that can be said is that there is a reasonable chance that the Court would permit government to adopt modest initiatives, so long as it was promoting goals associated with deliberative democracy.

Indeed the Court has been cautious, and self-consciously so, about laying down firm rules governing the role of the free speech principle on new and emerging technologies. It is aware that things are changing rapidly and there is much that it does not know.

Because issues of fact and value are in a state of flux, the Court has tended to offer narrow, case-specific rulings that supply little guidance and constraint for the future.[9]

But the free speech principle has an independent life outside the courtroom. It is often invoked, sometimes strategically but sometimes as a matter of principle, in such a way as to discourage government initiatives that might make the communications market serve democratic goals. Outside the law, and inside the offices of lobbyists, newspapers, radio stations, and recording studios as well as even in ordinary households, the First Amendment has a large *cultural* presence. This is no less important than its technical role in courts. Here the identification of the free speech principle with consumer sovereignty is becoming all the tighter. Worst of all, the emerging cultural understanding severs the link between the First Amendment and democratic self-rule.

Recall here Gates's words: "It's already getting a little unwieldy. When you turn on DirectTV and you step through every channel— well, there's three minutes of your life. When you walk into your living room six years from now, you'll be able to just say what you're interested in, and have the screen help you pick out a video that you care about. It's not going to be 'Let's look at channels 4, 5, and 7.'" Taken to its logical extreme, the emerging wisdom would identify the First Amendment with the dream of unlimited consumer sovereignty with respect to speech. It would see the First Amendment in precisely Gates's terms. It would transform the First Amendment into a constitutional guarantee of consumer sovereignty in the domain of communications.

Decades ago, I had some personal experience with the conception of the First Amendment as an embodiment of consumer sovereignty, and it may be useful to offer a brief account. From 1997 to 1998, I served on the President's Advisory Committee on the Public Interest Obligations of Digital Television Broadcasters. Our task was to consider whether and how television broadcasters should be required to promote public interest goals—through, for example, closed captioning for the hearing impaired, emergency warnings, educational programming for children, and free airtime for candidates.

About half the committee's members were broadcasters, and most of them were entirely happy to challenge proposed government regulation as intrusive and indefensible. One of the two co-chairs was the redoubtable Leslie Moonves, president of CBS. Moonves is an obviously intelligent, public-spirited man but also the furthest thing from a shrinking violet, and he is, to say the least, attuned to the economic interests of the television networks. Because of its composition, this group was not about to recommend anything dramatic. It was, on the contrary, bound to be highly respectful of the prerogatives of television broadcasters. In any case, the advisory committee was just that—an advisory committee—and we had power only to write a report and no authority to impose any duties on anyone at all.

Nonetheless, the committee was subject to a sustained, intense, high-profile, and evidently well-funded lobbying effort by economic interests, generally associated with the broadcasting industry, seeking to invoke the First Amendment to suggest that any and all public interest obligations should and would be found unconstitutional. An elegantly dressed and high-priced Washington, DC, lawyer testified before us for an endless hour, making outlandish claims about the meaning of the First Amendment. A long stream of legal documents was generated and sent to all of us—most of them arguing that (for example) a requirement of free airtime for candidates would offend the Constitution. Instead of offering careful empirical arguments about the possible effects of various approaches, we repeatedly heard a simple claim: "That would violate the First Amendment!" It did not much matter whether the relevant approach would, in fact, violate the First Amendment. (Most of the people in our group were not lawyers.)

At our meetings, the most obvious (omni)presence was Jack Goodman, the lawyer for the National Association of Broadcasters, the lobbying and litigating arm of the broadcast industry, which wields the First Amendment as a kind of protectionist weapon against almost everything that government tries to do. To say that Goodman and the association would invoke the free speech principle at the drop of a hat or the faintest step of a Federal Communications Commission official in the distance is only a slight exaggeration.

Of course all this was itself an entirely legitimate exercise of free speech. But when the President's Advisory Committee on the Public Interest Obligations of Digital Television Broadcasters already consists, in large part, of broadcasters, and when that same committee is besieged with tendentious and implausible interpretations of the First Amendment, something does seem amiss.

There is a more general point. The National Association of Broadcasters and others with similar economic interests typically use the First Amendment in precisely the same way that the National Rifle Association uses the Second Amendment. We should think of the two camps as jurisprudential twins. The National Association of Broadcasters is prepared to make self-serving and outlandish claims about the First Amendment before the public and courts, and pay lawyers and publicists a lot of money to help establish those claims. The National Rifle Association does the same thing with the Second Amendment. In both cases, those whose social and economic interests are at stake are prepared to use the Constitution, however implausibly invoked, in order to give a veneer of principle and respectability to arguments that would otherwise seem hopelessly partisan and self-interested.

Our advisory committee heard a great deal about the First Amendment, marginally relevant Supreme Court decisions, and footnotes in lower-court opinions, but exceedingly little—in fact close to nothing—about the pragmatic and empirical issues on which many of our inquiries should have turned. If educational programming for children is required on CBS, NBC, and ABC, how many children will end up watching? What would they watch or do instead? Would educational programming help them? When educational programming is required, how much do the networks lose in dollars, and who pays the tab—advertisers, consumers, network employees, or someone else? What would be the real-world effects on citizens and fund-raising alike of free airtime for candidates? Would such a requirement produce more substantial attention to serious issues? Would it reduce current pressures to raise money? What are the consequences of violence on television for both children and adults? Does television violence actually increase violence in the real world? Does it make children anxious in a way that creates genuine psychological harm? How, exactly, are the hard of hearing affected when captions are absent?

We can go further still. In the early part of the twentieth century, the due process clause of the Fourteenth Amendment was used to forbid government from regulating the labor market through, for example, legislation about minimum wages and maximum hours.[10] The Court thought that the Constitution allowed workers and employers to set wages and hours as they "chose," without regulatory constraints. This is one of the most notorious periods in the entire history of the Supreme Court. Judicial use of the Fourteenth Amendment for these purposes is generally agreed to have been a grotesque abuse of power. Most people now see that the underlying questions were democratic ones, not ones for the judiciary. The Court should not have forbidden democratic experimentation that would, plausibly at least, have done considerable good.

Indeed, a central animating idea in these now-discredited decisions was precisely that of consumer sovereignty—ensuring that government would not "interfere" with the terms produced by workers, employers, and consumers. (The word "interfere" has to be in quotation marks because the government was there already; the law of property, contract, and torts helps account for how much workers receive, how long they work, and how much consumers pay.) But in the twenty-first century, the First Amendment is serving a similar purpose in popular debate and sometimes in courts as well.

All too often, it is being invoked on behalf of consumer sovereignty in a way that prevents the democratic process from resolving complex questions that turn on issues of fact and value that are ill suited to judicial resolution. To say this is not to claim that the First Amendment should play no role at all. On the contrary, it does impose serious limits on what might be done. In emphasizing the limits of the free speech principle, I should not be taken to downplay the central importance of that principle in protecting democratic self-governance. But some imaginable initiatives, responding to the problems I have discussed thus far, are fully consistent with the free speech guarantee. They would promote its highest aspirations.

FREE SPEECH IS NOT AN ABSOLUTE

We can make some progress here by investigating the idea that the free speech guarantee is "an absolute" in the specific sense that government may not regulate speech at all. This view plays a large role in public debate, and in some ways it is a salutary myth. Certainly the idea that the First Amendment is an absolute helps to discourage government from doing things that it ought not to do. At the same time, it gives great rhetorical power to critics of illegitimate government censorship. That's good. But a myth, even if in some ways salutary, remains a myth, and any publicly influential myth is likely to create many problems.

There should be no ambiguity on the point: free speech is not an absolute. We have seen that the government is allowed to regulate speech by imposing neutral rules of property law, telling would-be speakers that they may not have access to certain speech outlets. But this is only the beginning. Government is permitted to regulate computer viruses, unlicensed medical advice, attempted bribery, perjury, criminal conspiracies ("let's fix prices!"), threats to assassinate the president, blackmail ("I'll tell everyone the truth about your private life unless you give me $100"), criminal solicitation ("might you help me rob this bank?"), child pornography, violations of the copyright law, false advertising, purely verbal fraud ("this stock is worth $100,000"), and much more.

Note that many of these forms of speech will not be especially harmful. A fruitless and doomed attempt to solicit someone to commit a crime, for example, is still criminal solicitation. A piti-fully executed attempt at fraud is still fraud. Sending a computer virus that doesn't actually work is still against the law, and the same is true of computer hacks of personal information.

Perhaps you disagree with the view, settled as a matter of current US law (and so settled in most other nations as well), that *all* these forms of speech are unprotected by the free speech principle. There is certainly a good argument that some current uses of the copyright law impose unnecessary and unjustifiable restrictions on free speech—and that these restrictions are especially troublesome in the Internet era.[11] But you are not a free speech absolutist unless you believe that *each* of these forms of speech should be protected by that principle. And if this is your belief, you are a most unusual person (and you will have a lot of explaining to do).

This is not the place for a full account of the reach of the First Amendment of the US Constitution.[12] But it is plain that some distinctions must be made among different kinds of speech. It is important, for example, to distinguish between speech that can be shown to be quite harmful and speech that is relatively harmless. As a general rule, the government should not be able to regulate the latter. We might also distinguish between speech that bears on democratic self-government and speech that does not; certainly an especially severe burden should be placed on any government efforts to regulate political speech. Less simply, we might want to distinguish among the *kinds of lines* that government is drawing in terms of the likelihood that government is acting on the basis of illegitimate reasons (a point to which I will return).

These ideas could be combined in various ways, and indeed the fabric of modern free speech law in the United States reflects one such combination. Despite the increasing prominence of the idea that the free speech principle requires unrestricted choices by individual consumers, the Supreme Court continues to say that political speech receives the highest protection, and that government may regulate (for example) commercial advertising, obscenity, and libel of ordinary people without meeting the especially stringent burden of justification required for political speech. But for present purposes, all that is necessary is to say that no one really believes that the free speech principle, or the First Amendment, is an absolute. We should be thankful for that.

THE FIRST AMENDMENT AND DEMOCRATIC DELIBERATION

The fundamental concern of this book is to see how unlimited consumer options might compromise the preconditions of a system of freedom of expression, which include unchosen exposures and shared experiences. To understand the nature of this concern, we will make most progress if we insist that the free speech principle should be read in light of the commitment to democratic deliberation. A central purpose of the free speech principle is to implement that commitment.

There are profound differences between those who emphasize consumer sovereignty and those who stress the democratic roots of the free speech principle. For the latter, government efforts to regulate commercial advertising are not necessarily objectionable. Certainly false and misleading commercial advertising is more readily subject to government control than false and misleading political speech. Democratic efforts to reduce the risks of smoking—as, say, through mandatory graphic warnings on the front of cigarette packs—are hardly off the table. If they would save lives, they might well be acceptable. For those who believe that the free speech principle has democratic foundations and is not fundamentally about consumer sovereignty, government regulation of television, radio, and the Internet is not *always* impermissible, at least so long as it is reasonably taken as an effort to promote democratic goals.

Suppose, for example, that government proposes to require television broadcasters (as indeed it now does) to provide three hours per week of educational programming for children. Or suppose that government decides to require television broadcasters to provide a certain amount of free airtime for candidates for public office or a certain amount of time on coverage of elections. For those who believe in consumer sovereignty, these requirements are quite troublesome, and they seem like a core violation of the free speech guarantee. For those who associate the free speech principle with democratic goals, these requirements are fully consistent with its highest aspirations. In many democracies—including, for instance, Germany and Italy—it is well understood that the mass media can be regulated in the interest of improving democratic self-government.[13]

There is nothing novel or iconoclastic in the democratic conception of free speech. On the contrary, this conception lies at the heart of the original understanding of freedom of speech in the United States. In attacking the Alien and Sedition Acts, for example, Madison claimed that they were inconsistent with the free speech principle, which he linked explicitly to the American transformation of the concept of political sovereignty. In England, Madison noted, sovereignty was vested in the king. But "in the United States, the case is altogether different. The People, not the Government, possess the absolute sovereignty."[14]

It was on this foundation that any "Sedition Act" must be judged illegitimate. "The right of electing the members of the Government constitutes . . . the essence of a free and responsible government," and "the value and efficacy of this right depends on the knowledge of the comparative merits and demerits of the candidates for the public trust." It was for this reason that the power represented by a Sedition Act ought, "more than any other, to produce universal alarm; because it is leveled against that right of freely examining public characters and measures, and of free communication among the people thereon, which has ever been justly deemed the only effectual guardian of every other right."[15]

In this way, Madison saw "free communication among the people" not as an exercise in consumer sovereignty, in which speech was treated as a kind of commodity, but instead as a central part of self-government, the "only effectual guardian of every other right."[16] Here Madison's conception of free speech was a close cousin of that of Justice Brandeis, who, as we saw in chapter 2, viewed public discussion as a "political duty" and believed that the greatest menace to liberty would be "an inert people."

A central part of the US constitutional tradition, then, places a high premium on speech that is critical to democratic processes, and centers the First Amendment on the goal of self-government. If history is our guide, it follows that efforts by government to promote a well-functioning system of free expression, as through extensions of the public forum idea, may well be acceptable. It also follows that government faces special burdens when it attempts to regulate political speech—burdens that are more severe than those it confronts when it attempts to regulate other forms of speech.

American history is not the only basis for seeing the First Amendment in light of the commitment to democratic deliberation. The argument can be justified by basic principle as well.[17] Consider the question whether the free speech principle should be taken to forbid efforts to make communications markets work a bit better from the democratic point of view. Let's return to our standard examples: educational programming for children, free airtime for candidates for public office, and closed captioning for the hearing impaired. (I am putting the Internet and social media to one side for now, because they raise distinctive questions.) Perhaps some of these proposals would do little or no good, or even harm, but from what standpoint should they be judged inconsistent with the free speech guarantee?

If we believe that the Constitution gives all owners of speech outlets an unbridgeable right to decide what appears on "their" outlets, the answer is clear: government could require none of these things. But why should we believe that? If government is not favoring any point of view, and if it is really improving the operation of democratic processes, it is hard to find a legitimate basis for complaint. Indeed, the Supreme Court has expressly held that the owners of shopping centers—areas where a great deal of speech occurs—may be required to keep their property open for expressive activity.[18] Shopping centers are not television broadcasters, but if a democratic government is attempting to build on the idea of a public forum so as to increase the likelihood of exposure to and debate about diverse views, is there really a reasonable objection from the standpoint of free speech itself?

In a similar vein, it makes sense to say that speech that is political in character, in the sense that it relates to democratic self-government, cannot be regulated without an especially strong showing of government justification—and that commercial advertising, obscenity, and other speech that is not political in that sense can be regulated on the basis of a weaker government justification. I will not attempt here to offer a full defense of this idea, which of course raises some tough questions. But in light of the importance of the question to imaginable government regulation of new technologies, there are three points that deserve brief mention.

First, an insistence that government's burden is greatest when it is regulating political speech emerges from a sensible understanding of government's own incentives. It is here that government is most likely to be acting on the basis of illegitimate considerations, such as self-protection or giving assistance to powerful private groups. Government is least trustworthy when it is attempting to control speech that might harm its own interests, and when speech is political, government's own interests are almost certainly at stake. This is not to deny that government is often untrustworthy when it is regulating commercial speech, art, or other speech that does not relate to democratic self-government. But we have the strongest reasons to distrust government regulation when political issues are involved.

Second, an emphasis on democratic deliberation protects speech not only when regulation is most likely to be biased but also when regulation is most likely to be harmful. If government regulates child pornography on the Internet or requires educational programming for children on television, it remains possible to invoke the normal democratic channels to protest these forms of regulation as ineffectual, intrusive, or worse. But when government forbids criticism of an ongoing war effort, the normal channels are in an important sense foreclosed by the very regulation at issue.

Controls on public debate are uniquely damaging because they impair the process of deliberation that is a precondition for political legitimacy.

Third, a stress on democratic deliberation is likely to fit, far better than any alternative, with the most reasonable judgments about particular free speech problems. However much we disagree about the most difficult speech problems, we are likely to believe that at a minimum, the free speech principle protects political expression unless government has exceedingly strong grounds for regulating it. On the other hand, forms of speech such as perjury, attempted bribery, threats, unlicensed medical advice, and criminal solicitation are not likely to seem to be at the heart of the free speech guarantee. An understanding of this kind certainly does not answer all constitutional questions. It does not provide a clear test for distinguishing between political and nonpolitical speech—a predictably vexing question.[19] (To those who believe that the absence of a clear test is decisive against the distinction itself, the best response is that any alternative test will lead to line-drawing problems of its own. Because everyone agrees that some forms of speech are regulable, line drawing is literally inevitable. If you're skeptical, try to think of a test that eliminates problems of this kind.) It does not say whether and when government may regulate art or literature, sexually explicit speech, or libelous speech. In all cases, government is required to have a strong justification for regulating speech, political or not.

But the approach I am defending does help to orient inquiry. When government is regulating false or fraudulent commercial advertising, libel of private persons, or child pornography, it is likely to be on firm ground. When government is attempting to control criminal conspiracy or speech that contains direct threats of violence aimed at particular people, it need not meet the stringent standards required for regulation of political dissent. What I have suggested here, without fully defending the point, is that a conception of the First Amendment that is rooted in democratic deliberation is an exceedingly good place to start.

FORMS OF NEUTRALITY

None of this means that the government is permitted to regulate the communications market however it wishes. To know whether to object to what government is doing, it is important to know what *kind* of line it is drawing.[20]

There are three possibilities here.

- The government might be regulating speech in a way that is *neutral with respect to the content of the speech at issue*. This is the least objectionable way of regulating speech. For example, government is permitted to say that people may not use loudspeakers on the public streets after midnight or that speakers cannot have access to the front lawn immediately in front of the White House. A regulation of this kind imposes no controls on speech of any particular content. Here's an Internet example: if government says that no one may use the website of CNN unless CNN gives permission, it is acting in a way that is entirely neutral with respect to speech content; so too with restrictions on sending computer viruses. The government bans the ILOVEYOU virus, but it also bans the IHATEYOU virus and the IAMINDIFFERENTTOYOU virus. What is against the law is sending viruses; their content is irrelevant.

- The government might regulate speech in a way that depends on the content of what is said, but without discriminating against any particular point of view. Suppose, for example, that government bans commercial speech on the subways but allows all other forms of speech on the subways. In the technical language of First Amendment law, this form of regulation is "content based" but "viewpoint neutral." Consider the old fairness doctrine, which required broadcasters to cover public issues and allow speech by those with opposing views. Here the content of speech is highly relevant to what government is requiring, but no specific point of view is benefited or punished.

The same can be said for the damages award against the Nuremburg Trials website; the content of the speech definitely mattered, but no particular point of view was being punished. The same award would be given against a website that treated antiabortion people in the same way that the Nuremburg Trials treated doctors. In the same category would be a regulation saying that in certain areas, sexually explicit speech must be made inaccessible to children. In these cases, no lines are being drawn directly on the basis of point of view.

The government might regulate a point of view that it fears or dislikes. This form of regulation is often called "viewpoint discrimination." Government might say, for instance, that no one may criticize a decision to go to war, no one may claim that one racial group is inferior to another, or no one may advocate violent overthrow of government. Here the government is singling out a point of view that it wants to ban, perhaps because it believes that the particular point of view is especially dangerous.

It makes sense to say that these three kinds of regulations should be treated differently, on the Internet as elsewhere. Viewpoint discrimination is the most objectionable. Content-neutral regulation is the least objectionable. If officials are regulating speech because of the point of view that it contains, their action is almost certainly unconstitutional. Government should not be allowed to censor arguments and positions merely because it fears or disapproves of them. If officials are banning a disfavored viewpoint, they ought to be required to show, at the very least, that the viewpoint really creates serious risks that cannot be adequately combated with more speech. Officials ought also be required to explain, in convincing terms, why they are punishing one point of view and not its opposite.

Content-neutral regulations are at the opposite extreme, and such regulations are often legitimate. If the government has acted in a content-neutral way, courts usually do not and should not intervene, at least if the basic channels of communications remain open, and if government has a solid reason for the regulation. Of course a gratuitous or purposeless regulation must be struck down even if it is content neutral. Suppose that government says that the public streets—or for that matter the Internet—may be used for expressive activity, but only between 8:00 p.m. and 8:30 p.m. If so, the neutrality of the regulation is no defense. But content-neutral regulations are frequently easier to justify; their very neutrality and hence breadth ensures that there is a good reason for them. The government is unlikely to ban expressive activity from 8:30 p.m. until 7:59 a.m. because so many people would resist the ban. The more likely regulation prohibits noisy demonstrations when people are trying to sleep, and there is nothing wrong with such prohibitions.

Now consider the intermediate case. When government is regulating in a way that is based on content but neutral with respect to point of view, there are two issues. The first is *whether the particular line being drawn suggests lurking viewpoint discrimination*—a hidden but detectable desire to ban a certain point of view. When it does, the law should probably be struck down. If government says that the most recent war, or abortion, may not be discussed on television, it is, as a technical matter, discriminating against a whole topic, not against any particular point of view, but there is pretty good reason to suspect government's motivations. A ban on discussion of the most recent war is probably an effort to protect the government from criticism.

The second and perhaps more fundamental issue is *whether government is able to invoke strong, content-neutral grounds for engaging in this form of regulation*. A ban on televised discussion of the most recent war should be struck down for this reason. The ban seems to have no real point, aside from forbidding certain perspectives from being expressed. But the government has a stronger argument if, for example, it is requiring broadcasters to offer three hours of educational programming for children. In that case, it is trying to ensure that television serves children—an entirely legitimate interest.

Of course, some cases may test the line between discrimination on the basis of content and discrimination on the basis of viewpoint. If government is regulating sexually explicit speech when that speech offends contemporary community standards, is it regulating on the basis of viewpoint or merely content? This is not an easy question, and many people have argued over the right answer. But an understanding of the three categories discussed here should be sufficient to make sense out of the bulk of imaginable free speech challenges—and should provide some help in approaching the rest of them as well.

PENALTIES AND SUBSIDIES

However we resolve that question, it remains true that government can do a lot of things to improve the system of free speech. Here it is important to make a further distinction, between "subsidies," on the one hand, and "penalties," on the other. In general, government is likely to have a great deal of trouble when it is imposing penalties on speech. Such penalties are the model of what a system of free expression avoids. Government will have more room to maneuver if it is giving out selective subsidies. Public officials are not required to give money out to all speakers, and if they are giving money to some people but not to others, they may well be on firm ground. But the distinction between the penalties and subsidies is not always obvious.

The most conspicuous penalties are criminal and civil punishments. If government makes it a crime to libel people over the Internet or imposes civil fines on television broadcasters who do not provide free airtime for candidates for office, it is punishing speech. The analysis of these penalties should depend on the considerations discussed thus far—whether political speech is involved, what kind of line the government is drawing, and so forth.

Somewhat trickier, but belonging in the same category, are cases in which government is *withdrawing a benefit to which people would otherwise be entitled*, when the reason for the withdrawal is the government's view about the appropriate content of speech. Suppose, for example, that government gives an annual cash subsidy to all speakers of a certain kind—say, those networks that agree to provide educational programming for children. But suppose that government withdraws the subsidy from those networks that provide speech of which the government disapproves. Imagine, for example, that the government withdraws the subsidy from networks whose news shows are critical of the president. For the most part, these sorts of penalties should be analyzed in exactly the same way as criminal or civil punishment. When benefits are being withdrawn, just as when ordinary punishment is being imposed, government is depriving people of goods to which they would otherwise be entitled, and we probably have excellent reason to distrust its motives. If government responds to dissenters by taking away benefits that they would otherwise receive, it is violating the free speech principle.

But a different issue is posed when government gives out selective subsidies to speakers. It often does this by, for example, funding some museums and artists but not others, and generally through the National Endowment for the Arts and the Public Broadcasting System. Imagine a situation in which government is willing to fund educational programming for children, and pays a station to air that programming on Saturday morning—without also funding situation comedies or game shows. Or imagine that government funds a series of historical exhibits on the Civil War without also funding exhibits on the Vietnam War, World War II, or the history of sex equality in America. What is most important here can be stated simply: *under current law in the United States (and generally elsewhere), government is permitted to subsidize speech however it wishes.*[21]

Government often is a speaker, and as such, it is permitted to say whatever it likes. No one thinks that there is a problem if officials endorse one view and reject another. And if government seeks to use taxpayer funds to subsidize certain projects and enterprises, there is usually no basis for constitutional complaint. The only exception to this principle is that if government is allocating funds to private speakers in a way that discriminates on the basis of viewpoint, there might be a First Amendment problem.[22] The precise nature of this exception remains unclear. But it would certainly be possible to challenge, on constitutional grounds, a decision by government to fund the Republican Party website without also funding the Democratic Party website.

Of course, this kind of discrimination goes far beyond anything that I will be suggesting here. What is important is that government has a great deal of room to maneuver insofar as it is not penalizing speech but instead subsidizing it.

A POWERFUL, PRUDENT FIRST AMENDMENT

This chapter has dealt with a wide range of free speech issues, some of them briskly, and it is important not to lose the forest for the trees. My basic claims are that the First Amendment in large part embodies a democratic ideal, that it should not be identified with the notion of consumer sovereignty, and that it is not an absolute. Some questions are hard; the use of social media to recruit terrorists is one of them. But the core requirement of the free speech principle is that with respect to politics, government must remain neutral among points of view. Content regulation is disfavored; viewpoint discrimination is almost always out of bounds.

These are enduring principles. A key task is to ensure that government complies with them, whatever the direction of the technologies over which communication occurs.

PROPOSALS

A well-functioning democratic order would be compromised by a fragmented system of communications. To some extent, democratic nations have already been compromised by such fragmentation. Having urged these points, I do not intend to offer any kind of blueprint for the future; this is not a policy manual. Recall too that some problems lack solutions. But surely things can be made better rather than worse. In thinking about what might be done by either private or public institutions, we need to have some sense of the problems that we aim to address, and of some possible ways of dealing with them.[1]

It is important to offer three clarifications. First, we are speaking of problems, not catastrophes, and the problems are accompanied by compensating benefits. Twitter and Facebook challenge but do not endanger democracy; on balance, they are good for it, and we should not wish them away. Second, the modern communications market should be taken as a whole, and I will explore some proposals that would apply to radio and television, not to websites or social media. Third, any improvements are likely to be incremental, and many of them will be quite modest—positive steps, not magic bullets, which are in any case in short supply. My main goal here is to explore the risks of polarization and fragmentation, not to say that with one or two steps, or ten, we can make those risks disappear.

If the discussion thus far is correct, there are three fundamental concerns from the democratic point of view:

● the value of exposure to materials, topics, and positions that people would not have chosen in advance, or at least enough exposure to produce a degree of understanding and curiosity about the truth

- the importance of a range of common experiences

- the need for attention to substantive questions of policy and principle, combined with a range of positions on such questions

Of course, it would be ideal if citizens were demanding and private providers were creating a range of initiatives designed to alleviate the underlying concerns. To a significant extent, they are; you can find evidence to that effect with just a little time online. In a free society, our emphasis should not be on government mandates but instead on purely private solutions. Current communications technologies create extraordinary and ever-growing opportunities for exposure to diverse points of view, and indeed increased opportunities for shared experiences and substantive discussions of both policy and principle. Private choices can lead to far more, not less, in the way of exposure to new topics and viewpoints, and also to more, not less, in the way of shared experiences. But to the degree that they fail to do so, it is worthwhile to consider how self-conscious efforts by private institutions, and perhaps public ones as well, might pick up the slack.

Any ideas about how to handle the situation require an understanding of how people are likely to react to topics and points of view that they have not selected. If people cannot develop an interest in unchosen topics, then exposure to those topics is unlikely to be worthwhile. If people will never listen to points of view with which they disagree, or if hearing them will simply increase polarization, there would be little point in exposing them to those points of view. If people would never learn from exposure to unchosen views and topics, we might as well build on the emerging capacity of companies to discern and predict tastes, and just allow people to see, hear, and get what they already like.

It is true that if you feel strongly, you might not learn anything from being exposed to contrary opinions. It is nonetheless realistic to say that most people are willing to listen to points of view that they have not selected. Many of us are fully prepared to develop an interest in topics that we have not chosen and in fact know nothing about. That is how we learn, and we are entirely aware of that fact. To work well, a deliberative democracy had better have many such people. It cannot possibly function without them. And if many people are able to benefit from wider exposure, it is worthwhile to think about ways to improve the communications market to their and our advantage.

I briefly discuss several possibilities here, including:

- deliberative domains

- disclosure of relevant conduct by networks and other large producers of communications

- voluntary self-regulation

- economic subsidies, including publicly subsidized programming and websites

- "must-carry" policies, designed to promote education and attention to public issues

- the creative use of links to draw people's attention to multiple views

- opposing viewpoint and serendipity buttons, designed particularly for Facebook, and perhaps suitable elsewhere as well

Different proposals would work better for some communications outlets than for others. Disclosure of public affairs programming is sensible for television and radio broadcasters, but not for websites. I will be examining must-carry requirements for television stations, but with respect to the Internet, such requirements would be hard to justify—and would almost certainly be unconstitutional. I will be arguing for the creative use of links on the Internet, although I will not suggest, and do not believe, that the government should require any links. Most important, the goals of the proposals could be implemented through private action, which (I reiterate) is the preferred approach by far.

DELIBERATIVE DOMAINS

It would be extremely valuable to have several widely publicized deliberative domains on the Internet, ensuring opportunities for discussion among people with diverse views. In chapter 4, we encountered Fishkin's deliberative opinion poll, attempting to describe public opinion not after telephone calls to people in their homes yield unreflective responses but as a result of extended conversations in groups of heterogeneous people. Fishkin has created a website with a great deal of valuable and fascinating material.[2] Along with many others, Fishkin has been engaged in a process of creating deliberative opportunities on the Internet—spaces where people with different views can meet and exchange reasons, and have a chance to understand, at least a bit, the point of view of those who disagree with them. The hope is that citizen engagement, mutual understanding, and better thinking will emerge as a result.

We can envision many variations on this theme, both real and online. Imagine a new website, deliberativedemocracy.com—or if you wish, deliberativedemocracy.org. (Neither name is yet taken; I've checked.) The site could easily be created by the private sector. When you come to the site, you might find a general description of goals and contents. Everyone would understand that this is a place where people of divergent views are invited to listen and speak. And once you're there, you would be able to read and (if you wish) participate in discussions of a topic of your choice by clicking on icons representing, for example, national security, relevant wars, civil rights, the environment, unemployment, foreign affairs, poverty, the stock market, children, gun control, labor unions, and much more. Many of these topics might have icons with smaller subtopics—under environment, there might be discussions of global warming, genetically engineered food, water pollution, and hazardous waste sites.

Each topic and subtopic could provide brief descriptions of agreed-on facts and competing points of view as an introduction and frame for the discussion. Private creativity on the part of users would undoubtedly take things in boundless unanticipated directions. Private managers of such sites would have their own norms about how people should interact with one another; deliberativedemocracy .com, for example, might encourage norms of civility.

Many experiments in deliberative democracy are now emerging, sometimes self-consciously, and sometimes through the kinds of spontaneous developments that occur on e-mail and e-lists. The Deliberative Democracy Consortium is noteworthy here. It offers a range of references, links, and materials.[3] For obvious reasons, there would be many advantages to a situation in which a few deliberative sites were especially prominent. If this were the case, deliberativedemocracy.org, for example, would have a special salience for many citizens, supplying a forum in which hundreds of thousands or even millions could participate, if only through occasional reading. But we should hardly be alarmed if a large number of deliberative websites were to emerge and compete with one another—a plausible description of what is starting to happen.

A VERY BRIEF NOTE ON CIVILITY

Speaking of civility, it is worthwhile to ponder in that connection the so-called Rapoport rules, which read:[4]

1. You should attempt to express your target position so clearly, vividly, and fairly that your target says, "Thanks, I wish I'd thought of putting it that way"

2. You should list any points of agreement (especially if they are not matters of general or widespread agreement)

3. You should mention anything you have learned from your target

4. Only then are you permitted to say so much as a word of rebuttal or criticism

The Rapoport rules are not exactly well-respected on social media or in political discussion generally. One reason is that life is short, and it can be time-consuming to follow the first three steps; you want to get on with it. Another reason is that if you're mad or even just charged up, you might not be in the best frame of mind to describe your target's position in a way that produces gratitude. On Facebook and Twitter, targets often react, reasonably enough, by insisting, "I never said anything like that!" And they didn't. The Rapoport rules are a bit fussy, but it would be terrific if people would move a bit more in their direction.

SUNLIGHT AS DISINFECTANT

The last decades have seen an extraordinary growth in the use of a simple regulatory tool: the requirement that people disclose what they are doing. In the environmental area, this has been an exceptionally effective strategy. Probably the most striking example is the Emergency Planning and Community Right-to-Know Act. Under this statute, firms and individuals must report to state and local government the quantities of potentially hazardous chemicals that have been stored or released into the environment. This has been an amazing and unanticipated success story. Mere disclosure, or the threat of it, has resulted in voluntary, low-cost reductions in toxic releases.[5]

Building on the basic idea, the Environmental Protection Agency has also created a public inventory for greenhouse gases, hoping and expecting that by itself, disclosure will have a beneficial effect. Right on its opening web page, the Occupational Safety and Health Administration prominently discloses every workplace death in the United States, promptly after it occurs, and it names names in the hope that publicity will increase safety.[6] (No employer wants to be named in that way on this site.) There is far more in this vein. Dozens of nations have joined the Open Government Partnership, which attempts to use openness as a spur to improving the performance of government (not least by reducing corruption).[7]

It should be no wonder that disclosure has become a popular approach to dealing with pollution. When polluters are required to disclose their actions, political or market pressures will lead to reductions, without any need for actual government mandates. Ideally, no requirements need to be imposed. People will disclose on their own—in part because of the public demand for relevant information. In the area of communications, voluntary disclosure should be preferred. Commendably, several of the leading information technology companies publish transparency reports. Twitter, for instance, discloses the number of government requests for information, requests for content takedown, and more.[8] Others such as Verizon and WhatsApp seem to disclose less information than their peers.[9] To the extent that important information is not forthcoming, disclosure requirements deserve consideration.

Consider the case of television. Suppose, for example, that certain programming might be harmful to children, and that certain other programming might be beneficial to society. Is there a way to discourage the bad and encourage the good without regulating speech directly? Disclosure policies suggest a promising approach, at least if it is possible to specify what is being disclosed. Thus the mandatory V-chip is intended to permit parents to block programming that they want to exclude from their homes; the V-chip is supposed to work hand in hand with a ratings system giving information about the suitability of programming for children of various ages.

Similarly, a provision of the 1996 Telecommunications Act imposes three relevant requirements. First, television manufacturers must include technology capable of reading a program-rating mechanism. Second, the Federal Communications Commission must create a ratings methodology if the industry does not produce an acceptable ratings plan within a year. Third, broadcasters must include a rating in their signals if the relevant program is rated. The ratings system has now been in place for many years, and it seems to have been, at the very least, a modest success, making it far simpler and easier for parents to monitor what children are seeing.

A chief advantage of disclosure policies is their comparative flexibility. Most important, they allow viewers to do as they wish. If viewers know the nature of programming in advance, they can impose market pressures by watching more or less; broadcasters are responsive to those pressures. People can also impose political pressures by complaining to stations or elected representatives, and here too it is possible to induce changes. From the democratic point of view, disclosure also has substantial virtues. A well-functioning system of deliberative democracy requires a certain degree of information, so that citizens can engage in their monitoring and deliberative tasks. A good way to enable citizens to oversee private or public action—and also assess the need for less, more, or different regulation—is to inform them of both private and public activity. The very fact that the public will be in a position to engage in general monitoring may well spur better choices on the part of those who provide television and radio programming.

Disclosure could be used in many different ways, suitable for different communications media. Television and radio broadcasters, cable television stations, information technology companies, and social media companies might, for example, voluntarily adopt disclosure policies of various sorts. The idea here, associated with Justice Brandeis, is that "sunlight is the best of disinfectants." And if such policies are not adopted voluntarily, modest legal requirements might be considered. The idea would be to ensure that anyone who is engaging in a practice that might produce harm, or do less good than might be done, should be required to disclose that fact to the public.[10] The disclosure might or might not alter behavior. If it does not alter behavior, we have reason to believe that the public is not much concerned about it. If the behavior does change, the public was, in all likelihood, sufficiently exercised to demand it.

As an illustration, consider a simple proposal: *television and radio broadcasters should be required to disclose, in some detail and on a quarterly basis, all their public service and public interest activities.* The disclosure might include an accounting of any free airtime provided to candidates, opportunities to speak for those addressing public issues, rights of reply, educational programming, charitable activities, programming designed for traditionally underserved communities, closed captioning for the hearing impaired, local programming, and public service announcements.

Astonishingly, most radio and television broadcasters have yet to disclose this information to the public, though the National Association of Broadcasters has done some information gathering. A hope, vindicated by similar approaches in environmental law, is that a disclosure requirement will by itself trigger improved performance by creating a kind of competition to do more and better, and enlisting various social pressures in the direction of improved performance.

I have referred several times to the old fairness doctrine, which required broadcasters to cover public issues and allow a right of reply for dissenting views. We have seen that this doctrine was repealed largely on the ground that it chilled coverage of public issues in the first instance. We have also seen that while the repeal was amply justified, it has had a downside insofar as it has increased fragmentation and hence polarization. But whether or not we think the old fairness doctrine was defensible, a disclosure requirement—tied to coverage of public issues and diversity of views—would be a far less intrusive way of accomplishing the most appealing goals of that doctrine. Such a requirement might well produce some movement toward more coverage of public issues and more attention to diverse perspectives. It is even possible that such a requirement would help to address the three problems identified at the beginning of this chapter.

It is also possible that any disclosure requirement would produce no movement at all. But notice that people did not anticipate that the Environmental Protection Agency's Toxic Release Inventory would by itself spur reductions in toxic releases, as it emphatically did. In order for voluntary improvements to occur, the disclosure requirements must be accompanied by economic or political pressure of some kind, perhaps from external monitors, or at least a degree of conscience on the part of producers. Disclosure is likely to do some good if there are external monitors, and if those monitors are able to impose costs on those with bad records.

The external monitors might include public interest groups seeking to "shame" badly performing broadcasters. They might include rivals who seek to create a kind of "race to the top" in the form of better performance. They might include newspaper reporters and websites. If public interest organizations and viewers who favor certain programming are able to mobilize, perhaps in concert with certain members of the mass media, substantial improvements might be expected. It is even possible that a disclosure requirement would help create its own monitors. And in view of the relative unintrusiveness of a disclosure requirement and the flexibility of any private responses, this approach is certainly worth trying.

At worst, little will be lost. At most, something will be gained, probably in the form of better programming and greater information about the actual performance of the industry. In light of the aspirations of most viewers, the possible result of disclosure will be to improve the quality and quantity of both educational and civic programming in a way that promotes the goals of a well-functioning deliberative democracy.

My emphasis here has been on the application of disclosure requirements to television and radio broadcasters. I do not suggest that such requirements should be imposed on websites. In view of the remarkable range and diversity of websites, no such requirements would make sense. What, exactly, would be disclosed by Amazon.com, startrek.com, foxsports.com, columbia.edu, or republic.com? Of course some disclosures and warnings might be provided voluntarily. For example, many websites already inform people of content unsuitable for children. Other disclosure practices could undoubtedly help both consumers and citizens. But for the purposes of my concerns here, those practices should not be compelled.

VOLUNTARY SELF-REGULATION AND BEST PRACTICES

A somewhat more ambitious approach, going beyond mere disclosure, would involve voluntary self-regulation by those who provide information. One of the most noteworthy trends of the last two decades, inside and outside the world of communications, has been in the direction of such self-regulation, which is designed to protect a range of social goals.[11] In the area of occupational safety, many employers follow agreed-on "best practices," designed to reduce the level of accidents and disease. Similar approaches are followed in the environmental area. The same idea might easily be adopted for democratic purposes. For example, television and radio stations might agree, perhaps via some kind of code of conduct, to attempt to provide a wide range of views on public issues so as to ensure that listeners encounter something other than a loud version of what they already think.

One of the motivating ideas behind voluntary self-regulation is that competition among producers, while usually wonderful, can sometimes be harmful from the viewpoint of the public as a whole.[12] Endless efforts to get people's attention may do long-term damage. Everyone knows that there has been an increasing trend toward "tabloidization," with mainstream newspapers and broadcasters emphasizing scandals and sensationalism. This trend predated the Internet, but it seems to have been accelerated by it. Often the news seems not to involve news at all. Sometimes it seems to be a continuation of the fictional drama that preceded it with detailed discussion of the "real-life events" mirrored in the fiction. Many journalists worry about this problem. As Robert

Frank and Phillip Cook warn, with reference to the effects of market forces:

> Increasingly impoverished political debate is yet another cost of our current cultural trajectory. Complex modern societies generate complex economic and social problems, and the task of choosing the best course is difficult under the best of circumstances. And yet, as in-depth analysis and commentary give way to sound bites in which rival journalists and politicians mercilessly ravage one another, we become an increasingly ill-informed and ill-tempered electorate.[13]

But an agreement among producers can break (or brake) this competition and hence perform some of the valuable functions of law—without intruding law into the domain of speech regulation.

With respect to television, consider the possibility of promoting democratic goals through voluntary approaches, as through a code of conduct to be issued and promoted by the National Association of Broadcasters, or perhaps by a wider range of those who produce television for the public. For many decades, in fact, the association did administer such a code. It did so partly to promote its economic interests (by raising the price of advertising), partly to fend off regulation (by showing that the industry was engaged in beneficial self-regulation, making government efforts unnecessary), and partly to carry out the moral commitments of broadcasters themselves. Notably, voluntary self-regulation has played a role in numerous areas of media policy, including, for example, cigarette advertising, children's advertising, family viewing, advertising of hard liquor, and fairness in news reporting.

In the 1980s, congressional concern about televised violence led to an intriguing new law creating an antitrust exemption for networks, broadcasters, cable operators and programmers, and trade associations, precisely in order to permit them to generate standards to reduce the amount of violence on television. As we have seen, a ratings system for television is now in place, and it should be treated as an instructive illustration of voluntary self-regulation—perhaps not wholly successful, but giving parents a general sense of the appropriateness of programming.

Even if any such new code did not apply to social media or websites (and in view of their nature and diversity, it certainly should not), it might address some of the problems discussed thus far. In light of the intensity of market pressures, it might be pie in the sky, but signatories could agree to cover substantive issues in a serious way, avoid sensationalistic treatment of politics, give extended coverage to public issues, and allow diverse voices to be heard. In fact, ideas of this kind long played a role in the television industry until the abandonment of the broadcasters' code in 1979. In view of the increasing range of options and the declining centrality of television broadcasters, there are undoubtedly limits to how much can be done through this route. But in many contexts, voluntary self-regulation of this kind has produced considerable good, and a code of some kind could provide a sort of quality assurance to the public.

If formal codes of conduct are not feasible—and they probably are not—we could imagine less formal efforts to establish and follow best practices. For providers of television and radio, such practices might deal with programming for children, emergency situations, and perhaps coverage of elections. It is also possible to imagine informal agreements or understandings among some websites, designed to protect children, ensure privacy, and promote attention to diverse views. If market forces are producing serious problems, we have every reason to encourage creative thinking in this vein.

SUBSIDIES

An additional possibility, also with an established history, would involve government subsidies. With respect to television and radio, many nations, including the United States, have relied on a combination of private and public funding. In the United States, PBS is designed to offer programming, including educational shows for children, that (it is believed) will find insufficient funding in the private domain. Interestingly, and contrary to common belief, most of PBS's funding comes from private sources, but the government does provide significant help. This is a genuine public–private partnership. And in many domains, taxpayer resources are given to assist those who produce artistic, cultural, and historical works of many different kinds.

The traditional rationale for a separate public broadcasting network has been weakened by the massive proliferation of options, including many, on both television and the Internet, that provide discussion of public issues and educational programming for children. This is not to say that the rationale has been eliminated. Tens of millions of Americans continue to rely on over-the-air broadcasting, and many of them benefit from and depend on PBS. Nor do I mean to suggest that in all respects, the situation is better now than it was when the universe of options was so much smaller. In a system with four channels, PBS had a kind of salience that it now lacks, and it is by no means clear that the current situation, with dozens or hundreds of available stations, is in every way an improvement for all children or adults. Public broadcasting continues to supply important services. But with many private outlets doing the same kind of thing, it does seem clear that the rationale for PBS in its current form is weaker than it once was.

What, if anything, might be done in addition or instead? One possibility is to use modest levels of taxpayer money to assist high-quality efforts in nonprofit, nongovernmental spaces on the Internet. Such spaces are now proliferating, and they are adding a great deal to our culture. Taxpayer funds are limited, of course, and there are claims on government resources with higher priority. My only point it that it is worth rethinking the PBS model. It is past time to consider new initiatives that make better sense in the new communications environment.

MUST CARRY: CONSTITUTIONAL DEBATES

Some of the most interesting developments in the law of speech involve "access rights," or must-carry rules. In fact, the public forum doctrine creates a kind of must-carry rule for streets and parks. These sites must be opened up for speech. You and I are entitled to have access to them. Is there any place for must-carry rules on television or radio, or is the whole idea a relic of the past?

To answer these questions, it is necessary to have some sense of the legal background. In the 1970s, the Supreme Court held that government has the authority to subject television and radio broadcasters to a kind of must-carry rule in the form of the old fairness doctrine, requiring attention to public issues and an opportunity for diverse views to speak.[14] At the same time, the Court firmly rejected the idea that private newspapers may be treated as public forums and subject to must-carry rules.[15] In the Court's view, the government could not force newspapers to give a "right of reply" to those who sought to combat a controversial statement of opinion or fact. The apparent difference between broadcasters and newspapers— fragile even in the 1970s, and fragile to the breaking point today—is that the former are "scarce," largely for technological reasons, and hence are more properly subject to governmental controls.

Now that the scarcity rationale is so much weaker, the continued viability of the fairness doctrine is exceedingly doubtful. If the Federal Communications Commission tried to reinstate the doctrine, the Court would probably strike it down. The Court has nonetheless upheld legislation that imposes must-carry rules on cable television providers.[16]

The relevant legislation, still on the books, requires cable providers to set aside a number of their channels for both "local commercial television stations" and "noncommercial educational television stations." Congress defended these requirements as a way of ensuring the economic viability of broadcasters, on whom many millions of Americans continue to rely. In finding the must-carry requirements constitutional, the Court noted, "Assuring that the public has access to a multiplicity of information sources is a governmental purpose of the highest order, for it promotes values central to the First Amendment." The Court also emphasized the "potential for abuse of . . . private power over a central avenue of communication," and stressed that the Constitution "does not disable the government from taking steps to ensure that private interests not restrict, through physical control of a critical pathway of communication, the free flow of information and ideas."[17]

In so saying, the Court was recalling Justice Brandeis's emphatically republican conception of the First Amendment. Indeed, Justice Stephen Breyer, in a separate opinion, made the link with Justice Brandeis explicit: the statute's "policy, in turn, seeks to facilitate the public discussion and informed deliberation, which, as Justice Brandeis pointed out many years ago, democratic government presupposes and the First Amendment seeks to achieve."[18]

Here, then, is an unambiguous endorsement of the idea that government has the power to regulate communications technologies in order to promote goals associated with deliberative democracy. Notably, Justice Breyer's general approach to the Constitution is in this vein; he reads the Constitution as a whole in terms of deliberative democracy.[19]

So far, so good. But for those interested in thinking about the implications of the Court's decision, there are many questions. How crucial was it to the Court's reasoning that the cable provider controlled access to cable stations? Suppose that government imposed must-carry rules on cbs.com, cnn.com, or foxnews.com—arguing that one or the other of these must ensure sufficient diversity of view, or cover issues of importance to local communities.

We might imagine a law requiring foxnews.com to give more attention to "liberal" positions—or that cnn.com ensure that when New Yorkers click on its site, they see stories that bear on New York in particular. I hope that everyone would agree that no such requirements would be sensible, and if they were imposed, they should be struck down (immediately) as unconstitutional. The sheer range of views on the Internet would make it impermissibly selective to single out foxnews.com for special obligations, and a general requirement, imposed on all sites, would be far too intrusive to be justifiable. Coverage of local issues is important, but the massive increase in options means that such coverage is readily available. It may take a few seconds to find it, but is that a serious problem?

"Must carry" has no legitimate role on the Internet. But it remains true that providers, including cnn.com and foxnews.com, do best if they give sympathetic and substantive attention to a number of views, not only one.

THE SCARCE COMMODITY OF ATTENTION

I have emphasized that one of the most important of all commodities is people's attention. This is what companies are endlessly competing to obtain. Much activity on the Internet by those interested in profits and other goods is designed to produce greater attention, even if only for a moment. If a company, or a political candidate, can get attention from three hundred thousand people for as little as two seconds, it will have accomplished a great deal.

As almost everyone has noticed, many Internet sites do not, and need not, charge a fee for users. You can get the content of many magazines and newspapers without paying a penny. Nor is the phenomenon limited to magazines and newspapers. If you want to learn about cancer, you can find out a great deal from numerous sources, entirely free of charge. Google.com charges nothing for its search service. Why is this? In most of these cases, advertisers are willing to foot the bill. What advertisers are buying is access, and usually brief access at that, to people's eyes—a small period of attention.

Here again we can see that those who use websites are commodities at least as much as they are consumers. They are what websites are selling to advertisers for a fee, and sometimes a large one. Targeting and customization are playing a large role here, as advertisers come to learn, with precision, how many and which people visit which sites, and from which advertisements.

Of course advertisements cannot guarantee sales. Most people who see an icon for Bloomingdales.com, Amazon.com, or Netflix .com will simply ignore it. But some will not; they will be curious and see what there is to see. Or they will file it away in some part of their minds for future use. If we combine an understanding of access rights and must-carry rules with an appreciation of the crucial role of attention, we might enlist advertisers' practices in the service of public interest goals. In other words, public-spirited actors, knowing that attention is valuable, might think of ways to capture that attention, not to coerce people, but to trigger their interest in material that might produce individual and social benefits. Links among sites are the obvious strategy here; I am focusing on voluntary linking decisions, not on government mandates.

Consider in this light a proposal: providers of material with a certain point of view might also provide links to sites with a dramatically different point of view. The *Nation*, a liberal magazine whose site features left-of-center opinions, might agree to display icons for the *Weekly Standard*, a conservative magazine, in return for an informal agreement from the *Weekly Standard* to display icons for the *Nation*. The icon itself would not require anyone to read anything. It would merely provide a signal to the viewer that there is a place where a different perspective might be consulted.

Of the thousands or millions of people who choose any particular site, not most, but undoubtedly a few would be sufficiently interested to look further. Best of all, this form of "carriage" would replicate many features of the public street and the general-interest intermediary. It would alert people to the existence of materials other than those that they usually read. We have seen that some sites do this already. The problem is that the practice remains unusual.

We could even foresee a situation in which many partisan sites offer links implicitly saying something like this: "We have a clear point of view, and we hope that more people will come to believe what we do. But we are also committed to democratic debate and discussion among people who think differently. To that end, we are offering links to other sites, in the interest of affording genuine debate on these issues." If many sites would agree to do this, the problem of fragmentation would be reduced.

In the current context, textual references to organizations or institutions are often hyperlinks, so that when a magazine such as the *National Review* refers to the World Wildlife Fund or the Environmental Defense Fund, it also allows readers instant access to their sites. As compared to icons, the advantage of the hyperlink approach is that it is less trouble for the owner and less intrusive on the owner's prerogatives—indeed, it is barely an intrusion at all.

In a similar vein, public-spirited bloggers would do well to offer links to those whose views are quite different from their own. Liberal blogs could more regularly link to conservative ones, and vice versa. Many bloggers offer "blogrolls" in which they list other blogs that they like or otherwise seek to publicize. As it turns out, liberal bloggers seem to list mostly or only liberal bloggers on their blogrolls, and conservative bloggers show the same pattern. It would be good to show greater diversity, through a norm by which both liberals and conservatives include at least a few high-quality blogs from people with whom they do not agree. We could easily imagine explicit or implicit "deals" among bloggers with competing opinions, producing mutual linking. Such arrangements would increase the likelihood that people would be exposed to different perspectives; they would also reflect a healthy degree of mutual respect.

I certainly do not suggest or believe that government should require anything of this kind. Some constitutional questions are hard, but this one is easy: any such requirements would violate the First Amendment. If site owners and bloggers do not want to provide icons or links, they are entitled to refuse to do so. What is most important is that we could easily imagine a situation in which icons and links are more standard practices, in a way that would promote the goals of both consumers and citizens, and do so without compromising the legitimate interests of authors or site owners.

OPPOSING VIEWPOINT AND SERENDIPITY BUTTONS

Social media are constantly changing, and what's important today might not be so tomorrow. There is some evidence of decentralization, as younger people sort themselves into diverse media. Nonetheless, Facebook does have a special role, not only in the United

States, but also worldwide. As of 2016, it had 1.6 billion active users—a significant percentage of the 7.4 billion people in the world. I have said some negative things about the News Feed, but like most of those 1.6 billion, I really like Facebook. It has a unique function in connecting people to people and also in connecting people to news. If its own conception of "core values" is not entirely right, at least it deserves immense credit for focusing on the issue of core values. How might Facebook do better?

In an intriguing essay, Geoffrey Fowler argues that Facebook should create opposing viewpoint buttons, allowing people to click on them and receive uncongenial perspectives. Fowler remarks, "Imagine if you could flip a switch on Facebook, and turn all the conservative viewpoints that you see liberal, or vice versa. You'd realize your news might look nothing like your neighbor's." He adds, "What I see is a missed opportunity for technology to break down walls during this particularly divided moment. With access to more information than ever online, how could other points of view be so alien?"[20] That's a terrific question.

The beauty of the opposing viewpoint button is that it would not force anything on anyone. You would push it if you like; you don't have to do so. Many people no doubt would decline. But options can be attractive—and they can also shape people's conception of what social media and information sources are for. With an opposing viewpoint button, Facebook, or any other provider, would be saying, *There are other positions out there. Want to have a look?* Many people would say yes.

We can imagine variations on this theme. Instead of opposing viewpoint buttons, Facebook might offer "serendipity buttons," exposing people to unanticipated, unchosen material on their News Feed. Perhaps the material could draw from news stories from prominent outlets, such as the *New York Times* and the *Wall Street Journal*. On a random basis, perhaps they could provide material on events in countries other than one's own. With serendipity buttons, Facebook users could think, I am here in large part to learn. What can I find out?

We could imagine serendipity buttons of many different types. Experimentation is the watchword here. An aggressive idea would be that users would receive serendipity or opposing viewpoints by default, subject to the right to opt out. With such a system, your News Feed might contain all sorts of surprises. Sure, you would see things from your friends, but you would also see other things; your News Feed would be a bit like a great city or a genuine newspaper. True, some users would not love that, and so Facebook might not love it either—but people could easily opt out. We could easily imagine a system of opposing viewpoints by default, with an opportunity to opt out as well. Facebook might not think that that is the best business model, but perhaps someone will give something like this a try. (Count me in.)

THE TYRANNY OF THE STATUS QUO

The tyranny of the status quo has many sources. Sometimes it is based on a fear of unintended consequences, as in the economists' plea, "The perfect is the enemy of the good"—a mantra of resignation to which we should respond, with Dewey, that "the better is the enemy of the still better." Sometimes it is grounded in a belief, widespread though palpably false, that things cannot be different from what they now are. (Things were different yesterday, and they will be different tomorrow.) Sometimes proposed changes seem to be hopelessly utopian, far too much so to be realistic. And sometimes they seem small and incremental, even silly, and do nothing large enough to solve the underlying problems.

The suggestions I have offered here are modest and incremental. They are designed to give some glimpses of the possibilities and do at least a little bit of good. Some of them merely build on existing practices. What is especially important in the current era is that we retain a sense of the grounds on which we can evaluate them. To those skeptical of the ideas outlined here, it makes sense to ask: If we seek to enlist current technologies in the service of democratic ideals, what kinds of practices would be better?

TERRORISM.COM

Since the terrorist attacks of September 11, 2001, many people in the United States, Europe, and elsewhere have been focused on a simple question: *Why do they hate us?* On the basis of the discussion thus far, we should now be able to see that part of the answer lies not in anything particular to religion, or even to the rhetoric of Osama bin Laden or ISIL, but in social dynamics and especially in the process of group polarization. And in fact, leaders of terrorist organizations show a working knowledge of group polarization. They try to isolate their "recruits." They want them to speak mostly to people who are already predisposed in the preferred direction. They know that information and psychology are essential to their goals. They want to control the information environment. For those who seek to disrupt their plans and keep people safe, information and psychology are also essential.

There is no natural predisposition toward terrorism, even among the most disaffected people in the poorest nations. Social dynamics—not poverty, poor education, and disadvantage—play the key role.[1] Online behavior, including uses of social media, is an important part of those dynamics.

RECLAIMING AMERICA

There is a discussion group on the Internet. It was started two years ago by about a dozen political activists who were concerned about the increasing public pressure for gun control and the perceived "emasculation" of the Second Amendment (which in the group's view, clearly bans almost all government restrictions on the sale of guns). But the group was also troubled by the growing authority of government, especially the national government, over the lives of ordinary people, and worried too about the threat to our "European heritage" and "traditional moral values" posed by uncontrolled immigration, terrorism, "Radical Islam," and the increasing social power of transgender "activists." The group's members were fearful that the Republican and Democratic parties had become weak-willed "twins," unable and unwilling to police national borders, or take on the "special interests" that were threatening to "take away our constitutional liberties." The group called itself Reclaim America.

The members of Reclaim America now number well over four thousand people, who regularly exchange facts and points of view, and who share relevant literature with one another. For a majority of the participants, the discussion group provides most of the information on which they base their judgments about political issues.

Over the last two years, the concerns of Reclaim America have been greatly heightened. Nearly 70 percent of the members carry firearms—some as a result of the group's conversations. Small but vigorous protests have been planned, organized, and carried out in three state capitals. A march on Washington, DC, is now in the works. Recent discussion has occasionally turned to the need for "self-protection" against illegal immigrants, terrorists, and the state, through civil disobedience and possibly selective "strikes" on certain targets in the public and private sectors. The motivation for this discussion is the widely disseminated view that the "FBI and possibly the CIA" are starting to take steps to "dismember" the group. One member has sent bomb-making instructions to all the other members of Reclaim America. No violence has occurred as yet. But things are unquestionably heading in that direction.

So far as I know, there is no Reclaim America. This story is not true. But it is not exactly false. It is a composite based on online behavior, sometimes less and often more extreme. Even if we limit ourselves to the United States, discussion groups and websites of this kind have been around for a long time. A number of years ago, the *Terrorist's Handbook* was posted on the Internet, including instructions on how to make a bomb (the same bomb, as it happens, used in the Oklahoma City bombing in 1995, which killed dozens of federal employees). On the National Rifle Association's "Bullet 'N' Board," a place for discussion of matters of mutual interest, someone calling himself "Warmaster" once explained how to make bombs out of ordinary household materials. Warmaster observed, "These simple, powerful bombs are not very well known even though all the materials can be easily obtained by anyone (including minors)." After the Oklahoma City bombing, an anonymous notice was posted not to one but instead to dozens of news groups on Usenet (a system of discussion forums), listing all the materials in the Oklahoma City bomb and exploring ways to improve future bombs.

TERRORISM ONLINE

Terrorists and hate groups have long been communicating online, sometimes about conspiracies and (this will come as no surprise) formulas for making bombs. (Often they use encryption on the dark web, the part of the Internet that is not searchable and frequently requires password authentication.) Members of such groups tend to communicate largely or mostly with one another, feeding their various predilections. The two students who launched the attack in Littleton, Colorado, in 1999 actually had an Internet site containing details about how to make a bomb. Omar Mateen, the terrorist who perpetrated the worst mass shooting in US history in 2016, reportedly used social media to post terrorism-related content before his attack and also to pledge allegiance to ISIL while he held hostages at an Orlando nightclub.

Al-Qaeda, ISIL, and others use social media to recruit people and propagate hatred. Consider the suggestion that after al-Qaeda's operational capabilities were degraded, it migrated "online, where it made a strategic move away from centrally coordinated attacks in favor of inspiring individuals (its online journal is called 'Inspire')."[2] Terrorist groups often receive and spread rumors, many of them false and even paranoid. In fact, spreading falsehoods is one of their daily activities, and they do that online. However government should trade off security, freedom of speech, and privacy, there is no question that the Internet is being used as a method for terrorists to communicate with one another. One specialist captures the point by noting, "New patterns of social connection that are unique to online culture have played a role in the spread of modern networked terrorism."[3] And terrorism experts Jon Cole and Benjamin Cole urge:

> The role of the Internet in globalizing Islamism is central to this relationship [between self-radicalizing cells and transnational terror networks] as it allows the widespread transnational community of Islamists to maintain contact with each other. . . . [T]he internet also provides access to violent media propaganda, and technical "know-how" to conduct acts of terrorism.[4]

Democratic governments in the United States, the United Kingdom, Germany, France, and elsewhere are entirely aware of this point.[5] In combating terrorism and violent extremism, they seek to disrupt self-radicalizing cells, and even more important, work to minimize their number. They do that by working with allies and friends in unfriendly places, and counteracting lies and propaganda. They are acutely aware of the dynamics that I have been discussing here, and the extent to which they can produce serious threats to human life.

They have tried multiple strategies, including suggestions that terrorists end up dying, and snark—sarcastic remarks implying that terrorists are dupes ("Blowing up mosques! Crucifying and executing Muslims! Plundering public resources! Suicide bombings inside mosques! Travel is inexpensive because you won't need a return ticket!"). More recently, they have been "using Facebook videos, Instagram ads and other social media that have been designed to convince young men and women that joining the militants' fight means breaking their mothers' hearts, tearing apart their families and leaving their loved ones to lives of emptiness."[6] They have also been alert to the importance of the messenger. According to Richard Stengel, the undersecretary of state for public diplomacy and public affairs, "We're not the most effective messenger for our message. There's no tweet from the U.S. State Department that's going to talk a young man out of joining ISIS."[7] In this light, it might well be most effective to undertake efforts "without an American imprint."

WHY THEY HATE US

Terrorist leaders for al-Qaeda, ISIL, and others act as *polarization entrepreneurs*. They create enclaves of like-minded people. They stifle dissenting views and take steps to ensure a high degree of internal solidarity. Consider the following account:

> Terrorists do not even consider that they may be wrong and that other views may have some merit. . . . They attribute only evil motives to anyone outside their group. The . . . common characteristic of the psychologically motivated terrorist is the pronounced need to belong to a group. . . . Such individuals define their social status by group acceptance. . . . Terrorist groups with strong internal motivations find it necessary to justify the group's existence continuously. A terrorist group must terrorize. As a minimum, it must commit violent acts to maintain group self-esteem and legitimacy. Thus, terrorists sometimes carry out attacks that are objectively nonproductive or even counterproductive to their announced goal.[8]

In fact, terrorist organizations impose psychological pressure to accelerate the movement in extreme directions. Thus,

> Another result of psychological motivation is the intensity of group dynamics among terrorists. They tend to demand

unanimity and be intolerant of dissent. With the enemy clearly identified and unequivocally evil, pressure to escalate the frequency and intensity of operations is ever present. The need to belong to the group discourages resignations, and the fear of compromise disallows their acceptance. Compromise is rejected, and terrorist groups lean toward maximalist positions. . . . In societies in which people identify themselves in terms of group membership (family, clan, tribe), there may be a willingness to self-sacrifice seldom seen elsewhere.[9]

In the particular cases of ISIL and al-Qaeda, there is a pervasive effort to link Muslims all over the globe, above all by emphasizing a shared identity—one that includes some and excludes others. Osama bin Laden tried to appeal "to a pervasive sense of humiliation and powerlessness in Islamic countries. Muslims are victims the world over . . . Bosnia, Somalia, Palestine, Chechnya, and . . . Saudi Arabia. . . . He makes the world simple for people who are otherwise confused, and gives them a sense of mission."[10] Hence there are cultlike features to the indoctrination effort: "The military training [in al-Qaeda camps] is accompanied by forceful religious indoctrination, with recruits being fed a stream of antiwestern propaganda and being incessantly reminded about their duty to perform jihad."[11]

In addition, the al-Qaeda terrorists are taught to believe that they are

not alone . . . but sacrificing themselves as part of a larger group for what they believe is the greater good. [The men are] recruited as teenagers, when self-esteem and separation from family are huge developmental issues. [The indoctrination] involves not only lessons in weaponry but [also] an almost cult-like brainwashing over many months. Among Muslims, the regimen typically includes extended periods of prayer and a distortion of the Koran.[12]

There is no question that terrorism is fueled by the dynamics that I have been exploring here—above all, group polarization and cascade effects. It is possible to go further. Many Internet sites and some communications outlets are specifically designed to promote terrorism or at the very least portray terrorists in a sympathetic light. We have seen that leaders of terrorist organizations themselves use social media to promote discussion among like-minded people and for recruitment purposes. Consider this example from Facebook:

"Islamic State of Iraq and Al-Sham Facebook Page," Facebook.com, Author's screenshot

It is important to see that terrorists and extremists often suffer from what political scientist Russell Hardin calls a "crippled epistemology."[13] They are not stupid; they are not poorly educated; and they do not suffer from mental illness. The problem is what they know. Actually they know very little, and much of it is false. What they know comes in large part from people who appeal to and amplify their preexisting inclinations. They hear louder echoes of their own voices. That can be a recipe for violence.

Social media play a major role here. According to the FBI:

> To an even greater degree than al-Qa'ida or other foreign ter-
> rorist organizations, ISIL has persistently used the Internet to
> communicate. From a homeland perspective, it is ISIL's wide-
> spread reach through the Internet and social media which
> is most concerning, as ISIL has aggressively employed this
> technology for its nefarious strategy. ISIL blends traditional
> media platforms, glossy photos, in-depth articles, and social
> media campaigns that can go viral in a matter of seconds. No
> matter the format, the message of radicalization spreads faster
> than we imagined just a few years ago.
>
> As a communication medium, social media is a critical tool
> for terror groups to exploit.... With the widespread horizon-
> tal distribution of social media, terrorists can identify vulner-
> able individuals of all ages in the United States—spot, assess,
> recruit, and radicalize—either to travel or to conduct a home-
> land attack. The foreign terrorist now has direct access into
> the United States like never before.[14]

In several terrorist attacks on US soil, the attackers pledged allegiance to ISIL on social media. In May 2015, two gunmen opened
fire outside a Prophet Mohammed cartoon contest in Garland,
Texas, a suburb of Dallas. Just before the attack, one of the gunmen tweeted, "May Allah accept us as mujahideen."[15] In December 2015, a married couple opened fire at a holiday office party in
San Bernardino, California, killing fourteen people. Siyed Rizwan
Farook and Tashfeen Malik had exchanged private messages about
jihad and martyrdom, and after the attack Malik posted a note on
Facebook on behalf of herself and her husband pledging allegiance
to Abu Bakr al-Baghdadi, a leader of ISIL.[16]

Though rare, "lone-wolf" terrorist attacks do occur, and online
platforms help to radicalize people, including potential and actual
attackers.[17] One study finds that after 9/11, online social networks
played a primary role in radicalization.[18] It concludes that

at the root of this change is technology. With the rise of Internet chat rooms, conspiracy websites, Facebook and Twitter, online activists can connect scattered people who are worried about everything from drone strikes to a one-world government and the pending imposition of martial law in the United States and tell them that they do not worry in isolation. Moreover, radicalization is often caused by an *affinity with online sympathizers.*[19]

ISIL has also sought to recruit people to travel to its self-proclaimed caliphate in Syria and Iraq. As of September 2015, roughly 250 Americans traveled or attempted to travel to Syria, with about 150 succeeding in doing so.[20] The average was about 10 Americans per month between 2014 and mid-2015 (according to FBI director James Comey, that figure declined sharply to about 1 person per month as of May 2016).[21] While the numbers are not large, a feature that ties these people together is that they are active in online jihadist circles, and are prolific posters on social media.[22]

Consider a journalistic account of how ISIL targeted a lonely twenty-three-year-old American woman on Twitter, e-mail, and Skype.[23] ISIL recruiters sought to isolate her from other viewpoints online and in her community, politely answering her questions while slowly indoctrinating her and pushing her toward more extreme perspectives. In online communications, the recruiters advised the woman not to go to a local mosque that disavowed ISIL, telling her that it had been infiltrated by the government. The isolation is deliberate. As one former extremist noted, "We look for people who are isolated," he said. "And if they are not isolated already, then we isolated them." The tactics tracked a manual on recruiting written by al-Qaeda in Iraq: keep in regular touch with potential recruits, empathize with their emotions ("listen to his conversation carefully," and "share his joys and sadness"), teach the basics of Islam, and only later introduce the concept of jihad.[24] The recruiters invited the young woman and her little brother to ISIL.

Without a family intervention and subsequent FBI involvement, the recruitment effort might have been successful.

In short, the Internet and social media facilitate recruitment from across the world, in virtual forums and among vulnerable, isolated persons. As Daniel Benjamin, former coordinator for counterterrorism at the US Department of State, put it, "If you look at the history of terrorism, the Internet is probably the most important technological innovation since dynamite, and it's enormously difficult to deal with all the different aspects."[25]

TWEETING TERRORISTS

To what extent does ISIL use Twitter, and does suspending accounts help to limit Twitter activity? As of late 2016, suspension of ISIL accounts has been the general rule, and it seems to have succeeded. But notwithstanding the company's continuing and at times aggressive efforts, others involved in terrorism continue to use Twitter.

Several years ago, researchers J. M. Berger and Jonathan Morgan created a kind of snapshot of ISIL supporters on Twitter.[26] From September to December 2014, they offered what they called a conservative estimate: ISIL supporters used at least forty-six thousand Twitter accounts. Among them, one in five users selected English as their primary language, and the average number of followers was a thousand (much higher than the ordinary Twitter user). During the time of the study, Twitter began suspending large numbers of accounts held by ISIL supporters. The researchers found that ISIL adapted to these suspensions in various ways, such as temporarily shifting to other social media platforms; creating small accounts to "fly under the radar" and uploading videos to file-sharing sites that could then be disseminated more broadly; and reconstituting some accounts with strong privacy settings to allow small groups of known supporters to follow sponsored tweets.

It is reasonable to think Twitter ought to suspend as many accounts supporting ISIL as possible. After all, doing so should reduce ISIL's reach, including to lone wolves. That is the right approach, and Twitter has followed it. But Berger and Morgan suggest a potential downside to doing so: loud and radicalizing echo chambers. After rounds of suspensions, Berger and Morgan attempted to re-create a network of similar size to study, but "there was substantial overlap in the accounts followed by the new seed accounts, pointing toward a much more inwardly focused network, even as the average number of followers increased." Berger and Morgan noted that suspending accounts might segregate ISIL supporters, which can reduce the number of moderating or deradicalizing influences—that is, it can close off potential exit ramps. It can also create a more insular internal network that could prove an even more radicalizing force: "The increased stridency and monotonic content may discourage some new members of the network from remaining. For others, there is a risk that the more focused and coherent group dynamic could speed and intensify the radicalization process."[27] The researchers conclude that these risks should be weighed against the potential benefits of disrupting ISIL's attempt to encourage lone-wolf attacks through social media. In my view, the benefits greatly exceed the risks—but there are risks.

In a subsequent study, Berger and another coauthor, Heather Perez, studied only English-language ISIL-supportive Twitter accounts from June to October 2015. They found that there were only about a thousand such identifiable Twitter accounts, with an average of three to four hundred followers. During the period studied, Twitter suspended about 1.8 percent of these users per day. Importantly, Berger and Perez discovered that the suspensions were effective in limiting the size and reach of the network. Targeted suspensions also devastated individual users who repeatedly created new accounts; such suspensions "typically had a very significant detrimental effect on . . . repeat offenders, shrinking both the size of their networks and the pace of their activity." Although Berger and Perez did not directly test how suspensions affect echo chambers, this second study demonstrated that "ISIS English-language social networks are extremely insular, meaning users mostly follow and interact with each other."[28]

As noted, ISIL appears to be essentially off Twitter as a result of the suspensions. Between mid-2015 and late 2016, Twitter suspended 360,000 accounts believed to be associated with terrorism.[29] To identify such accounts, Twitter uses its own technology, including proprietary spam-fighting tools, in addition to reports from users. It has also been reported that YouTube and Facebook have adopted automated systems to block or remove extremist content from their pages.

In response to Twitter's suspensions, one of ISIL's strategies was to use hashtags as a recruitment tool and means of spreading propaganda. But those who oppose ISIL, including democratic governments, might counteract this strategy through using the same hashtags to convey diverse messages, entirely inconsistent with those of ISIL. Among social media, Telegram may be one of ISIL's remaining options, and it is not easy to reach a large audience that way. But other terrorist organizations continue to attempt to use Twitter, and that presents a continuing challenge for those who seek to defeat them.

COUNTERING TERRORISM ON SOCIAL MEDIA

Terrorists' uses of the Internet and social media for recruitment, inspiration, and radicalization have put increasing pressure on both private institutions and governments to disrupt their online activities. As noted, the US government is engaging in many such efforts, trying to discredit their propaganda (which prominently includes lies and conspiracy theories), frequently by working with partners that are credible to those who are the targets of that propaganda. These efforts are extremely important in counteracting harmful informational and reputational cascades.

In 2016, Israel accused Facebook of complicity in Palestinian attacks on Israeli citizens.[30] Between October 2015 and June 2016, a wave of violence left over thirty Israelis and over two hundred Palestinians dead. Senior officials in the Israeli government objected that posts on Facebook encouraged and glorified lone-wolf attacks by Palestinians on Israelis, and that Facebook failed to take down such incendiary posts. On the basis of the same wave of violence, some twenty thousand Israelis filed a class action lawsuit in a New York state court, alleging that Facebook was complicit in such attacks.[31] It is important to emphasize, however, that Facebook has been highly active and largely successful in taking down pages and posts by terrorist organizations.

In January 2016, senior national security officials from the Obama administration traveled to Silicon Valley to meet with executives from Apple, Facebook, Twitter, and other tech firms to enlist their support in combating terrorist uses of social media.[32] After these meetings, the administration announced the creation of a new interagency task force led by the Department of Homeland Security, and charged with developing counterradicalization and intervention strategies. In February 2016, the Department of Homeland Security announced an expansion of its use of social media, including by monitoring people applying for various immigration benefits as well as those seeking asylum from Syria.[33]

Members of the US Congress have noticed the underlying concerns. In December 2015, the House passed a bill to combat terrorist use of social media.[34] The Senate introduced a similar measure.[35] Other bills would require social media companies to report terrorist activity on their platforms to law enforcement authorities (similar to how the law requires reporting of child pornography online).[36] To date, however, Congress has not enacted any such proposals.

Other democratic countries have enacted legislation to control access to online content that promotes terrorism. Under French law, for example, the government can block Internet sites that incite terrorist attacks or publicly glorify them.[37] As a result of a counterterrorism law enacted in June 2016, anyone who knowingly hinders the effectiveness of this practice faces penalties—five years in prison and a fine of seventy-five thousand euros.[38] Under another provision, ordinary Internet users who "habitually consult" messages, images, or representations that incite terrorism or glorify it apparently face criminal punishment of two years in prison along with a fine of thirty thousand euros. (There are exceptions for those viewing terrorist content for academic or scientific research, or to conduct criminal investigations.)[39] This is all in addition to a general provision of the French criminal code that prohibits anyone from directly inciting or glorifying terrorism, resulting in heavier sentences for those who do so online—seven years in prison and a fine of a hundred thousand euros.[40] Terrorist uses of the Internet and social media have generated intense debate as well as introspection in France. After the attacks of November 13, 2015, in Paris, a commission of inquiry called for reflection on the role and responsibilities of the media and social media in the event of terrorist incidents.[41]

There is no question that terrorist uses of social media will continue to adapt and evolve, and that it will endanger human lives. Public officials will continue to combat those uses. Private organizations, including tech firms, will often help. Some of the relevant actions do not raise free speech issues. At least under US constitutional law, actions by the private sector do not pose constitutional problems. Frequently what is involved is meeting dangerous speech with counterspeech, correcting the record or putting people on new paths.[42] When the government uses counterspeech, it creates no constitutional issue. But the intensifying international focus on terrorism, and al-Qaeda and ISIL in particular, poses a fresh challenge to the greatest American contribution to the theory and practice of free speech: the clear and present danger test. In both the United States and Europe, it is at least worth asking whether that test may be ripe for reconsideration.

CLEAR AND PRESENT DANGERS

As developed by Supreme Court Justices Holmes and Brandeis in the first decades of the twentieth century, the clear and present danger test forbids the government from regulating political speech unless the danger is both likely ("clear") and imminent ("present"). If a person were to say, "The US government should be overthrown,"

"The more acts of terrorism, the better," or "All Muslims should join ISIL," he could not be punished unless those statements were likely to produce imminent lawless action.

As it is usually understood, the clear and present danger test protects a lot of dangerous speech, including many forms of recruitment and propaganda for terrorist purposes. Holmes himself acknowledged this point, issuing a stern warning against "attempts to check the expression of opinions that we loathe and believe to be fraught with death." (It is worth lingering over the last three words.) The warning is a good one. Ordinarily, the best response to speech that government deems dangerous, or that actually is dangerous, is more speech, not censorship (as Brandeis emphasized).

But it is important to understand that the clear and present danger test has not always been with us. On the contrary, it was accepted relatively recently. In their time, Holmes and Brandeis were losers in dissent; the Supreme Court did not fully adopt their view until 1969. Both during and after World War I, the free speech principle was widely understood to allow the government to punish speech whenever it had a "bad tendency," meaning a tendency to produce harm. Dangerous speech was regulable; the free speech principle lacked anything like the robustness that it has today.

As the Supreme Court ruled in 1925, there would be no protection of speech whose "natural tendency and probable effect was to bring about the substantive evil which the legislative body might prevent."[43] Under this test, of course, terrorist recruitment activity would not be protected. And the same is true of a lot of political dissent—which means that the test did not and would not protect speech nearly enough. As late as 1951, the Supreme Court allowed regulation of speech even when the danger was neither clear nor present. In *Dennis v. United States*, the court upheld a conviction of people trying to organize the Communist Party to overthrow the US government.[44] The justices refused to understand the clear and present danger test to "mean that, before the Government may act, it must wait until the putsch is about to be executed, the plans have been laid and the signal is awaited."

In words that could easily be repeated in the context of terrorist recruitment and propaganda activity, the Court found it sufficient that the revolutionaries wanted to "strike when they thought the time was ripe." When the safety of the community was at grave risk, because of "an apparatus designed and dedicated to the overthrow of the Government, in the context of world crisis after crisis," the government could act to stop horrific harm, even if it was neither likely nor (strictly speaking) imminent. The central idea was that as the magnitude of the harm increased, it would be unnecessary to show that it was likely and imminent. In ordinary life, that idea makes a great deal of sense. If a certain action would produce a 5 percent chance that you will lose all your money, your child, or your life a year from now, you probably will not take that action, and you will do a great deal to make sure that it does not occur. So too in the context of regulation in general: if an activity poses a 10 percent chance of killing a hundred thousand people in ten years, there is a good argument that the activity should be prohibited, even if the danger is hardly clear and by no means imminent. Is it so obvious that speech should be treated differently? Always? In the context of risks of terrorism, posed by uses of social media? At the very least, no one should object if those who run social media voluntarily take down posts by terrorist organizations.

One of the greatest and most influential judges in US history, with the unlikely name of Learned Hand, rejected the clear and present danger test for another reason. He believed that the free speech principle simply did not protect explicit or direct incitement to violence, even if no harm was imminent. He thought that his approach gave appropriate space for freedom of speech: if you are merely agitating for change, the government cannot proceed against you. You are absolutely protected. But if you are expressly inciting people to commit murder, you aren't protected by the Constitution. Hand much preferred his approach to the clear and present danger test, which he thought squishy. By contrast, he defended his exemption of incitement as a "qualitative formula, hard, conventional, difficult to evade."[45] Under Hand's approach, the question of whether speech would be protected would be answered by reference to the nature of the speech—the actual words it includes—rather than by reference to its consequences. In that way, Hand rejected the approach favored by Holmes and Brandeis.

For decades, the Supreme Court has shown zero interest in Hand's formula. And most people have regarded the *Dennis* decision as an epic blunder, a product of the Red Scare, not to be taken seriously in a free society. Brandeis offered the best reason: "If there be time to expose through discussion the falsehood and fallacies, to avert the evil by the processes of education, the remedy to be applied is more speech, not enforced silence." In his view, "Only an emergency can justify repression."[46]

It is an appealing thought, and it is usually right. But is it convincing as applied to the recruitment and propaganda efforts of terrorist organizations? To their efforts on social media, which can dramatically amplify the capacity of speech in one place to cause violence elsewhere at some uncertain time? What if more speech does not work (and it often will not), and the result is that dozens, hundreds, or thousands of people are killed?

To be sure, there can be value in even the most extreme and hateful forms of speech: at the very least, people will learn what other people believe, and that is important. But it is fair to ask whether that benefit might be dwarfed by the cost, if those forms of speech create a genuine risk of large numbers of deaths. Hand himself argued that his narrow definition of incitement avoids subjectivity and overreach, and that it cannot be abused by the government to silence dissenters and unpopular causes. Under Hand's test, some forms of terrorist recruitment would be far out of bounds and therefore unprotected.

To minimize the danger to free speech, one possibility would be to consider combining Hand's approach with a form of balancing: if (and only if) people are explicitly inciting violence, by unambiguously calling for it, perhaps their speech does not deserve protection when (and only when) it produces a serious risk to public safety, whether imminent or not. Or perhaps the very idea of imminence could be broadened so as not to require dangers to materialize in, say, a day, a week, or even a month. That approach would essentially retain the high level of protection that is now given to political speech and dissent of all kinds. In the United States, it would be a narrow departure from current law. True, it is not clear that it would be the optimal approach. Contrary to Hand, some people might object that if speech is genuinely dangerous, it should not be protected even if it does not involve express incitement. Other people would urge that the clear and present danger test really is best, even if the underlying speech is "fraught with death." The question is whether that conclusion makes sense in the current era—and if it really does mean that people are going to die.

In free societies, it is almost always wrong to punish speech. But at the very least, the argument for the clear and present danger test is not quite as clear as it once was—and it might not be so well suited to the present.

11

#REPUBLIC

Much of what I have argued here is captured in some passages from two of the greatest theorists of freedom and democracy, Mill and Dewey. Recall once more Mill's words:

> It is hardly possible to overstate the value, in the present low state of human improvement, of placing human beings in contact with other persons dissimilar to themselves, and with modes of thought and action unlike those with which they are familiar. . . . Such communication has always been, and is peculiarly in the present age, one of the primary sources of progress.[1]

And now Dewey:

> The belief that thought and its communication are now free simply because legal restrictions which once obtained have been done away with is absurd. Its currency perpetuates the infantile state of social knowledge. For it blurs recognition of our central need to possess conceptions which are used as tools of directed inquiry and which are tested, rectified and caused to grow in actual use. No man and no mind was ever emancipated merely by being left alone.[2]

With these ideas in view, I have stressed the serious problems for individuals and societies alike that are likely to be created by the practice of self-insulation—by a situation in which many of us wall ourselves off from the concerns and opinions of our fellow citizens.

The ideal of consumer sovereignty, well represented in Facebook's core values and the supposedly utopian vision of complete personalization, would undermine democratic ideals. Rather than a utopian vision, the Daily Me is best understood as a kind of nightmare, the stuff of science fiction, carrying large lessons about some neglected requirements of democratic self-government. #Republic could be that nightmare—or it could exemplify the ideals for which Mill and Dewey spoke.

WITHIN AND WITHOUT ENCLAVES

A fully personalized speech market, consisting of countless niches, would make self-government less workable. In important ways it would reduce, not increase, freedom for the individuals involved. It would create a high degree of social fragmentation. It would spread falsehoods, some of them dangerous. It would make mutual understanding far more difficult among individuals and groups. To the extent that people are using the Internet in this way, they are disserving both themselves and their fellow citizens.

I have not said that this is the general pattern or that it is what most people are doing. Many people are curious, and they go online to see a wide range of topics and views. General-interest intermediaries also continue to play a large role. The Internet's public sphere is networked. But clustering is nonetheless common, and for politics, group polarization is a significant risk even if only a small number of people choose to listen and speak with those who are like-minded. A free society benefits from public domains offering a wide variety of topics and positions.

Nothing in these claims is inconsistent with the view that a free society makes spaces for freedom of choice and deliberating enclaves consisting of like-minded individuals. It should not be necessary to emphasize that freedom of choice is an individual and social good. Moreover, deliberating enclaves ensure that positions that would otherwise be silenced or squelched have a chance to develop. Individual members of such groups sometimes have a hard time communicating their views to the wider society, and if group members can speak among themselves, they can learn a great deal and ultimately contribute much more to their discussions with others.

Recall the importance of "second-order diversity"—the kind of diversity that comes when society benefits from many groups with clear practices and positions of their own.[3] If a nation allows many organizations to exist, and if each of them is fairly uniform, the nation may well benefit from the great range of views that will emerge. Facebook pages and Twitter accounts certainly promote second-order diversity. Note also that many people have concerns, objections, injuries, and fears that they may not voice, or even organize in their own minds, unless they learn that other people have them too. They may suffer from a form of "epistemic injustice," in which they are harmed in their very capacity to know, and not taken seriously as knowers.[4] They do not obtain a hearing for their experiences. Social media can counteract that injustice.

Although I have suggested that group polarization and cybercascades present serious dangers, both of these played an unquestionable role in movements that have and deserve widespread approval. To take just a few examples, consider the movement for same-sex marriage, the attack on apartheid in South Africa, the civil rights movement in the United States, and the assault on slavery itself. Group polarization fueled each and every one of these. Nor are group polarization and cascades merely matters of historical interest. Consider, for example, private conversations among political dissenters in authoritarian nations, cancer patients, science fiction enthusiasts, those concerned about infectious diseases, parents of children with physical or mental disabilities, poor tenants, and members of religious minorities. Insofar as social media make it easier to construct enclaves for communication among people with common experiences and complaints, they are a boon as well as a danger. It is far easier, for example, for people to discuss shared difficulties when they would otherwise feel quite isolated, and think, wrongly, that their condition is unique or in any case hopeless. In this way, enclave deliberation is highly desirable for the people involved and society as a whole.

The danger of deliberating enclaves should by now be familiar. Their members may move to positions that lack merit but are predictable consequences of the pressures produced by deliberation among the like-minded. (Baseless or even crazy views about how to deal with cancer are an example.) In the extreme case, enclave deliberation may even put social stability at risk (sometimes for better, usually for worse). Terrorism is itself a product of deliberation among like-minded people, and uses of social media to recruit terrorists raise serious challenges for free speech principles. We have seen that extremists often suffer from a kind of "crippled epistemology" in the form of exposure to a small subset of relevant information, coming mostly from other extremists.[5]

But it is not difficult to imagine a different kind of vision—one directly opposed to that offered by the Daily Me. Suppose that most people generally believe it important to seek out diverse opinions and learn about an assortment of topics. Suppose that the extraordinary opportunities provided by contemporary technologies are regularly used as an instrument of citizenship—mostly national but sometimes even global citizenship, in which people continually enlarge their own horizons, often testing their own views by learning about alternatives. We could easily imagine a general social practice to this effect, even a cultural shift toward a society in which people became broadly committed to using the Internet in this way. In some places, this shift is happening today.

We could also imagine a culture where aspirations of this kind were supported rather than undermined by private and public institutions. In such a culture, websites would frequently assist people in their desire to learn about other opinions—even opinions radically different from those of the websites' creators. In such a culture, it would be common to provide links to sites with a wide range of views. And in such a culture, government would attempt, perhaps only through moral suasion, to ensure that the system of communications is a help rather than a hindrance to democratic self-government.

CONSUMER AND CITIZEN

Many people think that a system of communications should be evaluated by asking whether it respects individual choice. On this view, the only real threat to free speech is censorship, conventionally understood. Speech is simply another commodity, to be chosen by consumers subject to the forces of supply and demand. With respect to ordinary consumer products, it seems natural to believe that the more people can "customize" or individuate their preferred products, the better things will be.

A well-functioning market for toasters, cars, chocolates, books, movies, and computers works better if it allows a large domain for individual choice—so that I will not have the same item that you have, unless this is what we want, in our individual capacities. For communications, as for cars and chocolates, one size does not fit all. Niche marketing is on the rise, and many people seem to think that the more niches, the better. We have seen, however, that insofar as the Internet increases consumer choice, it is not an entirely unmixed blessing for consumers. The consumption treadmill means that for many products, people's purchases of more and better goods will make them spend more, and possibly much more, without really making them a lot happier or improving their lives.

But the more fundamental problem is that a system of free expression should not be seen solely in terms of consumers and consumption at all. In a free republic, such a system is designed to maintain the conditions for democratic self-government—to serve citizens, not only consumers. Hence the public forum doctrine ensures that the streets and parks are open to speakers, even if many of us, much of the time and before the fact, would prefer not to hear what our fellow citizens want to say.

When the public forum doctrine was originally devised in the early twentieth century, avoiding streets and parks was far more difficult than it is today; hence the public forum doctrine had immense practical importance. But this is decreasingly true. It is now entirely possible to spend little time in public forums. Largely by happenstance, general-interest intermediaries of the mid- and late twentieth century—those who operate newspapers, magazines, and broadcasting stations—have done much of the historical work of traditional streets and parks. They promote exposure to issues and views that would otherwise escape attention, and that would not have been chosen before the fact. At the same time, they ensure a commonality of experience in a heterogeneous society.

In a free society, those who want to avoid general-interest intermediaries are certainly permitted to do so. No government agency compels adults to read or watch. Big Brother is not watching you, and he is not watching what you watch. Nonetheless, a central democratic goal is to ensure at least a measure of social integration—not merely of religious and racial groups, but across multiple lines, in a way that broadens human sympathies and enriches human life. A society with general-interest intermediaries, like a society with a robust set of public forums, promotes a shared set of experiences at the same time that it exposes countless people to information and opinions that they would not have sought out in advance. These features of a well-functioning system of free expression might well be compromised when individuals personalize their own communications packages—and certainly if they personalize in a way that narrows their horizons.

The problem of self-selection is compounded and complemented by the power of producers to create filters, so that people are given what they are likely to like, even if they have not chosen that. Algorithms are increasingly able to produce accurate filters, and they're getting better every day. As with self-selection, so too with algorithms: they make life easier and more convenient. If you're interested only in books about basketball, you shouldn't be sent advertisements for books about behavioral economics. But here as well, horizons can become narrowed, and people can get smaller.

I have emphasized throughout that a republic is not a direct democracy, and that a good democratic system contains institutions designed to ensure a measure of reflection and debate—not immediate responses to whatever people happen, at any particular moment in time, to say that they want. In this way, the original US Constitution was based on a commitment to a set of "filters" of a special kind—filters that would increase the likelihood of deliberation in government. The same commitment can be found in most democratic nations, which ensure against reflexive responses to popular pressures. Insofar as current technologies make it easier for people to register their short-term views and induce government to respond, they carry risks rather than promise. But insofar as those technologies make it easier for people to deliberate with one another and exchange reasons, they carry forward some of the animating ideals of the system of free expression.

We have seen as well that it is unhelpful and implausible to say that with respect to the Internet and other communications technologies, "no regulation" is the path for the future. Any system that protects property rights requires an active governmental role, and that role takes the form of regulation, among other things allowing "owners," owing their status as such to law, to exclude people seeking access. If site owners and operators are going to be protected against cyberterrorism and other intrusions on their property rights, government and law (not to mention taxpayers) will play a central role. The question is not whether we will have regulation but rather what kind of regulation we will have.

Free speech is never an absolute. Every democratic system regulates some forms of speech, not merely by creating property rights, but also by controlling a variety of forms of expression, such as perjury, bribery, threats, child pornography, and fraudulent commercial advertising (not to mention viruses sent by e-mail). The question is how we can regulate some kinds of speech while promoting the values associated with a system of free expression, emphatically including democratic self-government.

I have also stressed the relationship between freedom of expression and many important social goals. When information is freely available, tyrannies are unlikely to be able to sustain themselves; it is for this reason that the Internet is a great engine of democratic self-government. Social media can be especially valuable here. Drawing on the work of Amartya Sen, and with particular reference to contemporary technologies, I have suggested that freedom of expression is central to social well-being precisely because of the pressures that it places on governments. Recall Sen's finding that no society with a free press and open elections has ever experienced a famine. We should take this finding as a metaphor for the functions of freedom of expression in ensuring that governments serve the interest of their people, rather than the other way around. That can be seen as a strong point in favor of the democratic functions of social media.

BEYOND PESSIMISM, NOSTALGIA, AND PREDICTION

I have made three more particular suggestions. First, a communications system in which individuals have an unlimited power to customize and filter threatens to create excessive fragmentation. It would do this if different individuals and groups, defined in demographic, religious, political, or other terms, choose materials and viewpoints that fit with their own predilections while excluding topics and viewpoints that do not. This would undoubtedly produce—and is already producing—a more balkanized society. (Every year will have its own examples. Compare #BlackLivesMatter with #AllLivesMatter.) The danger is greatly heightened by the phenomenon of group polarization, through which deliberating groups move toward a more extreme point in the same direction indicated by their predeliberation judgments. Indeed, the Internet creates a large risk of group polarization, simply because it makes it so easy for like-minded people to speak with one another—and ultimately move toward extreme and sometimes even violent positions.

All too often, those most in need of hearing something other than echoes of their own voices are the least likely to seek out alternative views. The result can be cybercascades of a highly un-desirable sort, as false information spreads to thousands or even millions. We have seen evidence to this effect most vividly for ter-rorist organizations, but the point is far more general than that. Most broadly, recall Jacobs's remarkable prose-poem, *The Death and Life of Great American Cities*, celebrating serendipity, surprise, and unchosen encounters. Can social media be like Paris, Berlin, or San Francisco? Probably not. But they can certainly move in that direction.

Second, a system of unlimited filtering could produce too little in the way of shared information and experiences. When many or most people are focusing on the same topic, at least some of the time, we benefit from a kind of social glue. The point is all the more important in light of the fact that information is a public good—a good whose benefits are likely to spread well beyond the particu-lar person who receives it. General-interest intermediaries provide many advantages in this regard, simply because most of us obtain information that we spread to others, and from which they benefit.

Third, a system of unlimited filtering might well compromise freedom, understood both in terms of individual self-development and from the democratic point of view. For citizens in a republic, freedom requires exposure to a diverse set of topics and opinions. I have not suggested, and do not believe, that people should be forced to read and view materials that they abhor. But I do contend that a democratic polity, acting through democratic organs, tries to promote freedom, not simply by respecting consumer sovereignty, but by creating a system of communications that promotes expo-sure to a wide range of issues and views. Such a polity cares deeply about the truth.

Nothing that I have said should be taken as an empirical claim about the likely choices of individuals in the next decades and more. Most of us are happy or at least content to consult nonideo-logical sources; they are where we go for news. Many of us have a great deal of curiosity (an overlooked civic virtue), and we like to see materials that challenge us, and do not merely reinforce our existing tastes and judgments. This is demonstrated every day, not least by the truly astonishing growth of diverse sites on the Internet. I have emphasized that general-interest intermediaries continue to play a significant role, and many of them are doing extremely well online. No one can know what the system of communications will look like in the distant future.

What I have attempted to do is not to suggest grounds for nostalgia or general pessimism, and much less predict the future (in this context, an especially hopeless endeavor), but instead explore the relationship between current technologies and the central commitments of a system of democratic self-government. Rather than being diverted by pessimism, nostalgia, and speculation, we should move beyond all three in order to obtain a clearer understanding of our ideals and see what might be done to realize them.

FRANKLIN'S CHALLENGE

Recall Franklin's answer to the large crowd asking the US Constitution's authors what they had "given" to the public: "A republic, if you can keep it." Franklin's answer was an expression of hope, but it was also a reminder of a continuing obligation, even a dare. His suggestion was that any document committed to republican self-government depends for its effectiveness not on the decisions of the founders, and much less on worship of texts and authorities and ancestors, but instead on the actions and commitments of its citizenry over time. In drawing attention to the dangers posed by an "inert people," Justice Brandeis was merely carrying forward Franklin's theme.

My most general topic here has been the preconditions for maintaining a republic. We have seen that the essential factor is a well-functioning system of free expression—the "only effective guardian," in Madison's words, "of every other right." To be sure, such a system depends on prohibiting official censorship of controversial ideas and opinions. But it depends on far more than that.

It also depends on some kind of public domain, in which a wide range of speakers have access to a diverse public—and also particular institutions and practices, against which they seek to launch objections. It demands not only a law of free expression but also a culture of free expression, in which people are eager to listen to what their fellow citizens have to say. Perhaps above all, a republic, or at least a heterogeneous one, requires arenas in which citizens with varying experiences and prospects, and different views about what is good and right, are able to meet with one another and consult.

Current technologies are hardly an enemy here. They hold out far more promise than risk. Indeed they hold out great promise from the republican point of view, especially insofar as they make it so much easier for ordinary people to learn about countless topics, hold their governments accountable, and seek out endlessly diverse opinions. But to the extent that people are using social media to create echo chambers, and wall themselves off from topics and opinions that they would prefer to avoid, they are creating serious dangers. And if we believe that a system of free expression calls for unrestricted choices by individual consumers, we will not even understand the dangers as such.

Whether such dangers will materialize will ultimately depend on the aspirations, for freedom and democracy alike, by whose light we evaluate our practices. What I have sought to establish here is that in a free republic, citizens aspire to a system that provides a wide range of experiences—with people, topics, and ideas—that they would not have specifically selected in advance.

ACKNOWLEDGMENTS

All books have ancestors; this book has a father and a grandfather. The grandfather is *Republic.com*, published in 2001. That book quickly became dated, and it was followed by *Republic.com 2.0*, published in 2007. In the last ten years, much more has changed, above all with the rise of social media—hence this book.

For the previous books, whose mark is clearly visible in what is presented here, I received a great deal of help. For invaluable discussions, special thanks to my original editor, Thomas LeBien, and also to eight terrific colleagues and friends: Jack Goldsmith, Stephen Holmes, Martha Nussbaum, Eric Posner, Richard Posner, Geoffrey Stone, David Strauss, and the late Edna Ullmann-Margalit.

For this book, I am grateful to Eric Crahan and Peter Dougherty at Princeton University Press for wonderful suggestions and guidance, and Daniel Severson for truly superb research assistance, which included substantive ideas of many kinds. Heartfelt thanks as well to many people at Harvard's amazing Berkman Center for creative thinking of various sorts; I single out Sandra Cortesi, Briggs DeLoach, Rob Faris, and Urs Gasser for help of multiple kinds. Many thanks to Jack Goldsmith, a reader as well of both grandfather and grandchild, who provided terrific suggestions on how to improve the manuscript. I am grateful to Martha Minow, too, for support of many kinds, and in particular the Harvard Law School's Program on Behavioral Economics and Public Policy.

A more general thanks to the countless people over the years who have either worried with me about the risks of echo chambers or suggested, contrary to my arguments, that there is absolutely no reason for concern. Included among the first group are many friends and colleagues from the Obama administration—an extended family, truly—who have been concerned about political polarization. I have learned a lot from Jon Favreau, Dan Pfeiffer, Jen Psaki, Ben Rhodes, and David Simas. Barack Obama has himself been greatly focused on that problem, before and after assuming the presidency, and it is an honor to give thanks for illuminating discussions over the years, and in general, to my former University of Chicago colleague and White House boss.

Thanks finally to my wife, Samantha Power, who constructs the Daily Us, and who, more than anyone I have ever known, resists the echo chamber, and insists on unanticipated, unchosen exposures to both experiences and ideas.

NOTES

PREFACE

1. Aldous Huxley, *Brave New World* (New York: Harper and Brothers, 1932), 163.
2. John Stuart Mill, *Principles of Political Economy with Some of Their Applications to Social Philosophy*, 7th ed. (1848; repr., London: Longmans, Green and Co., 1909), bk. 3, ch. 17, para. 14. See also http://www.econlib.org/library /Mill/mlP.html (accessed August 23, 2016).

1. THE DAILY ME

1. See Nicholas Negroponte, *Being Digital* (New York: Vintage Books, 1995), 153. For a prescient discussion of "cyberbalkinization," see also Robert D. Putnam, *Bowling Alone: The Collapse and Revival of American Community* (New York: Simon and Schuster, 2000), 177–79, which draws in turn on an illuminating earlier paper, Marshall Van Alstyne and Erik Brynjolfsson, "Electronic Communities: Global Village or Cyberbalkans?" (working paper, MIT Sloan School, Cambridge, MA, 1996), http://web.mit.edu/marshall/www/papers /CyberBalkans.pdf (accessed August 23, 2016).
2. In a provocative 2011 book, Eli Pariser popularized a theory of "filter bubbles" in which he posited that due to the effects of algorithmic filtering, Internet users are likely to be provided with information that conforms to their existing interests and, in effect, is isolated from differing viewpoints. We continue to obtain evidence on the phenomenon. Eli Pariser, *The Filter Bubble: How the New Personalized Web Is Changing What We Read and How We Think* (New York: Penguin Press, 2011). A 2013 paper measures the effect of search personalization on Google, concluding that 11.7 percent of Google search results differed between users due to personalization—a finding that the authors describe as "significant personalization." Aniko Hannak, Balachander Krishnamurthy, Piotr Sapieżyński, David Lazer, Christo Wilson, Arash Molavi Kakhki, and Alan Mislove, "Measuring Personalization of Web Search," *Proceedings of the Twenty-Second International Conference World Wide Web* (New York: Association for Computing Machinery, 2013), 527, 528, http://dl.acm.org/citation .cfm?doid=2488388.2488435 (accessed August 23, 2016). In a similar vein, a 2015 paper takes initial steps toward visualizing filter bubbles in Google and Bing searches, finding that both search engines do create filter bubbles; the authors, however, note that it appears that filter bubbles may be stronger within certain topics (such as results of searches about jobs) than within others (such as results from searches about asthma). Tawanna R. Dillahunt, Christopher A. Brooks, and Samarth Gulati, "Detecting and Visualizing Filter Bubbles

in Google and Bing," *Proceedings of the Thirty-Third Annual ACM Conference: Extended Abstracts on Human Factors in Computing Systems* (New York: Association for Computing Machinery, 2015), 1851–56, http://dl.acm.org/citation .cfm?doid=2702613.2732850 (accessed August 23, 2016).

3. See Dan M. Kahan, Asheley R. Landrum, Katie Carpenter, Laura Helft, and Kathleen Hall Jamieson, "Science Curiosity and Political Information Processing," *Advances in Political Psychology* 38 (forthcoming) http://papers.ssrn .com/sol3/papers.cfm?abstract_id=2816803 (accessed August 29, 2016); Andrew M. Guess, *Media Choice and Moderation: Evidence from Online Tracking Data* (2016), https://dl.dropboxusercontent.com/u/663930/GuessJMP.pdf (accessed August 29, 2016).

4. See Cass R. Sunstein, *Infotopia: How Many Minds Produce Knowledge* (Oxford: Oxford University Press, 2006).

5. Shanto Iyengar, Gaurav Sood, and Yphtach Lelkes, "Affect, Not Ideology: A Social Identity Perspective on Polarization," *Public Opinion Quarterly* 76, no. 3 (2012): 405, http://pcl.stanford.edu/research/2012/iyengar-poq-affect-not -ideology.pdf (accessed August 29, 2016).

6. Ibid.

7. See Shanto Iyengar and Sean J. Westwood, "Fear and Loathing across Party Lines: New Evidence on Group Polarization," *American Journal of Political Science* 59, no. 3 (2015): 690.

8. Jane Jacobs, *The Death and Life of Great American Cities* (1961; repr., New York: Random House, 1993).

9. Ibid., 81, 95.

10. Putnam, *Bowling Alone*, 178.

11. See Robert Glenn Howard, "Sustainability and Narrative Plasticity in Online Apocalyptic Discourse after September 11, 2001," *Journal of Media and Religion* 5, no. 1 (2006): 25.

12. Adam Mosseri, "Building a Better News Feed for You," Facebook Newsroom, June 29, 2016, https://newsroom.fb.com/news/2016/06/building-a-better -news-feed-for-you/ (accessed August 29, 2016).

13. Adam D. I. Kramer, Jamie E. Guillory, and Jeffrey T. Hancock, "Experimental Evidence of Massive-Scale Emotional Contagion through Social Networks," *Proceedings of the National Academy of Sciences* 111, no. 24 (2015): 8788, http://www.pnas.org/content/111/24/8788.full (accessed August 29, 2016).

14. The point is emphasized in Andrew Shapiro, *The Control Revolution: How the Internet Is Putting Individuals in Charge and Changing the World We Know* (New York: PublicAffairs, 1999), from which I have learned a great deal, and many of whose concerns, including fragmentation and self-insulation, are the same as those stressed here.

15. Helen Margetts, Peter John, Scott Hale, and Taha Yasseri, *Political Turbulence: How Social Media Shape Collective Action* (Princeton, NJ: Princeton University Press, 2016), 5.

16. See Yochai Benkler, *The Wealth of Networks: How Social Production Transforms Markets and Freedom* (New Haven, CT: Yale University Press, 2006).
17. See Sunstein, *Infotopia*.
18. For a valuable general discussion, see C. Edwin Baker, *Advertising and a Democratic Press* (Princeton, NJ: Princeton University Press, 1997).
19. See Lawrence Lessig, *Free Culture: The Nature and Future of Creativity* (New York: Penguin Books, 2004); Benkler, *Wealth of Networks*.

2. AN ANALOGY AND AN IDEAL

1. Quoted in Alfred C. Sikes, *Fast Forward: America's Leading Experts Reveal How the Internet Is Changing Your Life* (New York: William Morrow, 2000), 210.
2. In some ways these developments are entirely continuous with other important social changes. The automobile, for example, was once criticized for "its extreme unsociability," especially compared with the railway, "which tended to gather together . . . all activity that was in any way related to movements of freight or passengers into or out of the city." George F. Kennan, *Around the Cragged Hill: A Personal and Political Philosophy* (New York: W. W. Norton and Company, 1993), 161, 160. Far more important in this regard has been what may well be the dominant technology of the twentieth century: television. In the words of political scientist Robert Putnam, the "single most important consequence of the television revolution has been to bring us home." And the result of the shift in the direction of home, Putnam adds, has been a dramatic reduction—perhaps as much as 40 percent—in activity spent on "collective activities, like attending public meetings or taking a leadership role in local organizations." Robert D. Putnam, *Bowling Alone: The Collapse and Revival of American Community* (New York: Simon and Schuster, 2000), 221, 229.
3. Elizabeth Dwoskin, "Pandora Thinks It Knows If You Are a Republican," *Wall Street Journal*, February 13, 2014, http://www.wsj.com/articles /SB10001424052702304315004579381393567130078 (accessed August 31, 2016).
4. Quoting Alvin Toffler in Sikes, *Fast Forward*, 208.
5. Hague v. Committee for Industrial Organization, 307 U.S. 496 (1939). For present purposes, it is not necessary to discuss the public forum doctrine in detail. Interested readers might consult Geoffrey R. Stone, Robert H. Seidman, Cass R. Sunstein, Mark Tushnet, and Pamela Karlan, *The First Amendment*, 4th ed. (New York: Wolters Kluwer Law and Business, 2012), 286–330.
6. See International Society for Krishna Consciousness v. Lee, 505 U.S. 672 (1992).
7. See Denver Area Educational Telecommunications Consortium, Inc. v. FCC, 518 U.S. 727, 803 (1996) (Justice Kennedy, dissenting).
8. See the excellent discussion in Noah D. Zatz, "Sidewalks in Cyberspace: Making Space for Public Forums in the Electronic Environment," *Harvard Journal of Law and Technology* 12, no. 1 (1998): 149–240.

9. See Merouan Mekouar, *Protest and Mass Mobilization: Authoritarian Collapse and Political Change in North Africa* (Abingdon, UK: Routledge, 2016). For a classic discussion, see also Timur Kuran, *Public Truths, Private Lies: The Social Consequences of Preference Falsification* (Cambridge, MA: Harvard University Press, 1997).

10. See Columbia Broadcasting System, Inc. v. Democratic National Committee, 412 U.S. 94 (1973).

11. For an especially illuminating elaboration of republican ideals, see Phillip Pettit, *Republicanism: A Theory of Freedom and Government* (Oxford: Oxford University Press, 1999).

12. See Gordon Wood, *The Radicalism of the American Revolution* (New York: Vintage Books, 1991).

13. For the best discussion of deliberative democracy from the standpoint of American history, see William Bessette, *The Mild Voice of Reason: Deliberative Democracy and American National Government* (Chicago: University of Chicago Press, 1984). There are many treatments of deliberative democracy as a political ideal. For varying perspectives, see Amy Gutmann and Dennis Thompson, *Democracy and Disagreement* (Cambridge, MA: Belknap Press, 1998); Jürgen Habermas, *Between Facts and Norms* (Cambridge, MA: MIT Press, 1997); Jon Elster, ed., *Deliberative Democracy* (New York: Cambridge University Press, 1998).

14. Aristotle, *Politics*, trans. Ernest Barker (Oxford: Oxford University Press, 1972), 123.

15. John Rawls, *A Theory of Justice* (Cambridge, MA: Harvard University Press, 1971), 358–59.

16. See Habermas, *Between Facts and Norms*, 940.

17. For a discussion of the preconditions for communication, see Jürgen Habermas, "What Is Universal Pragmatics?" in *Communication and the Evolution of Society*, trans. Thomas McCarthy (Boston: Beacon Press, 1979), 1, 2–4, 32.

18. As one illustration, many cities have created websites for citizens to report potholes. See, for example, City of Milwaukee, "How to Report Potholes," http://city.milwaukee.gov/commoncouncil/District7/How-to-Report-Potholes.htm#.V2lKlY7VxBU (accessed July 5, 2016). As another, San Francisco has a 311-Twitter service. See Susan Gunelius, "3 Smart Ways Governments Use Twitter and Facebook," Sprout Social, December 30, 2011, http://sproutsocial.com/insights/governments-twitter-facebook/ (accessed July 5, 2016).

19. To be sure, one of the central trends of the last century has been a decrease in the deliberative features of the constitutional design in favor of an increase in popular control. As central examples, consider direct primary elections, initiatives and referenda, interest group strategies designed to mobilize constituents and public opinion polling. To a greater or lesser extent, each of these has diminished the deliberative functions of representatives and increased accountability to public opinion at particular moments in time. Of course, any evaluation of these changes would require a detailed discussion. But from

the standpoint of the original constitutional settlement as well as democratic principles, reforms that make democracy less deliberative are at best a mixed blessing. Government by initiatives and referenda is especially troubling insofar as they threaten to create ill-considered law, produced by sound bites rather than reflective judgments by representatives, citizens, or anyone at all. For valuable discussion, see James S. Fishkin, *The Voice of the People: Public Opinion and Democracy* (New Haven, CT: Yale University Press, 1995).

20. Charles Louis de Secondat Baron de Montesquieu, *The Spirit of Laws* (1748; repr., New York: Cosimo Classics, 2011), bk. 8, ch. 16.

21. Quoted in Herbert J. Storing, ed., *The Complete Anti-Federalist* 2:369 (Chicago: University of Chicago Press, 1980).

22. Quoted in Joseph Gales, ed., *Annals of Congress* (1834), 1:763–64.

23. Marvin Meyers, ed., *The Mind of the Founder: Sources of the Political Thought of James Madison* (Hanover, NH: University Press of New England, 1981), 151–60.

24. Bill Gates, *The Road Ahead* (New York: Penguin Books, 1995), 167–68.

25. EW Staff, "Bill Gates Predicted the Future in January 2000," *Entertainment Weekly*, October 28, 2015, http://www.ew.com/article/2015/10/28/bill-gates-birthday-predicted-future (accessed September 1, 2016).

26. Quoted in Holman W. Jenkins Jr., "Google and the Search for the Future," *Wall Street Journal*, August 14, 2010, http://www.wsj.com/articles/SB10001424052748704901104575423294099527212 (accessed September 1, 2016).

27. John Dewey, *The Public and Its Problems: An Essay in Political Inquiry* (1927; repr., University Park: Pennsylvania State University Press, 2012), 154–55.

28. Abrams v. United States, 250 U.S. 616, 635 (Justice Holmes, dissenting).

29. Whitney v. California, 274 U.S. 357, 372 (1927) (Justice Brandeis, concurring).

30. See Cass R. Sunstein and Edna Ullmann-Margalit, "Solidarity Goods," *Journal of Political Philosophy* 9, no. 2 (2001): 129–49. The article is coauthored, but the central idea is Ullmann-Margalit's.

3. POLARIZATION

1. Quoted in Alfred C. Sikes, *Fast Forward: America's Leading Experts Reveal How the Internet Is Changing Your Life* (New York: William Morrow, 2000), 13–14.

2. Gregory J. Martin and Ali Yurukoglu, "Bias in Cable News: Persuasion and Polarization" (working paper no. 20798, National Bureau of Economic Research, Cambridge, MA, December 2014), http://www.nber.org/papers/w20798.pdf (accessed September 2, 2016).

3. See Shanto Iyengar and Richard Morin, "Red Media, Blue Media," *Washington Post*, May 3, 2006, http://www.washingtonpost.com/wp-dyn/content/article/2006/05/03/AR2006050300865.html (accessed September 2, 2016).

4. Marshall Van Alstyne and Erik Brynjolfsson, "Electronic Communities: Global Village or Cyberbalkans?" (working paper, MIT Sloan School,

Cambridge, MA, 1996), http://web.mit.edu/marshall/www/papers/CyberBalkans.pdf (accessed September 2, 2016).

5. For a fascinating discussion, see Ronald Jacobs, *Race, Media, and the Crisis of Civil Society: From Watts to Rodney King* (Cambridge: Cambridge University Press, 2000).

6. David Schkade, Cass R. Sunstein, and Reid Hastie, "What Happened on Deliberation Day?" *California Law Review* 95, no. 3 (2007): 915–40.

7. These include the United States, Canada, India, Bangladesh, New Zealand, Germany, India, and France. See Roger Brown, *Social Psychology*, 2nd ed. (New York: Free Press, 1986), 222. On Germany, see, for example, Johannes A. Zuber, Helmut W. Crott, and Joachim Werner, "Choice Shift and Group Polarization," *Journal of Personality and Social Psychology* 62, no. 1 (1992): 50–61. On New Zealand, see, for example, Dominic Abrams, Margaret Wetherell, Sandra Cochrane, Michael A. Hogg, and John C. Turner, "Knowing What to Think by Knowing Who You Are: Self-Categorization and the Nature of Norm Formation, Conformity, and Group Polarization," *British Journal of Social Psychology* 29, no. 2 (1990): 97–119.

8. See David G. Myers, "Discussion-Induced Attitude Polarization," *Human Relations* 28, no. 8 (1975): 699–714.

9. Brown, *Social Psychology*, 224.

10. David G. Myers and George D. Bishop, "The Enhancement of Dominant Attitudes in Group Discussion," *Journal of Personality and Social Psychology* 20, no. 3(1976): 286.

11. Ibid.

12. See Cass R. Sunstein, David Schkade, Lisa M. Ellman, and Andres Sawicki, *Are Judges Political? An Empirical Analysis of the Federal Judiciary* (Washington, DC: Brookings Institution, 2006).

13. See Elisabeth Noell-Neumann, *Spiral of Silence: Public Opinion—Our Social Skin* (Chicago: University of Chicago Press, 1984). See also Timur Kuran, *Private Truths, Public Lies: The Social Consequences of Preference Falsification* (Cambridge, MA: Harvard University Press, 1997).

14. For a look at how corroboration increases confidence and hence extremism, see Robert S. Baron, Sieg I. Hoppe, Chuan Feng Kao, Bethany Brunsman, Barbara Linneweh, and Diane Rogers, "Social Corroboration and Opinion Extremity," *Journal of Experimental Social Psychology* 32, no. 6 (1996): 537, 157–59n85.

15. For a conclusion that corroboration of one's views has effects on opinion extremity, see ibid., 541, 546–47, 557.

16. See Russell Spears, Martin Lea, and Stephen Lee, "De-individuation and Group Polarization in Computer-Mediated Communication," *British Journal of Social Psychology* 29, no. 2 (1990): 121–34; Abrams et al., "Knowing What to Think by Knowing Who You Are," 97, 112; Patricia Wallace, *The Psychology of the Internet* (Cambridge: Cambridge University Press, 1999), 73–76.

17. See John C. Turner, Michael A. Hogg, Penelope J. Oakes, Stephen D. Reicher, and Margaret S. Wetherell, *Rediscovering the Social Group: A Self-Categorization Theory* (New York: Basil Blackwell, 1987), 142.
18. Spears, Lea, and Lee, "De-individuation and Group Polarization."
19. See Wallace, *Psychology of the Internet.*
20. See Ross Hightower and Lutfus Sayeed, "The Impact of Computer-Mediated Communication Systems on Biased Group Discussion," *Computers in Human Behavior* 11, no. 1 (1995): 33–44.
21. Wallace, *Psychology of the Internet*, 82.
22. Chris Messina, "Groups for Twitter; or a Proposal for Twitter Tag Channels," Factory Joe, August 25, 2007, https://factoryjoe.com/2007/08/25/groups -for-twitter-or-a-proposal-for-twitter-tag-channels/ (accessed September 3, 2016).
23. On the different functions of hashtags, see Alice R. Daer, Rebecca F. Hoffman, and Seth Goodman, "Rhetorical Functions of Hashtag Forms across Social Media Applications," *Communication Design Quarterly Review* 3, no. 1 (2014): 12, 16.
24. Deen Freelon, Charlton D. McIlwain, and Meredith D. Clark, *Beyond the Hashtags: #Ferguson, #BlackLivesMatter, and the Online Struggle for Offline Justice* (Washington, DC: Center for Media and Social Impact, 2016), http:// archive.cmsimpact.org/sites/default/files/beyond_the_hashtags_2016.pdf (accessed September 3, 2016).
25. Quoted in ibid., 2.
26. Ryan J. Gallagher, Andrew J. Reagan, Christopher M. Danforth, and Peter Sheridan Dodds, "Divergent Discourse between Protests and Counter-Protests: #BlackLivesMatter and #AllLivesMatter" (unpublished manuscript, July 29, 2016), http://arxiv.org/pdf/1606.06820.pdf (accessed September 3, 2016).
27. Ibid., 13.
28. Sarita Yardi and danah boyd, "Dynamic Debates: An Analysis of Group Polarization over Time on Twitter," *Bulletin of Science, Technology, and Society* 30, no. 5 (2010): 316.
29. Libby Hemphill, Aron Culotta, and Matthew Heston, "Framing in Social Media: How the US Congress Uses Twitter Hashtags to Frame Political Issues" (unpublished manuscript, August 28, 2013), http://cs.iit.edu/~culotta /pubs/hemphill13framing.pdf (accessed September 3, 2016).
30. Soumitra Dutta and Matthew Fraser, "Barack Obama and the Facebook Election," *U.S. News and World Report*, November 19, 2008, http://www .usnews.com/opinion/articles/2008/11/19/barack-obama-and-the-facebook -election (accessed September 3, 2016).
31. Victoria Chang, "Obama and the Power of Social Media and Technology," *European Business Review*, May–June 2010, 16–21.
32. "Sweet to Tweet," *Economist*, May 6, 2010, http://www.economist.com/node /16056612 (accessed September 3, 2016).

33. Dutta and Fraser, "Barack Obama and the Facebook Election."

34. Pamela Rutledge, "How Obama Won the Social Media Battle in the 2012 Presidential Campaign," Media Psychology Blog, January 25, 2013, http://mprcenter.org/blog/2013/01/how-obama-won-the-social-media-battle-in-the-2012-presidential-campaign/ (accessed September 3, 2016).

35. *Donald J. Trump for President*, YouTube, https://www.youtube.com/Donaldtrump/about (accessed July 12, 2016).

36. For a work that offers an affirmative answer to the question in its own title, see Thomas W. Hazlett and David W. Sosa, "Was the Fairness Doctrine a 'Chilling Effect'? Evidence from the Postderegulation Radio Market," *Journal of Legal Studies* 26, no. 1 (1997): 279–301.

37. See Heather K. Gerken, "Second-Order Diversity," *Harvard Law Review* 118, no. 4 (2005): 1101–96.

38. See Miranda Fricker, *Epistemic Injustice: Power and the Ethics of Knowing* (Oxford: Oxford University Press, 2008).

39. See Caryn Christenson and Ann Abbott, "Team Medical Decision Making," in *Decision Making in Health Care: Theory, Psychology, and Applications*, ed. Gretchen B. Chapman and Frank A. Sonnenberg (Cambridge: Cambridge University Press, 2000), 267, 273–76.

40. Ibid., 274.

41. See Sunstein et al., *Are Judges Political?*

42. See David Schkade, Cass R. Sunstein, and Daniel Kahneman, "Deliberating about Dollars: The Severity Shift," *Columbia Law Review* 100, no. 4 (2000): 1139–76.

43. Diana C. Mutz, *Hearing the Other Side: Deliberative versus Participatory Democracy* (New York: Cambridge University Press, 2006).

44. See ibid., 76–77.

45. Ibid., 85.

46. Ibid., 74–76.

47. Ibid., 75.

48. See Charles G. Lord, Lee Ross, and Mark R. Lepper, "Biased Assimilation and Attitude Polarization: The Effects of Prior Theories on Subsequently Considered Evidence," *Journal of Personality and Social Psychology* 37, no. 11 (1979): 2098–109; Geoffrey D. Munro, Peter H. Ditto, Lisa K. Lockhart, Angela Fagerlin, Mitchell Gready, and Elizabeth Peterson, "Biased Assimilation of Sociopolitical Arguments: Evaluating the 1996 U.S. Presidential Debate," *Basic and Applied Social Psychology* 24, no. 1 (2002): 15–26; John W. McHoskey, "Case Closed? On the John F. Kennedy Assassination: Biased Assimilation of Evidence and Attitude Polarization," *Basic and Applied Social Psychology* 17, no. 3 (1995): 395–409.

49. See Geoffrey D. Munro and Peter H. Ditto, "Biased Assimilation, Attitude Polarization, and Affect in Reactions to Stereotype-Relevant Scientific Information," *Personality and Social Psychology Bulletin* 23, no. 6 (1997): 636–53.

50. Lord, Ross, and Lepper, "Biased Assimilation and Attitude Polarization."

51. See ibid.

52. See ibid.

53. Brendan Nyhan and Jason Reifler, "When Corrections Fail: The Persistence of Political Misperceptions," *Journal of Political Behavior* 32, no. 2 (2010): 303–30.

54. Ibid.

55. Ibid.

56. Ibid.

57. See Dan M. Kahan, Paul Slovic, Donald Braman, John Gastil, and Geoffrey L. Cohen, "Affect, Values, and Nanotechnology Risk Perceptions: An Experimental Investigation" (GWU Legal Studies Research Paper No. 261, 2007), http://papers.ssrn.com/sol3/papers.cfm?abstract_id=968652 (accessed September 3, 2016).

4. CYBERCASCADES

1. See, for example, Sushil Bikhchandani, David Hirshleifer, and Ivo Welch, "Learning from the Behavior of Others: Conformity, Fads, and Informational Cascades," *Journal of Economic Perspectives* 12, no. 3 (1998): 151–70; Andrew Daughety and Jennifer Reinganum, "Stampede to Judgment: Persuasive Influence and Herding by Courts," *American Law and Economics Review* 1, no. 1 (1999): 158–89.

2. See Timur Kuran and Cass R. Sunstein, "Availability Cascades and Risk Regulation," *Stanford Law Review* 51, no. 4 (1998): 683–768.

3. David Hirshleifer, "The Blind Leading the Blind," in *The New Economics of Human Behavior*, ed. Mariano Tomassi and Kathryn Ierulli (Cambridge: Cambridge University Press, 1999), 188, 204.

4. John F. Burnham, "Medical Practice à la Mode: How Medical Fashions Determine Medical Care," *New England Journal of Medicine* 317, no. 19 (1987): 1220–21.

5. See Timur Kuran, *Private Truths, Public Lies: The Social Consequences of Preference Falsification* (Cambridge, MA: Harvard University Press, 1997).

6. See Matthew J. Salganik, Peter Sheridan Dodds, and Duncan J. Watts, "Experimental Study of Inequality and Unpredictability in an Artificial Cultural Market," *Science* 311 (2006): 854–56.

7. Ibid., 855.

8. Ibid., 856.

9. Helen Margetts, Peter John, Scott Hale, and Taha Yasseri, *Political Turbulence: How Social Media Shape Collective Action* (Princeton, NJ: Princeton University Press, 2016).

10. Ibid., 98.

11. Ibid., 102.

12. Ibid., 198–99.

13. See Merouan Makouar, *Protest and Mass Mobilization: Authoritarian Collapse and Political Change in North Africa* (Abingdon, UK: Routledge, 2016).

14. George Johnson, "Pierre, Is That a Masonic Flag on the Moon?" *New York Times*, November 24, 1996, http://www.nytimes.com/1996/11/24/weekinreview/pierre-is-that-a-masonic-flag-on-the-moon.html (accessed September 4, 2016).

15. See Mark Granovetter, "Threshold Models of Collective Behavior," *American Journal of Sociology* 83, no. 6 (1978): 1420–43. For a vivid popular treatment, see Malcolm Gladwell, *The Tipping Point: How Little Things Can Make a Big Difference* (New York: Little, Brown and Company, 2000).

16. See Lisa Anderson and Charles Holt, "Information Cascades in the Laboratory," *American Economic Review* 87, no. 5 (1997): 847–62.

17. For a discussion of some of these examples, see ibid.; Granovetter, "Threshold Models," 1422–24.

18. Lev Muchnik, Sinan Aral, and Sean J. Taylor, "Social Influence Bias: A Randomized Experiment," *Science* 341, no. 6146 (2013): 647–51.

19. Ibid., 650.

20. See Jan Lorenz, Heiko Rauhut, Frank Schweitzer, and Dirk Helbing, "How Social Influences Can Undermine the Wisdom of Crowd Effect," *Proceedings of the National Academy of Sciences* 108, no. 22 (2011): 9020–25.

21. See ibid. Note, however, that even with diminished diversity, the crowd was still somewhat more accurate than a typical individual. This is a "soft" result, as the conclusion depends on the statistics used to analyze the data, but overall, groups were still wiser than individuals, though not always at conventional levels of statistical significance.

22. Ibid., 9024.

23. See R. Kelly Garrett, "Echo Chambers Online? Politically Motivated Selective Exposure among Internet News Users," *Journal of Computer-Mediated Communication* 14, no. 2 (2009): 265–85. See also R. Kelly Garrett and Natalie Jomini Stroud, "Partisan Paths to Exposure Diversity: Differences in Pro- and Counterattitudinal News Consumption," *Journal of Communications* 64, no. 4 (2014): 680–701; R. Kelly Garrett, "Selective Exposure: New Methods and New Directions," *Communication Methods and Measures* 7, no. 3–4 (2013): 247–56.

24. Garrett, "Echo Chambers Online?" 267.

25. Ibid., 266, 279.

26. Ibid., 280.

27. Ibid.

28. Matthew Gentzkow and Jesse M. Shapiro, "Ideological Segregation Online and Offline," *Quarterly Journal of Economics* 126, no. 4 (2011): 1799–1839.

29. Ibid., 1800.

30. See Andrew M. Guess, *Media Choice and Moderation: Evidence from Online Tracking Data* (2016), https://dl.dropboxusercontent.com/u/663930/GuessJMP.pdf (accessed August 29, 2016).

31. Ibid., 19.

32. Ibid., 28.

33. See Brendan Nyhan, "Relatively Few Americans Live in Partisan Media Bubble, but They're Influential," *New York Times*, September 7, 2016, http://www.nytimes.com/2016/09/08/upshot/relatively-few-people-are-partisan-news-consumers-but-theyre-influential.html (accessed August 29, 2016).

34. For a variety of studies, see Itai Himelboim, Stephen McCreery, and Marc Smith, "Birds of a Feather Tweet Together: Integrating Network and Content Analyses to Examine Cross-Ideology Exposure on Twitter," *Journal of Computer-Mediated Communication* 18, no. 2 (2013): 40–60; Elanor Colleoni, Alessandro Rozza, and Adam Arvidsson, "Echo Chamber or Public Sphere? Predicting Political Orientation and Measuring Political Homophily in Twitter Using Big Data," *Journal of Communication* 64, no. 2 (2014): 317–32; Jae Kook Lee, Jihyang Choi, Cheonsoo Kim, and Yonghwan Kim, "Social Media, Network Heterogeneity, and Opinion Polarization," *Journal of Communication* 64, no. 4 (2014): 702–22; Yonghwan Kim, Shih-Hsien Hsu, and Homero Gil de Zúñiga, "Influence of Social Media Use on Discussion Network Heterogeneity and Civic Engagement: The Moderating Role of Personality Traits," *Journal of Communication* 63, no. 3 (2013): 498–516; Bernhard Rieder, "The Refraction Chamber: Twitter as Sphere and Network," *First Monday* 17, no. 11 (2012): 170–86; Itai Himelboim, Marc Smith, and Ben Shneiderman, "Tweeting Apart: Applying Network Analysis to Detect Selective Exposure Clusters in Twitter," *Communication Methods and Measures* 7, no. 3–4 (2013): 195–223.

35. Miller McPherson, Lynn Smith-Lovin, and James M. Cook, "Birds of a Feather: Homophily in Social Networks," *Annual Review of Sociology* 27 (2001): 415–44.

36. Gueorgi Kossinets and Duncan Watts, "Origins of Homophily in an Evolving Social Network," *American Journal of Sociology* 115 (2009): 405–50.

37. Himelboim, McCreery, and Smith, "Birds of a Feather Tweet Together."

38. M. D. Conover, Jacob Ratkiewicz, Matthew Francisco, Bruno Goncalves, Filippo Menczer, and Alessandro Flammini, "Political Polarization on Twitter," *Proceedings of the Fifth International Association for the Advancement of Artificial Intelligence Conference on Weblogs and Social Media* (2011): 89–96, https://www.aaai.org/ocs/index.php/ICWSM/ICWSM11/paper/viewFile/2847/3275 (accessed September 6, 2016).

39. Ibid.

40. Yosh Haberstam and Brian Knight, "Homophily, Group Size, and Diffusion of Political Information in Social Networks: Evidence from Twitter" (working paper no. 20681, National Bureau of Economic Research, Cambridge, MA, 2014).

41. Note, however, that the researchers excluded from the sample those Twitter users who followed an even number of Democratic and Republican candidates.

42. Haberstam and Knight, "Homophily, Group Size, and Diffusion of Political Information," 17.

43. Ibid., 17–18.

44. Colleoni, Rozza, and Arvidsson, "Echo Chamber or Public Sphere?"

45. Eytan Bakshy, Solomon Messing, and Lada A. Adamic, "Exposure to Ideologically Diverse News and Opinion on Facebook," *Science* 348, no. 6239 (2015): 1130–32.

46. Ibid., 1132.

47. Eytan Bakshy, Solomon Messing, and Lada Adamic, "Exposure to Diverse Information on Facebook," Research at Facebook, May 7, 2015, https://research.facebook.com/blog/exposure-to-diverse-information-on-facebook/ (accessed September 6, 2016).

48. See, for example, Chris Cillizza, "Why Facebook's News Feed Changes Are Bad News for News, *Washington Post,* June 29, 2016, https://www.washingtonpost.com/news/the-fix/wp/2016/06/29/why-facebooks-news-feed-changes-are-bad-news/?tid=sm_tw_pp&wprss=rss_the-fix (accessed September 6, 2016).

49. Quoted in Eli Pariser, *The Filter Bubble: How the New Personalized Web Is Changing What We Read and How We Think* (New York: Penguin Press, 2011), 1.

50. Moshe Blank and Jie Xu, "News Feed FYI: More Articles You Want to Spend Time Viewing," Facebook Newsroom, April 21, 2016, http://newsroom.fb.com/news/2016/04/news-feed-fyi-more-articles-you-want-to-spend-time-viewing// (accessed September 6, 2016).

51. See, for example, Alessandro Bessi, Fabiana Zollo, Michela Del Vicario, Antonio Scala, Guido Caldarelli, and Walter Quattrociocchi, "Trend of Narratives in the Age of Misinformation," *PLOS ONE* 10, no. 8 (2015): 1–16, http://journals.plos.org/plosone/article/asset?id=10.1371%2Fjournal.pone.0134641.PDF (accessed September 6, 2016).

52. Michela Del Vicario, Alessandro Bessi, Fabiana Zollo, Fabio Petroni, Antonio Scala, Guido Caldarelli, H. Eugene Stanley, and Walter Quattrociocchi, "Echo Chambers in the Age of Misinformation" (unpublished manuscript, December 22, 2015), http://arxiv.org/pdf/1509.00189.pdf (accessed September 6, 2016).

53. Michela Del Vicario, Alessandro Bessi, Fabiana Zollo, Fabio Petroni, Antonio Scala, Guido Caldarelli, H. Eugene Stanley, and Walter Quattrociocchi, "The Spreading of Misinformation Online," *Proceedings of the National Academy of Sciences* 113, no. 3 (2016): 558.

54. Ibid., 554.

55. Ibid., 554–58.

56. Jeffrey Gottfried and Elisa Shearer, "News Use across Social Media Platforms," Pew Research Center, May 26, 2016, http://www.journalism.org/2016/05/26/news-use-across-social-media-platforms-2016/ (accessed September 6, 2016).

57. Amy Mitchell, Jeffrey Gottfried, and Katerina Eva Matsa, "Facebook Top Source for News among Millennials," Pew Research Center, June 1, 2015,

http://www.journalism.org/2015/06/01/facebook-top-source-for-political
-news-among-millennials/ (accessed September 6, 2016).

58. Allie VanNest, "Yahoo! Tops Twitter as Traffic Referral Source for Digital
    Publishers," Parse.ly, April 26, 2016, http://blog.parsely.com/post/3476
    /yahoo-tops-twitter-traffic-referral-source-digital-publishers/ (accessed September 6, 2016).

59. See Cass R. Sunstein, Sebastian Bobadilla-Suarez, Stephanie C. Lazzaro, and
    Tali Sharot, "How People Update Beliefs about Climate Change: Good News
    and Bad News," *Cornell Law Review* (forthcoming 2017), http://papers.ssrn
    .com/sol3/papers.cfm?abstract_id=2821919 (accessed September 28, 2016).

60. Dan M. Kahan, Hank Jenkins-Smith, and Donald Braman, "Cultural Cognition of Scientific Consensus," *Journal of Risk Research* 14 (2011): 147–74.

61. See Donald Braman, Dan M. Kahan, Ellen Peters, Maggie Wittlin, Paul Slovic,
    Lisa Larrimore Ouellette, and Gregory N. Mandel, "The Polarizing Impact of
    Science Literacy and Numeracy on Perceived Climate Change Risks," *Nature
    Climate Change* 2 (2012): 732.

62. See James S. Fishkin, *The Voice of the People: Public Opinion and Democracy*
    (New Haven, CT: Yale University Press, 1995).

63. For a superbly helpful overview, see "What Is Deliberative Polling®?" Center
    for Deliberative Democracy, http://cdd.stanford.edu/polls/docs/summary/
    (accessed September 6, 2016).

64. Fishkin, *Voice of the People*, 206–7.

65. Ibid.

66. James S. Fishkin and Robert Luskin, "Bringing Deliberation to the Democratic Dialogue," in *The Poll with a Human Face: The National Issues Convention Experiment in Political Communication*, ed. Maxwell McCombs and Amy
    Reynolds (Mahwah, NJ: Lawrence Erlbaum Associates, 1999), 23.

67. See ibid., 22–23. The findings showed a jump, on a scale of 1 to 4, from 3.51 to
    3.58, in the intensity of commitment to reducing the deficit; a jump, on a scale
    of 1 to 3, from 2.71 to 2.85, in the intensity of support for greater spending on
    education; and a jump, on a scale of 1 to 3, from 1.95 to 2.16, in the commitment to aiding American business interests abroad.

68. Ibid., 22–23. The findings showed an increase, on a scale of 1 to 3, from 1.40
    to 1.59, in the commitment to spending on foreign aid; they also showed a decrease, on a scale of 1 to 3, from 2.38 to 2.27, in the commitment to spending
    on Social Security.

69. For an early treatment, see Bruce Murray, "Promoting Deliberative Public
    Discourse on the Web," in *A Communications Cornucopia: Markle Foundation
    Essays on Information Policy*, ed. Roger G. Noll and Monroe E. Price (Washington, DC: Brookings Institution Press, 1998), 243.

70. Paul Matteucci, quoted in Alfred C. Sikes, *Fast Forward: America's Leading
    Experts Reveal How the Internet Is Changing Your Life* (New York: William
    Morrow, 2000), 15.

5. SOCIAL GLUE AND SPREADING INFORMATION

1. See Amartya Sen, *Poverty and Famines: An Essay on Entitlement and Deprivation* (Oxford: Oxford University Press, 1981).
2. See Amartya Sen, *Development as Freedom* (New York: Anchor Books, 1999).
3. Maeve Shearlaw, "Egypt Five Years On: Was It Ever a 'Social Media Revolution,'" *Guardian*, January 25, 2016, https://www.theguardian.com/world/2016/jan/25/egypt-5-years-on-was-it-ever-a-social-media-revolution (accessed September 7, 2016).
4. Michael Wines and Sharon LaFraniere, "In Baring Facts of Train Crash, Blogs Erode China Censorship," *New York Times*, July 28, 2011, http://www.nytimes.com/2011/07/29/world/asia/29china.html (accessed September 7, 2016).
5. Elihu Katz, "And Deliver Us from Segmentation," in *A Communications Cornucopia: Markle Foundation Essays on Information Policy*, ed. Roger G. Noll and Monroe E. Price (Washington, DC: Brookings Institution Press, 1998), 99, 105.
6. Ibid.
7. Ibid.
8. Cass R. Sunstein and Edna Ullmann-Margalit, "Solidarity Goods," *Journal of Political Philosophy* 9 (2001): 129–49. This is a joint article, but the central idea is Ullmann-Margalit's.
9. See Robert D. Putnam, *Bowling Alone: The Collapse and Revival of American Community* (New York: Simon and Schuster, (2000), 18–24.
10. See Chris Anderson, *The Long Tail: Why the Future of Business Is Selling Less of More* (New York: Hyperion, 2006).
11. Yochai Benkler, *The Wealth of Networks: How Social Production Transforms Markets and Freedom* (New Haven, CT: Yale University Press, 2006), 241–61.
12. Ibid., 242.
13. Ibid., 215.
14. Ibid., 247.
15. Ibid., 253, 257.
16. For a valuable discussion showing the complexity and diversity of networked public spheres in different nations (with attention to Egypt, Tunisia, and Bahrain), see Robert Faris, John Kelly, Helmi Noman, and Dalia Othman, "Structure and Discourse: Mapping the Networked Public Sphere in the Arab Region," 2016, http://www.arabnps.org/files/2016/03/ArabNPS.pdf (accessed September 7, 2016). In short, "In Egypt, we see polarized debates on Twitter that divide politically active users into three distinct and largely disconnected groups. In Bahrain, the antagonism between the government and opposition is manifest in a bipolar network structure on Twitter, and the debate is framed in sectarian language that appears intent on deepening the political divide. In comparison, the Twitter network in Tunisia appears to be much more integrated and the discourse between political opponents less hostile, despite the political rivalries there." Ibid., 2.

6. CITIZENS

1. Robert H. Frank and Philip J. Cook, *The Winner-Take-All Society: Why the Few at the Top Get So Much More Than the Rest of Us* (New York: Penguin Books, 1995), 201.
2. Dale Carnegie, *How to Win Friends and Influence People* (1936; repr., New York: Pocket Books, 1981), 110.
3. See Gary King, Jennifer Pan, and Margaret E. Roberts, "How the Chinese Government Fabricates Social Media Posts for Strategic Distraction, Not Engaged Argument" (unpublished manuscript, July 26, 2016), http://gking .harvard.edu/files/gking/files/50c.pdf (accessed September 7, 2016).
4. Ibid.
5. Ibid.
6. Ibid.
7. Timur Kuran, "Sparks and Prairie Fires: A Theory of Unanticipated Political Revolution," *Public Choice* 61, no. 1 (1989): 41–64, https://econ.duke.edu /uploads/assets/People/Kuran/Sparks%20and%20prairie%20fires.pdf (accessed September 7, 2016).
8. See Merouan Mekouar, *Protest and Mass Mobilization: Authoritarian Collapse and Political Change in North Africa* (Abingdon, UK: Routledge, 2016).
9. Alexis de Tocqueville, *Democracy in America* (1835; repr., New York: Alfred A. Knopf, 1987), 317.
10. John Dewey, "The Future of Liberalism," in *Dewey and His Critics*, ed. Sidney Morgenbesser (New York: Journal of Philosophy, 1977), 695, 697.
11. See Frank and Cook, *The Winner-Take-All Society*, 19.
12. See Albert O. Hirschmann, *The Passions and the Interests: Political Arguments for Capitalism before Its Triumph* (Princeton, NJ: Princeton University Press, 1967).
13. See Jon Elster, *Sour Grapes: Studies in the Subversion of Rationality* (Cambridge: Cambridge University Press, 1983).
14. Verisign, *The Domain Name Industry Brief* 13, no. 1 (2016), http://www .verisign.com/assets/domain-name-report-april2016.pdf (accessed September 8, 2016).
15. For a good discussion, see Robert H. Frank, *Luxury Fever: Weighing the Cost of Excess* (Princeton, NJ: Princeton University Press, 1998).
16. See ibid.
17. See ibid.

7. WHAT'S REGULATION? A PLEA

1. John Perry Barlow, "A Declaration of the Independence of Cyberspace," Electronic Frontier Foundation, February 8, 1996, http://homes.eff.org/~barlow /Declaration-Final.html (accessed July 31, 2016).
2. Richard Posner, *Catastrophe: Risk and Response* (Oxford: Oxford University Press, 2003), 85.

3. See *Internet Security Threat Report* 21 (2016), https://www.symantec.com /content/dam/symantec/docs/reports/istr-21-2016-en.pdf (accessed September 8, 2016).

4. Elinor Ostrom, *Governing the Commons: The Evolution of Institutions for Collective Action* (Cambridge: Cambridge University Press, 1990); Robert C. Ellickson, *Order without Law: How Neighbors Settle Disputes* (Cambridge, MA: Harvard University Press, 1991).

5. Friedrich Hayek, *The Road to Serfdom* (Chicago: University of Chicago Press, 1944), 38–39.

8. FREEDOM OF SPEECH

1. Virginia State Board of Pharmacy v. Virginia Citizens Consumer Council, 435 U.S. 748 (1976).

2. See 44 Liquormart v. Rhode Island, 517 U.S. 484 (1996) (Justice Thomas, concurring).

3. Citizens United v. Federal Election Commission, 558 U.S. 310 (2010).

4. See Buckley v. Valeo, 424 U.S. 1 (1979).

5. See, for example, Randall v. Sorrell, 126 S. Ct. 2479 (2006); McConnell v. Federal Election Commission, 540 U.S. 93 (2003).

6. See, for example, Thomas Krattenmaker and L. A. Powe, "Converging First Amendment Principles for Converging Communications Media," *Yale Law Journal* 104, (1995): 1719, 1725.

7. For discussions, see Lawrence Lessig, *Free Culture: The Nature and Future of Creativity* (New York: Penguin Books, 2004); Yochai Benkler, *The Wealth of Networks: How Social Production Transforms Markets and Freedom* (New Haven, CT: Yale University Press, 2006).

8. The old case, allowing government action, is Red Lion Broadcasting v. Federal Communications Commission, 395 U.S. 367 (1969).

9. See, for example, Denver Area Educational Telecommunications Consortium v. Federal Communications Commission, 518 U.S. 727 (1996). For a defense of the Court's caution, see Cass R. Sunstein, *One Case at a Time: Judicial Minimalism on the Supreme Court* (Cambridge, MA: Harvard University Press, 1999).

10. See Lochner v. New York, 198 U.S. 45 (1905).

11. See Lessig, *Free Culture*; Benkler, *Wealth of Networks*.

12. For an effort in this direction, see Cass R. Sunstein, *Democracy and the Problem of Free Speech* (New York: Free Press, 1995).

13. For an overview, see ibid., 77–81.

14. James Madison, "Report on the Virginia Resolution, January 1800," in *Writings of James Madison*, ed. Gaillard Hunt (New York: G. P. Putnam and Sons, 1906), 6:385–401.

15. Ibid.

16. Ibid.

17. I draw here on Sunstein, *Democracy and the Problem of Free Speech*, 132–36.
18. Pruneyard Shopping Center v. Robins, 447 U.S. 74 (1980).
19. For an attempt at an answer, see Sunstein, *Democracy and the Problem of Free Speech*, 121–65.
20. For the best discussion, see Geoffrey Stone, "Content Regulation and the First Amendment," *William and Mary Law Review* 25, no. 2 (1983): 189–252.
21. See Rumsfeld v. Forum for Academic and Institutional Rights, 126 S. Ct. 1297 (2006).
22. The murkiness of current law is illustrated by the Court's decisions in Rumsfeld v. Forum for Academic and Institutional Rights, in which the Court unanimously upheld the Solomon Amendment, withdrawing federal funding from educational institutions that refused to provide equal access to the US military, and in National Endowment for the Arts v. Finley, 524 U.S. 569 (1998), in which a sharply divided Court upheld a statute directing the National Endowment for the Arts, when making funding decisions, to consider "general standards of decency and respect for the diverse beliefs and values of the American public." In the National Endowment for the Arts case, the Court suggested that it would have ruled differently if the statute had discriminated on the basis of viewpoint.

9. PROPOSALS

1. For a valuable discussion, see R. Kelly Garrett and Paul Resnick, "Resisting Political Fragmentation on the Internet," *Daedalus* 104, no. 4 (2009): 108–20.
2. See Center for Deliberative Democracy, http://cdd.stanford.edu/ (accessed September 10, 2016).
3. See Deliberative Democracy Consortium, http://www.deliberative-democracy.net/ (accessed September 10, 2016).
4. They are described in Daniel C. Dennett, *Intuition Pumps and Other Tools for Thinking* (New York: Norton, 2013), 31–35.
5. See James T. Hamilton, *Regulation through Revelation: The Origin, Politics, and Impacts of the Toxic Release Inventory Program* (Cambridge: Cambridge University Press, 2005).
6. See Occupational Safety and Health Administration, https://osha.gov (accessed September 10, 2016).
7. See Open Government Partnership, www.opengovpartnership.org (accessed September 10, 2016).
8. See "Transparency Report," Twitter, https://transparency.twitter.com/ (accessed September 10, 2016).
9. See Nate Cardozo, Kurt Opsahl, and Rainey Reitman, *Who Has Your Back? Protecting Your Data from Government Requests*, Electronic Frontier Foundation, June 17, 2015, https://www.eff.org/files/2015/06/18/who_has_your_back_2015_protecting_your_data_from_government_requests_20150618.pdf (accessed September 9, 2016).

10. For a good discussion, see James T. Hamilton, *Channeling Violence* (Princeton, NJ: Princeton University Press, 1998).

11. See Neil Gunningham and Peter N. Grabosky, *Smart Regulation: Designing Environmental Policy* (Oxford: Clarendon Press, 1999).

12. See David M. Messick and Ann E. Tenbrunsel, eds., *Codes of Conduct: Behavioral Research into Business Ethics* (New York: Russell Sage Foundation, 1997).

13. See Robert H. Frank and Philip J. Cook, *The Winner-Take-All Society: Why the Few at the Top Get So Much More Than the Rest of Us* (New York: Penguin Books, 1995).

14. Red Lion Broadcasting Co. v. Federal Communications Commission, 395 U.S. 367 (1969).

15. Miami Herald Publishing Co. v. Tornillo, 418 U.S. 241 (1974).

16. Turner Broadcasting Co. v. Federal Communications Commission, 520 U.S. 180 (1997).

17. Ibid.

18. Ibid., 227 (Justice Breyer, concurring).

19. See Stephen Breyer, *Active Liberty: Interpreting Our Democratic Constitution* (New York: Vintage Books, 2005).

20. Geoffrey A. Fowler, "What If Facebook Gave Us an Opposing-Viewpoints Button?" *Wall Street Journal*, May 18, 2016, http://www.wsj.com/articles/what-if-facebook-gave-us-an-opposing-viewpoints-button-1463573101 (accessed September 9, 2016).

10. TERRORISM.COM

1. See Alan B. Krueger and Jitka Maleckova, "Education, Poverty, and Terrorism: Is There a Causal Connection?" *Journal of Economic Perspectives* 17, no. 4 (2003): 119–44; Alan B. Krueger, *What Makes a Terrorist? Economics and the Roots of Terrorism* (Princeton, NJ: Princeton University Press, 2008).

2. David Stevens and Kieron O'Hara, *The Devil's Long Tail: Religious and Other Radicals in the Internet Marketplace* (London: Hurst, 2015), 11.

3. Ibid., 49.

4. Jon Cole and Benjamin Cole, *Martyrdom: Radicalisation and Terrorist Violence among British Muslims* (London: Pennant Books, 2009), 269.

5. See Helene Cooper, "U.S. Drops Snark in Favor of Emotion to Undercut Extremists," *New York Times*, July 28, 2016, http://www.nytimes.com/2016/07/29/world/middleeast/isis-recruiting.html?hp&action=click&pgtype=Homepage&clickSource=story-heading&module=second-column-region&region=top-news&WT.nav=top-news (accessed September 11, 2016).

6. Ibid.

7. Quoted in ibid.

8. Quoting from "an essay from the US Army's Command & General Staff College in Fort Leavenworth, Kansas," see "The Basics: Combatting Terrorism," Terrorism Research Center, December 15, 2001, http://web.archive.org

/web/20011215003235/www.terrorism.com/terrorism/basics.shtml (accessed July 31, 2016).

9. Ibid.

10. Jeffery Bartholet, "Method to the Madness," *Newsweek*, October 22, 2001, http://europe.newsweek.com/method-madness-154003?rm=eu (accessed September 9, 2016).

11. Stephen Grey and Dipesh Gadher, "Inside Bin Laden's Academies of Terror," *Sunday Times* (London), October 7, 2001.

12. Margery Eagan, "It Could Be the Terrorist Next Door: Zealot Hides Behind His Benign Face," *Boston Herald*, September 13, 2001), http://bostonherald.com (accessed September 11, 2016).

13. See Russell Hardin, "The Crippled Epistemology of Extremism," in *Political Extremism and Rationality*, ed. Albert Breton, Gianluigi Galeotti, Pierre Salmon, and Ronald Wintrobe (Cambridge: Cambridge University Press, 2002), 3, 16.

14. "Social Media," FBI, https://www.fbi.gov/about-us/nsb/social-media (accessed July 4, 2016).

15. Holly Yan, "ISIS Claims Responsibility for Texas Shooting but Offers No Proof," CNN, May 5, 2015, http://www.cnn.com/2015/05/05/us/garland-texas-prophet-mohammed-contest-shooting/ (accessed September 11, 2016).

16. Jerry Markon, "Homeland Security to Amp Up Social Media Screening to Stop Terrorism, Johnson Says," *Washington Post*, February 11, 2016, https://www.washingtonpost.com/news/federal-eye/wp/2016/02/11/homeland-security-to-amp-up-social-media-screening-to-stop-terrorism-johnson-says/ (accessed September 11, 2016).

17. See Georgetown University, Security Studies Program, National Security Program Critical Issue Task Force, "Report: Lone Wolf Terrorism," June 27, 2015, http://georgetownsecuritystudiesreview.org/wp-content/uploads/2015/08/NCITF-Final-Paper.pdf (accessed September 11, 2016).

18. Mark Hamm and Ramon Spaaij, "Lone Wolf Terrorism in America: Using Knowledge of Radicalization Pathways to Forge Prevention Strategies," February 2015, 7, https://www.ncjrs.gov/pdffiles1/nij/grants/248691.pdf (accessed September 11, 2016).

19. Ibid., 11.

20. Soufan Group, "Foreign Fighters: An Updated Assessment of the Flow of Foreign Fighters into Syria and Iraq," December 2015, 19, http://soufangroup.com/wp-content/uploads/2015/12/TSG_ForeignFightersUpdate3.pdf (accessed September 11, 2016).

21. See Del Quentin Wilber, "FBI Says Fewer Americans Now Try to Join Islamic State," *Los Angeles Times*, May 11, 2016, http://www.latimes.com/nation/la-na-comey-fbi-20160511-snap-story.html (accessed September 11, 2016).

22. Testimony of Professor Peter Bergen, describing how 80 percent of the 62 identified Americans who traveled to Syria to join ISIL were active users in online jihadist circles. See Jihad 2.0: Social Media in the Next Evolution of

Terrorist Recruitment: Hearing Before the Senate Committee on Homeland Security and Governmental Affairs, 114th Cong., 2015.

23. Rukmini Callimachi, "ISIS and the Lonely Young American," *New York Times*, June 27, 2015, http://www.nytimes.com/2015/06/28/world /americas/isis-online-recruiting-american.html?_r=0 (accessed September 11, 2016).

24. Ibid.

25. Testimony of Ambassador Daniel Benjamin, US Government Efforts to Counter Violent Extremism: Hearing Before the Senate Subcommittee on Emerging Threats and Capabilities of the Senate Committee on Armed Services, 111th Cong. 822, 2010, https://www.gpo.gov/fdsys/pkg/CHRG-111shrg63687/html /CHRG-111shrg63687.htm (accessed September 11, 2016).

26. J. M. Berger and Jonathan Morgan, "The ISIS Twitter Census: Defining and Describing the Population of ISIS Supporters on Twitter" (analysis paper no. 20, Brookings Project on U.S. Relations with the Islamic World, 2015), http:// www.brookings.edu/~/media/research/files/papers/2015/03/isis-twitter -census-berger-morgan/isis_twitter_census_berger_morgan.pdf (accessed September 11, 2016).

27. Ibid., 58

28. J. M. Berger and Heather Perez, "The Islamic State's Diminishing Returns on Twitter: How Suspensions Are Limiting the Social Networks of English-Speaking ISIS Supporters" (occasional paper, Program on Extremism, George Washington University, 2016), https://cchs.gwu.edu/sites/cchs.gwu.edu/files/downloads /Berger_Occasional%20Paper.pdf (accessed September 11, 2016), 9, 4.

29. Richard Adhikari, "Twitter Steps Up Counterterrorism Efforts," August 24, 2016, http://www.technewsworld.com/story/83832.html (accessed September 28, 2016).

30. See David Wainer, "Israel Accuses Facebook of Complicity in West Bank Violence," *Bloomberg*, July 3, 2016, http://www.bloomberg.com/news/articles /2016-07-03/israel-accuses-facebook-of-contributing-west-bank-violence (accessed September 11, 2016).

31. See Michael E. Miller, "Does Facebook Share Responsibility for an American Peace Activist's Brutal Murder in Israel?" *Washington Post*, October 30, 2015, https://www.washingtonpost.com/news/morning-mix/wp/2015/10 /30/does-facebook-share-responsibility-for-an-american-peace-activists -brutal-murder-in-israel/ (accessed September 11, 2016). See also Harriet Salem, "Facebook Is Being Sued by 20,000 Israelis for Inciting Palestinian Terror," *Vice News*, October 27, 2015, https://news.vice.com/article/facebook-is -being-sued-by-20000-israelis-for-inciting-palestinian-terror (accessed September 11, 2016).

32. See Greg Miller and Karen DeYoung, "Obama Administration Plans Shake-up in Propaganda War against ISIS," *Washington Post*, January 8, 2016, https:// www.washingtonpost.com/world/national-security/obama-administration -plans-shake-up-in-propaganda-war-against-the-islamic-state/2016/01/08

/d482255c-b585-11e5-a842-0feb51d1d124_story.html (accessed September 11, 2016).

33. Markon, "Homeland Security to Amp Up Social Media Screening."

34. H.R. 3654: Combat Terrorist Use of Social Media Act of 2015, 114th Cong., 2015, https://www.govtrack.us/congress/bills/114/hr3654/text (accessed September 11, 2016).

35. S. 2517: Combat Terrorist Use of Social Media Act of 2016, 114th Cong., 2016, https://www.govtrack.us/congress/bills/114/s2517/text (accessed September 11, 2016).

36. S. 2372, 114th Cong., 2015, http://www.feinstein.senate.gov/public/index .cfm?a=files.serve&File_id=9BDFE0CA-FB12-4BEB-B64D-DC9239D93070. See also H.R. 4628: Requiring Reporting of Online Terrorist Activity Act, 114th Cong., 2016, https://www.congress.gov/bill/114th-congress/house-bill /4628/text (accessed September 11, 2016).

37. See Daniel Severson, "Encryption Legislation Advances in France," Lawfare, April 14, 2016, https://www.lawfareblog.com/encryption-legislation -advances-france (accessed September 11, 2016).

38. Code pénal, Article 421-2-5-1 (Fr.), https://www.legifrance.gouv.fr /affichCodeArticle.do;jsessionid=13656F1B72B860E871B8F8C57C2E53D9 .tpdila20v_2?idArticle=LEGIARTI000032633494&cidTexte=LEGI TEXT000006070719&dateTexte=20160711&categorieLien=id&oldAction=& nbResultRech= (accessed September 11, 2016).

39. Code pénal, Article 421-2-5-2 (Fr.), https://www.legifrance.gouv.fr /affichCodeArticle.do;jsessionid=13656F1B72B860E871B8F8C57C2E53D9 .tpdila20v_2?idArticle=LEGIARTI000032633496&cidTexte=LEGI TEXT000006070719&dateTexte=20160711&categorieLien=id&oldAction=& nbResultRech= (accessed September 11, 2016).

40. Code pénal, Article 421-2-5 (Fr.), https://www.legifrance.gouv.fr /affichCodeArticle.do;jsessionid=13656F1B72B860E871B8F8C57C2E53D9 .tpdila20v_2?idArticle=LEGIARTI000029755573&cidTexte=LEGI TEXT000006070719&dateTexte=20160711&categorieLien=id&oldAction= (accessed September 11, 2016).

41. See "Adoption et publication du rapport," Assemblée Nationale, http://www2 .assemblee-nationale.fr/14/autres-commissions/commissions-d-enquete /moyens-pour-lutter-contre-le-terrorisme/a-la-une/adoption-du-rapport (accessed July 11, 2015).

42. For a journalist account, see Cooper, "U.S. Drops Snark."

43. Gitlow v. New York, 268 U.S. 652, 671 (1925).

44. Dennis v. United States, 341 U.S. 494 (1951).

45. Letter from Learned Hand to Zechariah Chafee Jr., January 2, 1921, reprinted in Gerald Gunther, "Learned Hand and the Origins of Modern First Amendment Doctrine—Some Fragments of History," *Stanford Law Review* 27 (1975): 719, 770.

46. Whitney v. California, 274 U.S. 357 (1927).

11. #REPUBLIC

1. John Stuart Mill, *Principles of Political Economy with Some of Their Applications to Social Philosophy*, 7th ed. (1848; repr., London: Longmans, Green and Co. 1909), bk. 3, ch. 17, para. 14. See also http://www.econlib.org/library/Mill/mlP.html (accessed September 11, 2016).
2. John Dewey, *The Public and Its Problems: An Essay in Political Inquiry* (1927; repr., University Park: Pennsylvania State University Press, 2012), 168.
3. See Heather K. Gerken, "Second-Order Diversity," *Harvard Law Review* 118, no. 4 (2005): 1101–96.
4. See Miranda Fricker, *Epistemic Injustice: Power and the Ethics of Knowing* (Oxford: Oxford University Press, 2008).
5. See Russell Hardin, "The Crippled Epistemology of Extremism," in *Political Extremism and Rationality*, ed. Albert Breton, Gianluigi Galeotti, Pierre Salmon, and Ronald Wintrobe (Cambridge: Cambridge University Press, 2002), 3 16.

INDEX

ABC, 152, 179, 181, 198
abortion, 66, 81, 90, 191–92, 208–9
accountability, 9, 24, 46, 50, 138–39, 262, 268n19
activists, 80, 82, 178, 234–35, 242
advertising: Facebook and, 4; freedom of speech and, 193, 198, 200–202, 205–6; improving, 224, 229–30; Internet and, 28; Pandora and, 33; polarization and, 63; public forums and, 34; radio and, 28; republicanism and, 257–58; spreading information and, 146, 152–53; television and, 28; V-chip and, 219
Affordable Care Act (ACA), 81, 129
African Americans, 59, 66, 70, 79–80, 100, 109, 135, 154, 163, 259
AIDS, 110
algorithms, 3, 15, 21–22, 28–29, 32, 122–24, 257, 265n2
Alien and Sedition Acts, 203
All Lives Matter movement, 59, 80–82, 259
Al-Qaeda, 236, 238–39, 242, 247
Amazon, 22, 31–33, 150, 188, 222, 229
American Civil War, 51, 211
American Prospect magazine, 184
Anderson, Chris, 149–50
AOL, 171
Apple, 246
Arab Spring, 38–39, 138, 162
architecture of control, 1–2, 4, 6
architecture of serendipity, 5
Aristotle, 46
Arpanet, 182–83
artificial intelligence (AI), 3, 5, 21
AT&T, 183–84
Attention and Effort (Kahneman), 18
Auletta, Ken, 31

authoritarianism, x, 11, 38, 73, 98, 108, 160, 165, 254
automobiles, 8, 26, 186, 267n2

backfiring corrections, 93–97, 111
balkanization, 66, 70, 73, 89, 111, 259
Barlow, John Perry, 178
baselines, 23–24
Beatles, 104
behavior: architecture of serendipity and, 5; behavioral science and, 17–18, 59, 103, 160; browsing habits and, 5, 21–22, 116, 124; Carnegie and, 160; citizens and, 160–62, 167–68; consumers and, 26; cybercascades and, 98–99, 103, 109, 114–18, 123–24, 130; emotion and, 16–17, 82, 96–97, 242; Facebook and, 16; general-interest intermediaries and, 17–18 (*see also* general-interest intermediaries); group, 5; legal issues and, 220–21; manipulation and, 17, 28–29, 95, 164; mass media and, 19; minimization of effort and, 18; monopolistic, 28–29, 195; online, 22, 65, 83, 98, 116–17, 130, 234–35; polarization and, 59, 61, 65–66, 83; recruitment tactics and, 9, 63, 68, 192, 212, 234, 236, 239–43, 245, 248–50, 255; regulation and, 187, 195; republicanism and, 257, 263; social media and, 22, 65, 83, 98, 116–17, 130, 234–35; special-interest intermediaries and, 20; terrorism and, 234–35
Benkler, Yochai, 153–55
Bergen, Peter, 283n22
Berger, J. M., 243–44
Berners-Lee, Tim, 183